S0-ASN-988

CONTEMPORARY PUBLIC POLICY PERSPECTIVES AND BLACK AMERICANS

Recent Titles in
Contributions in Afro-American and African Studies
Series Advisers: John W. Blassingame and Henry Louis Gates, Jr.

CONTEMPORARY PUBLIC POLICY PERSPECTIVES AND BLACK AMERICANS

Issues in an Era of Retrenchment Politics

Edited by
MITCHELL F. RICE
and
WOODROW JONES, JR.

CONTRIBUTIONS IN AFRO-AMERICAN AND AFRICAN STUDIES,
NUMBER 77

GREENWOOD PRESS
WESTPORT, CONNECTICUT · LONDON, ENGLAND

ROBERT MANNING
STROZ'₋₋ ₋ ₋RARY

JUL 2 1985

Tallahassee, Florida

Library of Congress Cataloging in Publication Data

Main entry under title:

Contemporary public policy perspectives and black
  Americans.

  (Contributions in Afro-American and African studies,
ISSN 0069-9624 ; no. 77)
  Bibliography: p.
  Includes index.
  1. Afro-Americans—Government policy—Addresses,
essays, lectures.   2. Afro-Americans—Economic conditions
—Addresses, essays, lectures.   3. Afro-Americans—Social
conditions—1975– —Addresses, essays, lectures.
I. Rice, Mitchell F.   II. Jones, Woodrow.   III. Series.

E185.8.C78   1984   323.1'196073   84-717
ISBN 0-313-23711-5 (lib. bdg.)

Copyright © 1984 by Mitchell F. Rice and Woodrow Jones, Jr.

All rights reserved. No portion of this book may be
reproduced, by any process or technique, without the
express written consent of the publisher.

Library of Congress Catalog Card Number: 84-717
ISBN: 0-313-23711-5
ISSN: 0069-9624

First published in 1984

Greenwood Press
A division of Congressional Information Service, Inc.
88 Post Road West
Westport, Connecticut 06881

Printed in the United States of America

10 9 8 7 6 5 4 3 2 1

To
CECELIA
COLIN
MELISSA
and
KAMILAH

Contents

Figures

Tables

Acknowledgments

We would like to acknowledge the assistance of Coleen K. Nelson in preparing this book. She performed and provided a wide variety of tasks and indispensable support services, including the difficult task of typing the manuscript. We are also indebted to Dr. James T. Sabin, Vice President, Editorial, at Greenwood Press, who provided the opportunity and the patience necessary to complete this book.

CONTEMPORARY
PUBLIC POLICY
PERSPECTIVES
AND
BLACK AMERICANS

1
Mitchell F. Rice
Woodrow Jones, Jr.

Introduction: Public Policy and Black Americans

Public policy determines what governments do or fail to do, or "whatever governments choose to do or not to do," for their citizens.[1] Studying public policy has become important in our examination and analysis of government and politics. Political scientists, policy analysts and other scholars and interested students of the political system have become increasingly concerned with the allocation and the resulting distribution of benefits and burdens of societal resources, or "who gets what, when, where and how."[2] The major concern of this book is whether recent public policy objectives are meeting the needs of America's black population.

During the last few years the changing nature of public policies has reflected a lack of concern for racial issues in the society. As issues become colorless, the development of general social and economic programs for black Americans has not been a primary target of the national government. In part this change in attitude toward issues affecting blacks can be attributed to the decline in violence, the perception that things are getting better, the devolution of federal authority, and the changing strategies of black leadership. The result of this complex set of factors has been continued neglect of black concerns in new policy areas.

Contemporary public policies toward blacks differ from previous policies. Whereas previous public policies focused on the poverty conditions of the black community and the poor, contemporary public policies have racial impact without clear racial goals. New issues and controversies have replaced the major issues that were considered a permanent interest of blacks. While the results from previous policies are still felt intensely and are of continuing importance to blacks, attention must now be directed toward other policy areas. In addition, policymakers operate on an assumption that continuation of previous policy efforts aimed at blacks and the poor is not needed. Further, the assumption suggests that prior programmatic efforts to help the black community were unsuccessful and costly, so retrenchment from federal authority and responsibility is justifiable. This assumption presents a new crisis for the black community.

PRESENT ECONOMIC AND POLITICAL CONDITION OF BLACKS

Despite positive changes in the black political landscape, the economic conditions of Black America have deteriorated since the "Great Society" programs of the 1960s. The eroding economic base of the cities has resulted in one out of four blacks' being below the poverty line. This condition has further resulted in poor and overcrowded housing, poor health and a high level of crime in the black community. With black unemployment more than double that of whites, there is little hope for improvement in the overall economic condition of blacks. As of June 1982 the black unemployment rate was more than double that of whites—18.5 percent as opposed to 8.2 percent. Nearly 41 percent of black families had no one employed. In black families with children under eighteen years of age this figure increased to 44.2 percent.[3] Further, a closer examination of the current economic status of blacks shows a widening negative gap when compared to the 1970s. By 1980, slightly less than 20 percent of the black population made $25,000 or more as compared with 1978, when nearly 23 percent of the black population was at this income level. A similar decrease can be noted for the moderate ($10,000 to $24,999) income level. At the lowest (less than $10,000) income level, the proportion of black families increased from 36.5 percent in 1970 to 40.4 percent in 1980.[4] Compounding these problems is the increase in the number of black households headed by females. In 1980 a female was head of household in 42 percent of all black families, and more than half of black households headed by females had incomes below the 1980 poverty-level figure of $8,385. The median income for such families in 1980 was $7,425.[5] The growing increase in the number of black households headed by single females has serious ramifications for the economic conditions of black Americans.

Yet in examining median incomes of blacks and whites over the twenty-year period from 1960 to 1980, there have been some significant economic changes for *segments* of the black population. These changes are most visible in black families where both husband and wife are employed. In 1980, black families with both spouses in the labor force (about one-third of all black families) earned a median income of $22,795. This compares with 84 percent of the median income for white families where both spouses are working. Where the black female did not work, the median income decreased to $12,419, which is 64 percent of the median income of similar white families. Nearly 25 percent of all black families were in this category. In 1960 the median income for all black families was 55 percent that of whites. By 1975 the ratio had been reduced by

7 percentage points, and from 1975 to 1980 the ratio increased by 3 percentage points.[6]

The more positive political conditions of blacks have been fueled by electoral gains from mayoralty campaigns in large cities. The upsurge in the number of black voters has resulted in a growing atmosphere of expectation for some changes. The number of voting-age blacks increased by 44 percent from 1970 to 1980—from 12 million to 17 million. By 1982, four states (California, Illinois, New York and Texas) had a black electorate of 1 million or more, and thirteen states had a black electorate of 500,000 to 999,000. Blacks in the 1980 presidential election were the only major demographic group to show an increase in voting over the 1976 presidential election. The black vote over this period for this election increased by 2 percent.[7] The 1982 congressional elections produced a record number of twenty-one black members in the U.S. House of Representatives,[8] but in the same year blacks suffered a major disappointment with the narrow defeat of Mayor Tom Bradley's bid to become the first black governor of California. In 1983, however, blacks were elected for the first time as mayors of the cities of Chicago, Philadelphia and Charlotte. Despite overall black electoral gains, black victories at the polls represent only one step toward influencing the public policy process in a substantial and systematic way. These electoral gains must be translated into policies that produce social and economic equity.

Although the number of blacks holding elective public office has increased, blacks are still greatly underrepresented when compared to their total population.[9] Further, it has been noted that when blacks are elected their votes come primarily from the black population. Whites tend not to support a black candidate when a victory for the candidate may mean control of an institution.[10] Despite a few exceptions, this observation would seem to be applicable to major city, state and federal elective offices. Moreover, the distribution of blacks in administrative and appointive public service positions still remains small. The absence of blacks in positions that are important for the implementation of public policy is apparent,[11] and without high ranking administrative heads, blacks find themselves without advocates for the programs that affect them directly.[12] The impressions of black political progress will continue to be just as illusionary as those of economic progress if public policy decisions do not take into account their full impact on black Americans. Perhaps what is needed, as President Eddie N. Williams of the Joint Center for Political Studies argues, is that "every public policy should include a 'civil rights impact statement.' "[13]

PUBLIC POLICY AND RACIAL POLITICS

The debate over the definition of "public policy" is extensive. The term is often used to denote a particular governmental response. For example, education policy, or policy toward health care, or the specific policy of a governmental institution are all similar in their use of the term "policy." Yet each provides us with different perceptions of how we should define public policy. On the one hand, public policy can be viewed as an *intention* of governmental action.[14] On the other hand, public policy is often viewed as the actual *outcome* of governmental decision-making.[15] In both cases definitional problems arise when the term "public policy" is applied to the black community.

Because every definition is derived from one of the dominant approaches to the study of public policy, each definition suffers from the limitations of each paradigm. Our definition views policy as *a set of decisions directed at the accomplishment of some defined goal*.[16] For example, the federal government chose to establish the Headstart program to accomplish a specific goal: educational achievement for minorities. Consequently, "public policy" is *an intentional pattern of decisions by government for solving public problems*. The outcomes of such governmental intentions are manifest in policy developments on specific issues, regulations, and statements by public officials.

In studying public policy it is important to note the uniqueness of racial politics in American society. Power, issue politics, and ideology are often perceived differently by blacks, and this divergence reflects the unique social and political history that structures the position of blacks in the United States.[17] However, policies directed toward specific racial groups are not labeled *racial* policies. For example, historically, policies concerning health, housing and poverty have been directed not to specific racial groups but to the poor. Still, the racial significance of a policy is noted by the affected population.

Public policy can also be merely symbolic. The Full Employment Act of 1978 is an example of a policy that had no real program. Although there was much lamenting over the needs of the urban black community, the federal government took no real action and established no goals. Finally, many problems faced by blacks are structurally created problems that cannot be resolved by governmental action. For example, policies that came out of the 1974 energy crisis had a dynamic impact on the economic condition of the black community, but the federal government was unable to respond to them. The disjointed nature of public policy may in part be explained by the diverse assumptions manifest in the various approaches to the study of racial public policy.

APPROACHES TO THE STUDY OF RACIAL PUBLIC POLICY

There are three general approaches to an analysis of racial public policy: the ethnic politics approach, the institutional racism approach, and the policy analysis approach. The ethnic politics approach is primarily concerned with the historical process by which ethnic groups were able to integrate into the context of urban politics. The institutional racism approach focuses on the process of institutional exclusion of blacks from the mainstream of American life. The policy analysis approach investigates the values, goals and outcomes of specific governmental responses to black problems. Each approach offers its own definition and methodology for explaining black problems.

The Ethnic Politics Approach

The dominant model applied to all urban minority groups is the ethnic politics model. The argument presented is that ethnic group integration is inevitable in a pluralistic democracy.[18] Ethnic integration is founded on economic development and electoral competition. The economic development of cities provides the context in which newly arrived immigrants are able to translate unskilled labor into political and economic power. Active participation in electoral politics assures political power, and the opportunity for assimilation into the economic structure.[19]

The growth of ethnic power results in policies and programs that are geared toward ethnic interest. This assertion is grounded in historical experiences and a number of assumptions. First, the political resources of ethnic groups are related to their size and concentration. In the electoral framework of older cities, size and concentration allowed for bargaining for policy gains with votes. Second, the congruence in values among ethnics promotes common goals and policy preferences. Thus, as participation and political rewards increase, all public policies tend to have an ethnic dimension.

In contrast to the political experience of other ethnic groups, blacks have not assimilated into the same pattern of political power. The concentration of blacks in poorer communities has not resulted in acquisition of power. Further, blacks have experienced periods of conflictual goals because of divergent ideological interests within the black community. The lack of clear goals and organization has undermined the translation of these resources into public policy. Finally, the present gains in electoral power have not been translated into access to pluralist politics.

The Institutional Racism Approach

The institutional racism approach acknowledges the racial discrimination that is practiced in the society. Discrimination stems from the historical relationship between members of minority groups and dominant institutions.[20] The subtle forms of racial discrimination are manifest in a variety of ways. They can be overt or covert practices. Invariably, the intent of institutional racism is to provide selective rewards for blacks and to maintain inequality of political resources.[21]

Institutional racism presents problems in conceptualization that are the result of several value assumptions about the intentions of policy-making institutions. First, there is the assertion that the selectivity bias of most institutions promotes racism. Admission standards, apprenticeship requirements and experience standards all tend to be effective tools for undermining access to positions of power.

Second, the working environment and opportunity structure of most institutions make it difficult for blacks to acquire policy positions. Social class, social conduct and social networks all inhibit the opportunity structure for blacks in positions of power. Third, these institutions contribute to the racial status quo through their operating procedures and policies. Each of these assumptions suffers from the difficulty of empirical testing. If institutional procedures are mostly covert, how can we verify their existence?

The problems of verification undermine the explanatory power of the institutional racism approach.[22] Yet the pervasive impact of racism in housing, health care and education lends credibility to the idea that there are at least systematic biases: The proclivities and partialities of the political process that facilitate the quest for power by certain strata and hinder that of others are evident. However, the rigorous extrapolation to the institutional level of analysis has not been accomplished in most studies using this approach. Further, implicit within this approach is a theory of racism which has not been fully developed. What factors determine the racism of these institutions and not others? What is the source and intent of this racism? These and many other questions tend to limit the usefulness of this approach to black politics.

The Policy Analysis Approach

The approach that is most utilized in the social sciences is policy analysis. Policy analysis differs from the ethnic and institutional racism in that it focuses on resolving policy problems. In its most general sense, it implies the use of intuition and judgment and encompasses not only examination of policy by analyzing its component parts but also the design and synthesis of new alternatives.[23] Policy analysis tries to examine the cause and to explicate specific alternatives and recommendations. Previous approaches primarily advocated a particular solution to a problem, but the policy analysis approach attempts to improve decision-making by exploring a range of alternatives.

Policy analysis is an applied science that uses a multitude of methods from different disciplines. As an applied approach to the study of black problems, there are a number of explicit assumptions. First, the expressed intention of policy analysis is to provide value-free analysis of social problems. Values are implicit in that they are the main test of whether an analytical problem has been resolved. Second, policy analysis suggests that all actions on the part of governmental authorities must be measured to determine goal attainment. Invariably the analyst measures not by the value standards of the community but by the analyst's standards. Finally, the policy analysis approach is devoid of ideological considerations. The ideological goals of the government and of the clients of governmental service are not taken into account. In essence, using various techniques, the analyst assesses each alternative and recommends a policy that will provide the best solution.

One advantage of the policy analysis approach is that it allows manageable comparisons between policy arenas. The framework makes it possible to take a policy arena such as health and explore its ramifications with respect to the black community. By contrast, the narrowness of the institutional racism and ethnic politics approaches prevents both normative and empirical analyses. Unlike those two approaches, the policy analysis approach explores the legitimacy and credence given to various policy proposals and the weight of countervailing economic and political forces in the policy process.

PURPOSE AND OVERVIEW OF THIS VOLUME

Between the illusion of progress and the reality of current events lies the essence of racial public policy. This volume presents original essays that provide policy perspectives on selected contemporary issues as they relate to blacks in an era of retrenchment politics and with respect to their resultant benefits and burdens on the black community. No theory of racial public policy is set forth, and there is no attempt to examine all public policies that are of significance to the black community.

The policy perspectives presented here include discussions on the areas of the urban crisis, public employment, minority business enterprise, energy, the military, the police, affirmative action, economics, health, the future and ethics. At the same time, opportunities for individual achievement by blacks are scrutinized in order to place policy issues in the context of equity.

Chapter 2, by William E. Nelson, Jr., Lawrence Mosqueda and Philip Meranto, examines the urban policy pursued by the Reagan administration and suggests that the urban crisis in the United States is alive and well and deepening in terms of its impact on the black urban population. The authors attribute the urban crisis in the black community to Reaganomics and see retrenchment politics in the form of "supply-side economics" as aimed directly at blacks and the poor. They conclude that Reaganomics is a racial policy and that "the Reagan administration is the most racist in recent history."

In Chapter 3, Lenneal J. Henderson, Jr., and Michael B. Preston examine the intricate relationship between black Americans and public employment from a public interest theory perspective. They observe that blacks have been and are disproportionately more dependent on public employment than their other ethnic counterparts. Yet they point out that blacks remain behind in parity based on their population in several critical functional categories and that black public employees are laid off at a much higher rate than whites. The authors offer several recommendations for improving black public employment.

Black business enterprise is the subject of Chapter 4. After a brief look at black business in a black economy and a profile of black business, Lenneal J. Henderson, Jr., discusses the negative and positive impacts of recent business-oriented public policies on the black community and then focuses on strategic characteristics of black businesses and how public policy in general and black business policy in particular can benefit black businesses.

In Chapter 5, Huey L. Perry analyzes black input and representation in the formulation and administration of national energy policy. From two perspectives he pays particular attention to the black role in the energy policy process during the development and implementation of the Carter administration's comprehensive energy plan. The first perspective examines black input into the congressional energy policy making process; the second perspective examines black input in the Department of Energy's administration process. Perry concludes that black input in the total energy policy process during the Carter administration was mixed.

Chapter 6, by Patricia M. Shields, focuses on how military policy affects black servicemen. The author examines the military recruitment process in reference to blacks and looks at the effects of such internal policies as promotion and occupational assignment on black servicemen. Shields believes that the all-volunteer system has increased the number of blacks in the military and that this increase has led to a concern over a "Black Army." The chapter concludes that despite increased black participation in the military, blacks are promoted more slowly and receive poor occupational and training assignments.

Satisfaction with the job the police are doing is the topic of Chapter 7. Mark S. Rosentraub and Karen Harlow compare and contrast the attitudes of black citizens toward urban police departments over a period of three decades—the 1960s, 1970s and 1980s—arguing that during that time black attitudes toward police have remained just about the same. The authors conclude that conditions for a partnership of police and blacks necessary to fight crime do not exist. They suggest that this remains the major challenge for both the police and the black community in the years ahead.

In Chapter 8, J. Owens Smith examines discrimination and affirmative-action policy from both jurisprudential and policy perspectives. The major U.S. Supreme Court cases of the 1970s in the area of affirmative action are analyzed and discussed. The chapter also examines the legal and policy questions that critics of affirmative action have raised concerning meritocracy. Here Smith discusses three questions: (1) Does meritocracy confer protected rights on individuals? (2) Does meritocracy give an individual a legitimate claim to governmentally supported benefits? and (3) Does affirmative action confer "property" or "liberty" interest rights on the individual based on merit? Smith argues that if the courts continue to weaken affirmative action through reverse discrimination rulings, they will re-create the conditions and restrictions that the Civil Rights Act of 1964 was designed to remove, and that the constitutional, statutory, educational and employment rights of blacks will be violated.

In Chapter 9, James B. Stewart analyzes the impact of U.S. economic policy on black Americans. His principal thesis is that economic policy has exploited and continues to exploit the purchasing power of blacks. A brief historical review of the black economic experience is followed by a focus on contemporary economic policy and black Americans. The author concludes that blacks must articulate and pursue a comprehensive economic plan to improve the black economic position.

In Chapter 10, Woodrow Jones, Jr., and Mitchell F. Rice examine health care in the black community. They point out that inadequate health care has always been a problem in the black community and that cutbacks and block grant consolidations in the area of health by the Reagan administration will exacerbate the health care crisis in the black community. They implicitly argue that more funding, not less, is needed to develop a comprehensive plan for the equitable distribution of health services to the black community.

In Chapter 11, Louis C. Green looks at the long-range consequences of social policy on black America. He employs the phrase "black economic development" to mean both the long-range *objectives* of black Americans and the *process* by which these objectives are attained. Two future scenarios and their relationships to black economic development are examined. The author concludes that for public policy to be useful to black economic progress there must be long-term planning and goal-setting.

In Chapter 12, Mylon Winn presents an ethical perspective on how black administrators can address the different and opposing expectations they may encounter while performing their professional duties. He notes that black administrators must develop and maintain ethical virtues that rest on responsiveness and administrative integrity. Although these virtues sometimes oppose one another, he observes that black administrators can reconcile the differences by becoming highly skilled in mediation. Winn argues that mediation skills would allow black administrators to articulate their life experiences and produce more effective results in the policy process and in administration.

The value of these articles is that they demonstrate and emphasize the significance of the study of public policy by the black community. Through discussion and analysis a better understanding of the distributional effects of policy may be traced within an ethnic or racial context. It is hoped that this volume will serve to stimulate a new investigation of public policy as it relates to black Americans.

NOTES

1. Thomas R. Dye, *Understanding Public Policy* (Englewood Cliffs, N.J.: Prentice-Hall, 1975), p. 1.

2. Ellen F. Paul and Philip A. Russo, Jr., "Public Policy and Values," in Ellen F. Paul and Philip A. Russo, Jr. (eds.), *Public Policy: Issues, Analysis and Ideology* (Chatham, N.J.: Chatham House, 1982), p. 1.

3. See U.S. Department of Labor, Bureau of Labor Statistics, *Employment and Earnings* 29 (7) (Washington, D.C.: Government Printing Office, 1982).

4. For a concise discussion on these points, see Henry E. Felder, "Black Family Income, 1960–1980," *Focus* 11 (8) (August 1983): 3, 7.

5. Ibid.

6. Ibid.

7. See Eddie N. Williams, "Perspective," *Focus* 10 (9) (September 1982): 2, 4–5; and *Joint Center for Political Studies*, "Black Voter Registration, 1982," *Focus* 11 (6) (June 1983): 8.

8. Thomas Cavanagh, "Black Gains Offset Losses in '82 Elections," *Focus* 10 (11 & 12) (November/December 1982): 3–4, 8. Cavanagh further notes that the 1982 elections increased the number of black state legislators to 337 nationwide. Also see note 9.

9. As of July 1981 there were 5,014 elected black officeholders at all levels of government. This included 343 black officials in both federal and state legislatures; 2,863 city and county officials; 549 law enforcement officials; and 1,259 education officials. Of the total, 3,070 are located in the South. See U.S. Bureau of the Census, *Statistical Abstract of the United States, 1982–83* (Washington, D.C.: Government Printing Office, December 1982). By mid–1983 the number of black mayors had increased to 224, from 82 in 1973. See ibid., p. 7.

10. Joint Center for Political Studies, "Blacks, Demographic Change and Public Policy," Conference Report, *Focus* 10 (11 & 12) (November/December 1982): 1–4.

11. The Civil Rights Commission as reported by the Joint Center for Political Studies has issued a report showing that only 4.1 percent of the Reagan administration's top policy-making appointive positions in the executive branch are held by blacks. This compares to 12.2 percent at the end of President Carter's term. See Joint Center for Political Studies, *Focus* 11 (7) (July 1983): 7.

12. Over the years, numerous works have pointed out that public agencies have been unresponsive and insensitive to their black clientele. See, e.g., Douglas Fox, *The Politics of City and State Bureaucracy* (Pacific Palisades, Calif.: Goodyear, 1974); Paul Jacobs, *Prelude to Riot* (New York: Random House, 1967); Michael Lipsky, "Street Level Bureaucrats and the Analysis of Urban Reform," in George Fredrickson (ed.), *Neighborhood Control in the 1970s: Politics, Administration and Citizen Participation* (New York: Chandler, 1973); Mitchell F. Rice, "Inequality, Discrimination and Service Delivery: A Recapitulation for the Public Administrator," *International Journal of Public Administration* 1 (Winter 1979): 409–33; Gideon Sjoberg et al., "Bureaucracy and the Lower Class," *Sociology and Social Research* 50 (April 1966): 325–337; Steven Waldhorn, "Pathological Bureaucracies," in Virginia Ermer and John H. Strange (eds.), *Blacks and Bureaucracy: The Problems and Politics of Change* (New York: Thomas Y. Crowell, 1972).

13. Eddie N. Williams. "Perspective," *Focus* 11 (8) (August 1983): 2.

14. For a discussion of various definitions of the term public policy, see James E. Anderson, *Public Policy-Making* (New York: Praeger, 1975), pp. 2–4.

15. See Charles O. Jones, *An Introduction to the Study of Public Policy* (North Scituate, Mass.: Duxbury, 1977), pp. 3–5.

16. See Charles S. Bullock III, James E. Anderson, and David W. Brady, *Public Policy in the Eighties* (Monterey, Calif.: Brooks/Cole, 1983).

17. See Milton Gordon, *Assimilation in American Life* (New York: Oxford University Press, 1964), chaps. 5 and 6.

18. See Egdar Litt, *Ethnic Politics in America* (Glenview, Ill.: Scott, Foresman, 1970). On this point, see also Nathan Glazer and Daniel P. Moynihan, *Beyond the Melting Pot* (Cambridge, Mass.: M.I.T. Press, 1963).

19. Marguerite R. Barnett and James A. Hefner, *Public Policy for the Black Community* (New York: Alfred, 1976).

20. For further discussion on this point, see Edward S. Greenberg, Neal Milner and David J. Olsen, *Black Politics* (New York: Holt, Rinehart & Winston, 1971).

21. See David M. Gordon, *Problems in Political Economy: An Urban Perspective* (Lexington, Mass.: D. C. Heath, 1971).

22. See Barnett and Hefner, *Public Policy for the Black Community*, p. 8.

23. See Frank Fisher, *Politics, Values and Public Policy: The Problems of Methodology* (Boulder, Colo.: Westview, 1980).

2

William E. Nelson, Jr.
Lawrence Mosqueda
Philip Meranto

Reaganomics and the Continuing Urban Crisis in the Black Community

INTRODUCTION

At two recent conferences a vigorous debate emerged concerning whether there is an "urban crisis" in the United States. In both instances some commentators argued that despite the endless attention paid to urban problems in the media and elsewhere, U.S. cities continue to function, and reasonably well. It was suggested that critics who continue to focus on problems are themselves a problem, and that they have manufactured the image of a crisis. Thus, an urban crisis does not exist in reality, but only in the hue and cry of disgruntled academics and other negative critics of American society. One theme of this chapter is that there is indeed an urban crisis in America and that the crisis is deepening in terms of its impact on the black urban population.

During the late 1960s and early 1970s, city after city experienced devastating black rebellions. It was obvious that a crisis existed. The outbreak of unprecedented black urban violence and destruction was so serious that President Lyndon Johnson appointed a national commission to investigate the causes and remedies of the situation. The basic finding of the Kerner Commission was that the underlying causes of the black urban rebellions were rooted not in extremist or outside agitators "but in the multitude of social problems which characterized the black populations in central cities."[1] The recommendations centered on enactment of special social-service programs to aid black inner-city residents. Because during most of the 1970s there were no black urban rebellions of note in American cities, a casual observer might conclude that enough progress had been made to eliminate the reasons for rebellions. However, five and a half months into 1980 an explosive black urban rebellion occurred in Miami, Florida. By the time events had settled down to an uneasy and tense situation, 17 people had died, scores had been injured, 1,200 people had been arrested and $100 million worth of property had been damaged. The Miami rebellion was followed by four other revolts during the summer of 1980, raising again the question of why. What is occurring inside the centers of American cities at the beginning of the 1980s?

From both quantitative and qualitative perspectives, there is evidence that the social conditions which gave rise to the black urban rebellions of the 1960s have worsened by the 1980s and are becoming even more serious. For example, in 1960 some 4.7 percent of the white population and 8.6 percent of the black population was unemployed. By 1976 these figures had risen to 5.9 percent for whites and 15.9 percent for blacks.[2] In the winter of 1982 the federal government estimated that 6,000 people were joining the ranks of the unemployed each week.[3] At the end of 1981, unemployment stood at record post–World War II levels. The rate for adult males was 8.9 percent, for blacks 17.4 percent, for black teenagers 42.2 percent, for all teenagers 21.7 percent and for Hispanics 11.1 percent. Unemployment problems among young people have become dramatically worse since 1960. Table 2.1 shows that from 1960 to 1970, teenage unemployment grew significantly for all minority groups and for whites. Black teenage females experienced a 51 percent rate of unemployment in 1976, surpassing black male unemployment.

Thus, teenagers of most races, especially blacks, approached the end of the 1970s in a situation much worse than that of 1960 in terms of obtaining a job, gaining work experience and having hope for being employed in the future. For example, until recently in the city of Detroit many teenagers looked forward to relatively secure and well-paying jobs in the auto plants that employed their parents. It had not been unusual for one of the auto firms to call a Detroit high school and request as many as 500 graduates at a time to fill openings. Traditionally, blacks have been employed by the auto industry in great numbers, but

Table 2.1
Teenage Unemployment, 1960–1976

	Males 1960	Males 1970	Males 1976	Females 1976
Blacks	12%	21%	48%	51%
Mexican Americans	14	15	24	27
Puerto Ricans	15	18	55	38
Native Americans	17	18	35	36
Whites	10	11	15	19

Source: U.S. Commission on Civil Rights, *Social Indicators of Equality for Minorities and Women* (Washington, D.C., August 1978), p. 32.

in recent years auto workers with ten to fifteen years experience have been laid off indefinitely, and there is little possibility that young workers will be hired in the foreseeable future. As of February 1982, approximately 246,000 auto workers were on layoff industry-wide, with additional layoffs being announced weekly by the major auto corporations. Roger Witherspoon points out that "young adults from 18 to 34 constitute the fastest-growing group of suicidal Americans" and that between 1970 and 1975 the suicide rate rose 20 percent among black males of all ages and 33 percent for black teenagers ages 15 to 19.[4] That a significant number of young people would actually kill themselves suggests a nightmare dimension to the "American dream."

This increase in unemployment for whites, all minorities and teenagers in particular is even more problematic in view of the high rate of inflation in the American economy. As of June 1979, inflation was continuing at an annual rate of 13 percent. The consumer price index stood at 216.6, meaning that a market basket of goods and services that cost $100 in the base year of 1967 cost $216.00 in June 1979. In its 1979 report to the President and Congress, the National Advisory Council on Economic Opportunity found that the continuing combination of inflation and unemployment was making "the suffering of the poor more severe than ever. Many of the very poorest families *have to go into debt* to provide themselves with the basic necessities of life." The council also found that because of high inflation in the cost of necessities—food, housing, energy, medical care—households in the lowest 10 percent income group are spending 119 percent of their after-tax income on these basics. The report stated that the double burden of high unemployment and high inflation was not significantly eased by such public aid programs as unemployment insurance and food stamps. "Unemployment is still a potential catastrophe for individuals and families, and a source of expensive social disruption for the country as a whole."[5] Given this impact of high inflation and high unemployment, it is not surprising that despite the much-heralded "War on Poverty" and other urban reform programs, there has been no decline in the number of poverty-stricken people over the last decade. Using a very conservative definition of poverty, the U.S. Department of Commerce reported about 15 million poor people in the North and West in 1967, and the same number in 1975.[6]

Other definitions of poverty indicate that the number of people involved is much higher—somewhere between 24 million and 36 million—depending on the definition of poverty utilized.[7] Given the increased unemployment and steep rise in inflation, we suspect that there has been an absolute increase in the number of people who were poverty-stricken in the summer of 1980 compared to the summer of 1969. Michael Harrington observes:

[If] . . . the Eighties are likely to see difficult economic weather and inadequate political responses, at least in the first years of the decade, then one comes to a gloomy assessment of the future of the poor. Under those circumstances, there would well be more poor people in 1984 than there were twenty years earlier, when Lyndon Johnson declared that unconditional war on poverty.[8]

Another dimension of the urban crisis is the alarming increase in violent crimes (murder, rape, robbery, aggravated assault) committed in America's cities. In all large cities such crimes have increased significantly over the past two decades. For example, the incidents of violent crime per 100,000 people went from 243 in 1960 to 1,644 in 1977 in New York City; from 207 to 1,528 in Boston; from 569 to 1,836 in Detroit; from 620 to 941 in Chicago; from 800 to 1,902 in Newark; and from 618 to 1,869 in St. Louis.[9] Since 1977, crime has continued to increase in these and other major cities. This trend indicates not only an increase in conditions that motivate individuals to commit violent crimes but also a growing fear of crime on the part of the general population in cities.

The Kerner Commission report uncovered several basic causes of the urban uprisings during the 1960s. It concluded: "The most fundamental [cause] is the racial attitude and behavior of white Americans toward black Americans . . . . White racism is essentially responsible for the explosive mixture which has been accumulating in our cities since the end of World War II."[10] Although some progress has been made on the racial front in response to the black struggle of the 1960s, a new wave of racism is emerging today. For example, the Ku Klux Klan and the Nazi Party have become increasingly active in cities across the nation. This overall atmosphere is raising once again the issue of the precarious position of blacks in the inner cities of the United States. A recent statement by Vernon Jordan, past president of the National Urban League, captures some of the dimensions of this atmosphere.

If there is any overall description to give of 1980 as it was in black America, it is that it was a year of storm warnings, a year when long simmering problems started boiling to the surface, a year in which all the latent forces of the past decade became fully visible . . . . With a faltering economy to contend with, the new administration has proposed to the American people a mixture of reducing government expenses, raising the military budget, and cutting taxes, all at the same time . . . . It is within this proposal that much of the potential danger for blacks and the poor lie, for obviously if the budget cuts are to be made, a prime target will be social service programs that serve the poor.[11]

When these social-service program cuts (discussed later in this chapter) are added to the trends already noted, it becomes clear that the quality of urban life for millions of Americans is worsening. This is particularly the case for blacks and other minorities, but it is also becoming the case for blue-collar and white-collar workers.[12]

By the end of 1981, many public opinion polls revealed that a majority of the American people believed they were worse off than one year before. There was a continuing decline with no apparent solution in sight, especially in the older cities of the Northeast and the Midwest. The economic plight of these cities is having an acute effect on black inner-city residents.

THE BLACK URBAN CRISIS WITHIN A STAGNATING AMERICAN ECONOMY

Several recent studies of American inner cities have concluded that the urban conditions noted above may not be rooted in local conditions alone. Local job opportunities, unemployment rates, the poverty level and the overall economic atmosphere in many inner cities have increasingly become a function of national/international capitalist economic trends.[13] It is not unusual for the board of directors of a large transnational corporation or bank in New York City to make critical decisions concerning employment conditions in Buffalo, Cleveland, or Gary. Plant closings and relocations to the Sunbelt (or out of the country entirely) have become common, and local workers or community residents are unable to affect these basic decisions. Corporations and banks seeking higher profits display little loyalty to the cities that were their major sources of capital accumulation during the industrialization of American society.[14]

Over most of the post–World War II period (1945 to 1970), the American economy experienced considerable prosperity, fueling the metropolitan process that dominated the period. This meant an increase in real wages for many inner-city and suburban workers, who experienced an economic advance in their standard of living. However, black workers and other minorities did not experience the same advance as white workers, and the black struggle of the 1960s was in part a quest for a fair share of the growing American pie. However, by "early 1971 the United States was forced to renege on its commitment under an international treaty to convert foreign-held dollars to gold, and the dollar had to be devalued twice in rapid succession." These events were followed by twenty-seven bank failures from 1974 to 1976, including "two banks with assets of over a billion dollars."[15]

These events signaled the beginning of a new stage in the postwar economy, a stage that is characterized by (1) continuing stagnation in production and capital accumulation in all the capitalist economies in the world, (2) high inflation, (3) near depression and growing rates of unemployment, (4) an ever-mounting debt and (5) the specter of bankruptcy. According to editors of the *Monthly Review*:

What all this signifies is the petering out of the forces that generated the long postwar prosperity wave. In one industry after another there developed a sizable world-wide excess of capacity relative to demand . . . . Protectionism and cartels are once more on the agenda . . . . In short, in the past decade and so far in the present one, the world of capitalist economy has once again entered a stage of stagnation with no change in sight.[16]

The condition of economic stagnation, along with the severe competition from foreign capitalist economies, is undercutting the position of American workers, particularly black workers, in factories and industries. For example, the competition of the Japanese auto and steel industries is a large factor in the decline of the American counterpart industries. This competition has put both black workers and white workers on the unemployment lines.

The combination of these and other economic factors has also made it increasingly difficult for factories and industries in the United States to accumulate capital at the high levels of the postwar period. One response to this difficulty has been the Sunbelt migration phenomenon, which gathered momentum during the 1970s. Brad Heil argues that this shift is not rooted in technological change but that it is "predominantly the development of working class power (i.e., high wage welfarism) in the Northern regions which ultimately causes capital to seek geographic shifts." [17] He also points out that Northern working-class forces have been relatively successful in gaining concessions from capital compared to Southern workers. In order to escape the continuing costs of these concessions during this period of economic stagnation, the large capital interests located in the Northeast and the Midwest are increasingly shifting operations to the Sunbelt (and overseas). The attraction is "a region marked by a politically centralized ruling class, a limited welfare system, right-to-work laws, low unionization rates, cheap and highly exploitable labor, and a disproportionate share of federal expenditures." [18] This shift of capital operations and the threat of more plant closings is putting pressure on workers in Northern cities to accept a wide variety of concessions in their contracts or face the prospects of unemployment.

So the current economic situation confronting many urban residents in the North, particularly black residents, is problematic and uncertain. Further, it has been noted that, as a group, blacks are slow to migrate to the areas where most new job growth is taking place, and that when blacks do migrate to these areas it is after the areas have experienced their economic peak. This lag in relocation has been attributed to racism and job discrimination.[19] According to Ernest J. Wilson, major black organizations should make American industrial policy a priority item on their agenda of national policy concerns, because as industrial policy rhetoric and debate is converted to real policy, the policy outcomes will significantly affect black employment and economic opportunities now and in the future.[20]

REAGANOMICS, URBAN POLICY AND THE URBAN CRISIS

Ronald Reagan campaigned for the presidency on a platform that promised to balance the national budget, significantly cut federal taxes and increase defense spending. He interpreted the outcome of the 1980 presidential election as a mandate from "the people" to implement a program that would revolutionize the administrative and fiscal role of the federal government. However, a careful analysis of the election casts doubt on the accuracy of this interpretation.

The 1980 election recorded the lowest turnout of voters since 1948. Some 48 percent of eligible voters did not turn up at the polls. Of the voters who did turn out, only 51 percent voted for Reagan, and only a very small percentage of those were black. These figures do not add up to a mandate. The absence of an ideologically based policy consensus as a result of the election is underscored by a poll conducted by *Time* magazine shortly after the election which revealed that 63 percent of the voters believed Reagan won because the American people rejected Jimmy Carter, and for no other reason.[21] Only 24 percent of the *Time* respondents believed that the election results represented a mandate for more conservative policies.[22] A more recent study indicated that 38 percent of Reagan's supporters cited the reason "It is time for a change" and that only 11 percent voted for him because of his ideologically conservative views.[23]

Despite the shaky political foundation on which his administration was built, President Reagan introduced a series of radical budgetary reforms designed to drastically alter the distribution of wealth in American society. The theoretical underpinning of his economic policy shifts was supply-side economics, which called for sharp reductions in government spending coupled with significant tax cuts. Supply-side theorists predicted that reduced government spending when combined with general tax cuts would reduce inflation by controlling deficit spending, encouraging investment in new equipment by private industry and stimulating saving by the American people in general.

As implemented by the Reagan administration, supply-side economics has amounted to a grand scheme for transferring wealth from the public to a select segment of the private sector of the American economy. During the first three months of his administration, President Reagan proposed federal spending cuts of $48.6 billion for fiscal year 1982. The lion's share of these cuts would be made in entitlement programs, which serve to provide a small measure of economic security for many black Americans. Among the programs that would be drastically affected by the proposed cuts were food stamps and child nutrition. These were to be cut by $1.7 billion and $2.1 billion respectively. Federal aid to elementary and secondary education was to be cut by 25 percent, and the termination of the Comprehensive Employment and Training Act (CETA) public service employment programs and the Legal Services Corporation was proposed. In addition, the Reagan administration proposed to reduce the number of individuals receiving Aid to Families with Dependent Children (AFDC) payments by tightening up eligibility requirements. A disproportionate percentage of blacks are recipients of these programs. Assistance to unemployed workers would be curtailed through termination of public employment service employees and a reduction of federal grants that permit states to provide extended benefits to the unemployed. Benefits to workers hurt by foreign competition established under the Trade Adjustment Act would be eliminated, producing additional savings in socially related expenditures. Table 2.2 lists the major cuts in programs that would have an adverse effect on blacks and the poor. President Reagan focused the preponderance of his budget cuts on programs for blacks, the poor and the politically disorganized while exempting programs for the rich and politically powerful from major reductions. Initial plans to curtail social secu-

Table 2.2
Major Cuts in Programs for the Poor Required by Reconciliation Bill for Fiscal Year 1982

Program and Number of Participants Before Budget Cuts	Description of Program	Fiscal 1982 Baseline *	Fiscal 1982 Cuts	How Principal Savings Achieved
		(in billions of dollars)		
Compensatory Education (5.2 million)	Funds to school districts educating children from low income families	$4.0	-$.4	Spending limited to $3.48 billion, but program was not included in Reagan-backed block grant.
Pell Grants (2.6 million)	Grants to low and middle income college students; pays up to one-half of educational costs.	$3.2	-$.5	Spending limited to $2.65 billion. Education Department to determine how to reduce program costs.
CETA Public Service Jobs (822,000)	Grants to state and local governments to provide jobs to low income unemployed.	$3.8	-$3.8	Program eliminated.
CETA Job Training and Youth Programs (2.8 million)	Grants to state and local governments to provide job training to low-income youths and unemployed.	$2.6	-$.6	Spending for job limited to $1.43 billion. Youth employment and training capped at $576.2 million, but not consolidated with other programs as Reagan proposed.
Medicaid (18.3 million)	State-federal program to pay for medical care for the poor.	$18.5	-$1.1	Federal payments to state reduced; however, the Reagan-backed cap on contributions to states was not imposed.
Housing Assistance (2.4 million units)	Rent subsidies for low income families; assistance to public housing projects.	$28.6	-$11.6	Number of subsidized housing units cut; higher rental contribution from tenants required.
Food Stamps (22.6 million)	Coupons, good for food purchase, issued to low-income households.	$12.3	-$1.7	Income eligibility limited inflation adjustment delayed; benefits to working poor reduced.
Supplemental Feeding for Women, Infants and Children (WIC) (2.2 million)	Food packages (eggs, dairy products and fruits) provided to low-income mothers and children deemed to be at "nutritional risk."	$1.0	+$.02	Spending not cut, but limited to $1.017 billion.
School Feeding Programs (26 million)	Subsidies for meals served at schools; additional subsidies for meals served to children from low-income families.	$4.5	-$1.4	Federal subsidies for school meats cut; income eligibility limited; special milk program eliminated; summer feeding program restricted.

Table 2.2—*Continued*

Program and Number of Participants Before Budget Cuts	Description of Program	Fiscal 1982 Baseline	Fiscal 1982 Cuts	How Principal Savings Achieved
		(in billions of dollars)		
Aid to Families with Dependent Children (AFDC) (11.1 million)	Matching grants to state programs of cash support to low-income families with children.	$6.6	-$1.2	Benefits to working recipients reduced; states allowed to establish "workfare" programs.
Energy Assistance (11.7 million households)	Grants to states for distribution to welfare recipients and other low-income persons for help with energy bills.	$2.2	-$.4	Spending limited to $1.875 billion. Program converted into block grant.
Supplemental Security Income (SSI) (4.2 million)	Cash grants to low income aged, blind or disabled persons; benefits supplemented by states.	$7.8	-$.05	Accounting methods tightened.
Unemployment Insurance (3 million)	Federal-state insurance program providing 26 weeks of benefits to the unemployed; extended benefits available for an additional 13 weeks under certain conditions.	$21	-$.2	Nation-wide extended benefits program eliminated; restriction placed on conditions under which states can provide extended benefits.
Title XX Social Services	Grants to states for providing services such as day care, foster care and family planning.	$3.1	-$.7	Spending limited to $2.4 billion; program not included in Reagan-backed block grants.
Legal Services (1.5 million)	Grants to local legal aid clinics providing assistance to low-income persons in civil cases.	$.34	?	Program not included in Reagan-backed block grant; funding to be set by separate legislation.
Community Services Administration	Grants to local community action agencies for social services to low-income persons.	$.59	-$.2	Agency abolished; program converted into separate block grant, authorized at $389.4 million.
Social Security Minimum Benefits (3 million)	Ensures that Social Security recipients receive at least $122 a month, regardless of past earnings.	——	-$.7	Provision eliminated.

Source: Congressional Budget Office, Congressional Quarterly, Inc. *Current American Government,* Spring 1982, pp. 32–33.

*The baseline is, generally, the Congressional Budget Office's projection of the amount needed to maintain the existing program level in fiscal 1982, based on the 1981 spending level adjusted for inflation.

rity benefits sharply were abandoned after spokespersons for the elderly voiced sharp opposition and threatened a massive political rebellion.

The budget area most securely protected by President Reagan and his political allies was the military budget. Not only were reductions in the military budget to be off limits, but considerable emphasis would be given to bringing from Congress record increases in military expenditures. President Reagan's plans called for increased expenditures amounting to 7 percent (over inflation) a year, or $1.6 trillion over the next five years. If approved by Congress, this would amount to the largest peacetime military buildup in the history of the nation. The administration's shopping list of new weapons included Stealth warplanes, Trident submarines, two nuclear aircraft carriers, mobile land-based MX missiles and the production of at least one hundred B-1 bombers. Many critics of the Reagan budget pointed out the contradiction between his objective of reducing government spending and his plans to sharply increase defense expenditures. These critics noted that President Reagan's proposals for defense would totally wipe out the effects on government spending produced by his domestic cuts and that his budget plans in general should be modified.[24]

President Reagan was not persuaded by the arguments of critics that his plans for ''rearming'' the United States should be modified, so an emphasis on vast expenditures in the area of defense remained one of the cornerstones of Reaganomics. The decision by the Reagan administration to invest heavily in defense represents a major commitment by the federal government to shift the nation's resources from the public sector to the private sector. Over the next five years, Reaganomics will produce staggering windfall profits for defense-related industries, while simultaneously siphoning off resources that could be used to solve a wide range of domestic problems in the black community in particular and the nation in general.

Tax-cutting measures proposed by the Reagan administration and passed by Congress constitute additional instruments for transferring wealth from the public sector to the private sector. These measures were clearly designed to allow the rich and the powerful to increase their wealth at the public's expense. One proposal provided a three-year 25 percent across-the-board reduction in tax rates. The chief beneficiaries of this reform are taxpayers in the upper-income bracket saddled with high tax rates. Thus a wage earner with a wife and two dependent children earning $25,000 in 1982 would pay $305 less in taxes, while a similar couple making $100,000 would pay $2,137 less.

But the tax rate proposal was just the tip of the iceberg. Additional loopholes for the rich included a reduction in the maximum tax rate from 70 percent to 50 percent, an increase in the real estate exemption tax from $175,000 to $600,000, an increase in the tax-free gift allowance from $3,000 to $10,000, a reduction in the oil windfall-profits tax from 30 percent to 15 percent by 1982, a tax exemption for Americans living abroad on the first $15,000 of earned income and a provision that would allow business and industry to accelerate depreciation allowances for investment in equipment, machinery and buildings.[25]

In an unprecedented step, the Reagan tax measure included a provision that allowed companies to sell unused portions of their depreciation tax credits to other companies. In addition, a special tax loophole was designed for 2,500 floor traders on the commodities exchanges in Chicago, allowing them special exemptions worth $100,000 per floor trader. While depicting his tax cut package as an economic incentive for the average citizen, Reagan yielded to intense lobbying by special interests to make the tax bill an effective instrument for transferring public resources to the wealthy and the privileged. In a moment of candor, Budget Director David Stockman admitted that the tax bill was a giveaway to the rich, labeling the measure a Trojan horse that actually reflected the old Republican trickle-down theory of granting primary benefits to wealthy individuals and large corporations. "It's kind of hard to sell 'trickle-down' . . . so the supply-side formula was the only way to get a tax policy that was really 'trickle-down.' Supply-side is 'trickle-down' theory." [26]

REAGAN'S IMPACT ON THE PLIGHT OF THE INNER CITY

Reaganomics has already had a devastating impact on the cities. One serious consequence has been a widening of the income gap between blacks and the poor located in the inner cities and the affluent living in the suburbs. The Reagan budget axe has fallen most heavily on the programs dating back to the Roosevelt era designed to supplement the income of the poor. A recent study by the Congressional Budget Office revealed that 60 percent of the reductions in assistance to state and local governments produced by the Reagan reforms came from programs designed to aid low-income individuals. [27] The study found that the net effect of the Reagan cuts was to reduce the incomes of the poorest families by an average of three-tenths of 1 percent and to increase the incomes of affluent families by 8.4 percent. Deep slashes by the Reagan administration in the food stamp program will mean that welfare families "will lose 5 to 10 percent of their total incomes on average if they have no earnings, and up to 20 percent of their incomes if they are employed." [28] These drops in income will not be offset by federal tax cuts, since the lowest income group would receive only $2.3 billion in tax benefits (out of a total of $82 billion in 1983) while losing $6.9 billion in other benefits because of President Reagan's budget cuts. [29]

The growing income gap between blacks and the poor and the affluent has been due only in part to growing unemployment. Not only has Reaganomics been unable to reduce unemployment, it has contributed significantly to the economic woes of rank-and-file American workers. [30] High interest rates, produced by deficit spending, have sent shockwaves through the automobile, steel, rubber, and other industries, resulting in massive layoffs. Reaganomics has cut deeply into unemployment compensation for unemployed workers. At the same time, increased eligibility requirements under new Reagan administration regulations have prevented many unemployed workers from qualifying for other welfare benefits. In the Greater Cleveland area, for example, these regulations have resulted in the dropping of 17,000 persons from the federal welfare rolls, leaving Cuyahoga County officials the choice of providing benefits through scarce county funds or denying these individuals any form of government assistance.[31] Traditionally, the federal government has served as provider of last resort, but with the termination of CETA public employment programs and cutbacks in medicaid, low-income housing subsidies and other programs, black low-income central city residents are increasingly turning to state and local governments to save them from the most deleterious consequences of Reaganomics.

State and local governments have not responded effectively to the requests of citizens for increased assistance because they too have been victimized by Reaganomics. The shift in federal resources from the public sector to the private sector has meant a substantial decline in grants-in-aid from the federal government to state and local governments. For the first time since 1946, grants to cities and states by the federal government dropped from $95.9 billion in 1981 to $86.8 billion in 1982.[32] According to a recent report, cities and states absorbed $13 billion, or 37 percent, of the $35.2 billion in budget cuts voted for the past fiscal year.[33] This severe drop in federal funding has produced major dislocations in the budgets and administrative routines of state and local governments. To cope with reduced federal funding, most major cities have had to reduce real service expenditure levels for virtually every service they offer.[34] Human services programs have been especially vulnerable. Facing a loss of $460 million in federal funds, New York City reduced its education budget by $49 million and its day-care and senior citizens center budgets by $15 million, and reduced or eliminated benefits for 104,000 persons.[35] New York Governor Hugh Carey warned that "the days of wine and roses are over" for the citizens of the state.[36]

Cities are also experimenting with other emergency measures. Most major cities are beginning to impose user charges and fees for such services as libraries and recreational centers. The size of city payrolls is being reduced through massive layoffs of city employees. Capital improvement projects in many cities have ground to a halt because sufficient funds to complete them are not available. As a last resort, city officials are imposing new taxes on citizens and businesses within their jurisdictions.[37] These emergency measures have a direct impact on black residents. Low-income and unemployed blacks can least afford to pay user charges and fees, and as a result they are denied the benefits of many services.

Reaganomics has had a catastrophic effect in cities with high levels of unemployment and declining populations, many of which have a large black population. Although beset with the most severe economic problems, these cities have suffered the largest decline of federal aid. A recent study by the Joint Economic Committee of the Senate shows that these cities are not just losing a greater absolute amount of federal aid because they receive more federal aid but are also losing a *higher percentage* of federal aid than the aid lost by cities that are better off.[38] In effect, cities that were experiencing economic trouble before Reaganomics are being compelled to endure the highest proportion of the reduction in federal assistance sparked by Reaganomics. The continuation of this trend will spell disaster for high-cost, low-income citizens living in the declining inner cities of the Midwest, the North and the East. The prospects of relief do not appear promising. Decline in the ratings of municipal bonds will make raising money from the private sector extremely difficult for most cities.[39] And it will be difficult for these cities to turn to state governments for assistance, since state governments are facing their own budgetary crises, many of them induced by Reaganomics.[40]

Further, at the state level in 1981 some 29 states were operating within 5 percent "break-even" on their budgets. Aggregate surpluses of state and local governments declined from $10.1 billion in 1977 to $0.8 billion in 1980. Oregon and Washington had already cut government services drastically, with tenured faculty losing jobs at some state colleges and universities. The days of budget surpluses for most states appear to be over, the only exceptions being Alaska and possibly three or four other energy-producing states. So state governments do not appear to be in a position to offer financial assistance to city governments.

The reaction of the nation's mayors to President Reagan's plans has been mixed, with divisions reflecting party lines. Democratic mayors have complained that the administration's New Federalism policies have ignored pressing urban problems. At the January 1982 meeting of the U.S. Conference of Mayors, Chairperson Mayor Helen Boosalin of Lincoln, Nebraska spoke for several mayors when she said: "The President's State of the Union address on Tuesday [January 16, 1982] did not include the current state of the cities. It failed to address the problems that mayors face today."[41] Commentator Daniel Shorr provided a similar response. Noting that the Reagan administration expects that its programs will work in the long run, Shorr offered the observation that "people do not eat in the long run, they eat today." President Reagan offered little more than his sympathy for those who were unemployed and caught in the recession of 1981–1982.

Insofar as the Reagan administration has articulated an urban policy of any kind, it proposed to establish seventy-five "urban enterprise zones" in depressed cities by 1985. Within these zones, a combination of reduced federal (and perhaps state and local) taxes, in combination with a waiver of the minimum-wage laws, would be offered as an incentive to private firms to locate in depressed areas. This idea fits comfortably into the administration's philosophies. First, it would not require direct expenditures of funds or significant administrative oversight. Second, it is a perfect expression of "trickle-down" economic theory. The firms moving into enterprise zones would provide jobs and other benefits for blacks, the poor and other minorities who live in depressed areas. It should be noted that some underdeveloped nations (for example, Haiti) have created such zones in the past in an attempt to lure U.S. industries. In those zones, health and safety regulations, wage agreements and taxes are waived.

The "urban enterprise zone" proposal brought opposition from Democratic officials. The proposal to waive minimum-wage requirements is especially bothersome to liberals as well as to some labor union leaders. Full-time employment at current minimum-wage levels results in a yearly income below the government's official poverty standard. In an important respect, however, the proposal is in the tradition of past urban policies. From urban renewal through the Community Development Act, a central strategy for "saving the cities" was to provide incentives for private investment.

CONCLUSION: REAGAN AND THE BLACK COMMUNITY

Given their high concentrations in central cities, black Americans have been especially hard hit by President Reagan's policies. Unemployment rates and poverty rates, while high for whites, are even higher for blacks, and the policies of the Reagan administration exacerbate this situation. President Reagan and his aides have noted several times that he is "hurt" by implications that he or his policies are racist. However, as economist Robert Lekachman notes, "racism should be evaluated less by motive than by consequence. By this test, the Reagan administration is the most racist in recent history."[42]

What are some of President Reagan's racial policies and their consequences? Is Lekachman's judgment too harsh? Clearly, Reagan is uncomfortable with any domestic policy that is located in Washington, D.C. Reagan's philosophy of government logically leads to restoration of the ideology of "states' rights." States' rights historically has been a code word for local and regional segregationist policies. Without a doubt, decentralization of racial policies will erase many of the gains achieved since the 1954 *Brown v. Board of Education* Supreme Court decision.

President Reagan's commitment to a lesser role for the federal government is founded not only on his view of federalism but also on his view that voluntary compliance in a market economy should replace government coercion. It is his strong belief that the marketplace is the proper mechanism for achieving opportunity and that civil rights and affirmative-action policies interfere in a "freemarket." In his political past, President Reagan often expressed reservations about the Civil Rights Act of 1964 and affirmative-action programs. In his view, any individual who is unsuccessful in a properly functioning economy has to carry the blame for his or her own failures.

A legitimate question can be asked about this philosophy. Is the administration actually committed to the goals of equality, and does it honestly believe that voluntary actions will promote racial equality, or are these beliefs merely gimmicks to justify a reversal of policy? Congressman Gus Hawkins of California has expressed doubts about the motivations of some administration officials:

It isn't that these people are just against affirmative action. They oppose all anti-discrimination laws. One has to understand this in order to understand their system of operating. They don't believe in the theory that those who discriminate should be punished. In fact, it is useful to them to continue discrimination. This is how they intend to stay in office—by playing groups against one another, dividing them politically and exploiting them economically.[43]

In fact, President Reagan's view of the marketplace presupposes and requires a class-based society that accepts racial and social class inequalities. It is his belief that such inequalities result from difference in talent, willingness to work or other characteristics, but not from "discrimination." Based on an analysis of this philosophy, Congressman Hawkins expressed the belief that Reagan himself is not intentionally racist in his motivations.

In a December 17, 1981, news conference, President Reagan was asked to comment on the case of *United Steelworkers v. Weber*, the landmark U.S. Supreme Court decision that upheld the constitutionality of voluntary racial quotas to achieve affirmative action in the private sector. The President indicated that he was not familiar with the case. The reporter asking the question explained that it concerned a "voluntary agreement to conduct affirmative action programs for training minorities and moving them up through the work force." The President answered, "Well, if this is something that simply allows the training and the bringing up so there are more opportunities for them in voluntary agreement between the union and management, I can't see any fault with that. I'm for that."[44] Later, after consultation with Assistant Attorney General for Civil Rights William Bradford Reynolds, he announced that he was opposed to programs that have quotas or numerical goals, targets or timetables.[45]

President Reagan's commitment to "voluntary" action has been evident in other administrative policies. During the first year of the Reagan administration, the Justice Department filed only one school desegregation suit and no housing suits.[46] Previous federally initiated litigation was the target of efforts to withdraw the government's intervention. Republican politicians and White House officials "intervened to block or weaken six civil rights suits" by the end of 1981.[47]

An especially revealing case arose over busing controversies in the Seattle, Washington, school district. Since 1978, Seattle schools had operated under a voluntary, not court-imposed, desegregation plan. Later, voters in a referendum in the entire state of Washington voted to prohibit busing for the purpose of integration. When Seattle filed a legal challenge to the law, the Carter administration joined the city's suit. But on appeal to the state supreme court, the Justice Department under President Reagan reversed itself and supported the state in attempting to block the Seattle plan. The attorney for the Seattle school district protested that the Seattle case was not an appropriate one on which to switch sides. "The plan is working," he said, "It had popular support in the community and it was voluntary."[48] The Seattle case seemed to indicate clearly that the new administration would oppose busing in any form, even when communities *wanted* to undertake it.

Many of President Reagan's appointees have expressed opposition to stron, civil rights enforcement. For example, Secretary of Education Terrell Bell wrote to Senator Paul Laxalt of Nevada and stated, "It seems that we have some [civil rights] laws that we should not have, and my obligation to enforce them is against my own philosophy."[49] An even clearer statement was made by Deputy Attorney General Robert D'Agostino, who is the chief assistant in the Justice Department's Civil Rights Division. Under the Carter administration, the Justice Department had filed a school desegregation and housing suit against Yonkers, New York. After the suit was dropped by the Reagan administration, D'Agostino reflected on one aspect of the suit, which had contended that a disproportionate number of black students had been placed in special programs for the emotionally disturbed. D'Agostino said, "Blacks, because of their family, cultural and economic background, are more disruptive in the classroom on the average. It seems they would benefit from programs for the emotionally disturbed."[50]

The Reagan administration has taken several actions that seriously undermine civil rights programs. For example, in 1981 it moved to prohibit class-action suits under Title VII of the 1964 Civil Rights Act.[51] In January 1982 the President unilaterally rescinded past administration and court decisions that had denied tax exempt status to educational institutions practicing racial segregation. When a storm of criticism erupted, President Reagan claimed that he actually opposed tax exemption for such institutions but that it was properly a matter for Congress to decide. The President could have reinstated the eleven-year-old tax rule by a stroke of the pen. Benjamin Hooks of the National Association for the Advancement of Colored People (NAACP) has called President Reagan's Internal Revenue Service ruling on tax exemption for segregated academies "nothing short of criminal." He also notes that it is a "sign of encouragement to racist and reactionary groups in this country."[52] In May 1983, by a 8 to 1 vote (with Justice William H. Rehnquist dissenting) the U.S. Supreme Court rebuffed the Reagan administration in *Bob Jones v. United States*. The Court ruled that the Internal Revenue Service can deny tax exemptions to schools and colleges that violate "fundamental public policy."[53] The administration has also decided to move entirely out of the housing arena with regard to racial segregation. In late 1981, Justice Department officials were instructed not to employ the "effects test" when looking at housing discrimination. To initiate or intervene in housing or zoning segregation suits, Justice Department officials will have to prove "intent" to discriminate—an all but impossible task.[54]

The primary defenders of the Reagan administration's racial policies have come from the administration itself. Other close observers have almost uniformly condemned the activities of the administration. Thomas Atkins, general counsel for the NAACP, has stated that "The Department of Justice has become a department of injustice as it relates to victims of discrimination . . . . I have difficulty thinking of a single civil rights matter in which I would welcome participation of the U.S. Department, that that's a tragedy."[55] President Reagan's attempts to undo the civil rights gains of the last two decades are having tragic results for Black America—a situation that has not been entirely lost on the Reagan administration. In anticipation of possible urban disorders, Attorney General William French Smith established an "early warning system" in 1981 to anticipate and deal with racial and civil disturbances.[56] This move by the attorney general's office is indicative of the basic underlying policies of the Reagan administration. The overall consequences of these policies are to depress the quality of life for urban blacks and other minority groups. Should those attacked fight back, the strong arm of an increasingly militarized government stands ready to quell any rebellion.

NOTES

1. *Report of the National Advisory Commission on Civil Disorders* (New York: Bantam, 1968), p. 8.

2. U.S. Commission on Civil Rights, *Social Indicators of Equality for Minorities and Women* (Washington, D.C., August 1978), pp. 31–34.

3. *Denver Post*, January 9, 1982, p. 1.

4. "Suicide Is on the Rise in Kids and Teens," *Cleveland Plain Dealer*, Fall 1981.

5. *Report of the National Advisory Council on Economic Opportunity* (Washington, D.C., June 1979), p. 3.

6. U.S. Department of Commerce, *Social Indicators* (Washington, D.C.: Government Printing Office, 1977), p. 467.

7. See, e.g., David M. Gordon, *Problems in Political Economy: An Urban Perspective*, 2d ed. (Lexington, Mass.: D. C. Heath, 1977), pp. 295–301.

8. Michael Harrington, *The Other America* (New York: Penguin, 1981), p. 214.

9. Marcus Pohlmann, *Urban Colonialism*, Manuscript, College of Wooster, February 1982, p. 107.

10. *Report of the National Advisory Commission*, p. 10.

11. *Rocky Mountain News* (Denver), January 15, 1981, p. 46.

12. For a discussion on the impact of the urban crisis on public sector workers, see Marty Landsberg, Jerry Lembcke and Bob Marotto, Jr., "Public Employees: Digging Graves for the System," in *U.S. Capitalism in Crisis* (New York: Union for Radical Political Economics, 1978), pp. 294–305.

13. See, e.g., Edward Greer, *Big Steel: Black Politics and Corporate Power in Gary, Indiana* (New York: Monthly Review, 1979); Dan Georgakas and Marvin Surkin, *Detroit, I Do Mind Dying. A Study in Urban Revolution* (New York: St. Martin's, 1975); and William K. Tabb and Larry Sawers, *Marxism and the Metropolis: New Perspectives on Urban Political Economy* (New York: Oxford University Press, 1978).

14. On this point, see Dennis R. Judd, *The Politics of American Cities* (Boston: Little, Brown, 1979), p. 218.

15. "The Deepening Crisis of U.S. Capitalism," *Monthly Review*, October 1981, p. 2.

16. Ibid., p. 8.

17. Brad Heil, "Sunbelt Migration," in *U.S. Capitalism in Crisis*, p. 87.

18. Ibid., p. 92.

19. On this point, see Joint Center for Political Studies, "Blacks, Demographic Change and Public Policy," *Focus* 10 (11 & 12) (November/December 1982): 2–3.

20. See Ernest J. Wilson, "Blacks and the Industrial Policy Debate," *Focus* 11 (April 1983): 3.

21. *Time*, February 2, 1981, p. 22.

22. Ibid.

23. Tom J. Farer, "The Making of Reaganism," *New York Review of Books*, January 21, 1982, p. 44.

24. See *U.S. News and World Report*, December 29, 1980, pp. 27–28; and *Time*, February 22, 1982, p. 19.

25. See *Newsweek*, August 10, 1981, p. 18.

26. William Grieder, "The Education of David Stockman," *Atlantic Monthly*, December 1981, p. 47.

27. See *New York Times*, February 28, 1982, p. 19.

28. Ibid.

29. Ibid.

30. See *Time*, February 8, 1982, p. 19.

31. See *Cleveland Plain Dealer*, February 13, 1982, p. 1.

32. See *U.S. News and World Report*, January 8, 1982, p. 26.

33. Ibid.

34. "Emergency Interim Survey of Fiscal Condition of 48 Large Cities," Staff Study prepared for the Joint Economic Committee of the Senate, January 1982, p. 5.

35. See *U.S. News and World Report*, January 8, 1982, p. 27.

36. See *Denver Post*, January 28, 1982, p. F1.

37. See *U.S. News and World Report*, January 8, 1982, pp. 27–28.

38. See "Emergency Interim Survey," p. 5.

39. *U.S. News and World Report*, January 8, 1982, p. 28.

40. Ibid.

41. *Denver Post*, January 30, 1982, p. 3A.

42. Robert Lekachman, *Greed Is Not Enough: Reaganomics* (New York: Pantheon, 1982), p. 8.

43. Quoted from Max Benavidez, "A View from the Hill: Conversation with Gus Hawkins," *Equal Opportunity Forum*, January 1982, p. 32.

44. *Denver Post*, January 4, 1982, p. 1A.

45. For an examination of Reynolds' affirmative-action philosophy, see Charles Morgan, "The Saga of William Bradford Reynolds," *Equal Opportunity Forum*, January 1982, p. 24–26.

46. See *St. Louis Post-Dispatch*, December 6, 1981, p. 1.

47. Ibid., December 7, 1981, p. 1.

48. Ibid., December 8, 1981, p. 3.

49. Ibid., December 6, 1981, p. 2.

50. Ibid.

51. *Equal Opportunity Forum*, p. 26.

52. *Rocky Mountain News*, January 10, 1982, p. 25.

53. Cheryl M. Fields, "Tax Exemption Denied Schools Practicing Bias," *Chronicle of Higher Education*, June 1, 1983, p. 5.

54. *St. Louis Post-Dispatch*, December 6, 1981, p. 1.

55. *The Guardian*, June 1, 1983, p. 5.

56. *Rocky Mountain News*, May 29, 1981, p. 32.

3

Lenneal J. Henderson, Jr.
Michael B. Preston

Blacks, Public Employment and Public Interest Theory

INTRODUCTION

This chapter examines the intricate interrelationship between black Americans and public employment.[1] As a benefit, public employment is a multidimensional resource to black Americans providing (1) direct gainful employment to blacks with federal, state and local governments; (2) a flow of disposable income to black public employees; (3) retirement, health, disability, sick, annual and other *income security* benefits to eligible black public employees; and (4) exposure to and utilization of the organizational resources of government such as information, technology, money and varying amounts of such intangible resources as authority, legitimacy and coercion.

In addition to these direct benefits, black employees enjoy such indirect benefits as: (1) varying access to organizational networks, including labor and employee associations, government contractors, professional associations and voluntary associations; (2) employee protection through labor policies and laws prevailing in the public sector, such as the Civil Service Reform Act of 1978; and consequently (3) direct access to procedures and processes for petitioning governmental intervention in the event of a dispute over the interpretation and enforcement of such laws and policies.[2]

Most public employees enjoy these benefits. However, blacks have depended disproportionately on government employment because racism has impeded their ability to penetrate stable and lucrative occupations in commercial and industrial organizations. As a result, the benefits bestowed on public employees are relatively more substantial and indispensable to blacks. Although racial discrimination permeates public agencies, blacks have been more successful in finding even menial employment in the public sector. Consequently, given the public sector bias in black employment patterns, blacks also depend disproportionately on government for economic as well as political benefits.

Economic and political benefits associated with public employment are subject to the vagaries of public policy.[3] Public policy formulation, determination and implementation are controlled by corporate, nonprofit, political, administrative and international events and decisions that transcend the national black community. Yet the distributive and redistributive consequences of public policy formulation, determination and implementation, particularly for public employment, are closely related to the nature, extent and efficacy of black political participation.[4] However, as Browning, Marshall and Tabb indicate in their study of minority mobilization, "the level of local black electoral mobilization is also a function of local resources, namely, resources associated with relative size of the black population that would support black interests."[5] Such an assertion implies that public employment is a type of "local resource" convertible into political resources. As a result, the achievement of income, income security, organizational resources and other benefits through public employment can enhance political activity. Enhanced political activity provides blacks with an increasing number of opportunities to influence public policy and thereby to affect "the public interest."

BLACK PUBLIC EMPLOYMENT AND PUBLIC INTEREST THEORY

According to Peter Steiner, theories of the public interest are concerned with the way in which demands for public activity arise, are articulated and are legitimized. He says, "Definitions of the public interest distinguish between collective and individual action on the one hand and public (governmental) action on the other."[6] Both sets of actions encourage provision of some goods and discourage provision of other goods. Thus, these goods encouraged by collective or individual actions and provided by government are *public goods*.[7]

Although the public interest considers government-provided bridges, roads, housing, health care, food and other goods and services as "public goods," it frequently perceives public employment generated to provide these goods as secondary or incidental, not inherently a "good." Indeed, a perennial tension exists between the public's desire to have government provide goods and services of varying types and the governmental employment necessary to provide these goods and services. But as Stokey and Zeckhauser argue, "by their very nature, public goods will not be produced if the risk is left to individuals acting in isolation, even when it is to everyone's advantage to have them produced and hence clearly best for the group as a whole."[8] Succinctly, public employment is less popular and "legitimized" than the goods and services it provides.

A key hypothesis in this chapter is that public employment policies without a clear, strong and legitimated relationship to what is perceived by the American public as "the public interest," particularly as it relates to blacks, raise four interrelated policy issues:

1. Public perception of interest in providing or preserving public employment, or employment opportunity through public means, for blacks or, more generally, "the disadvantaged"

2. The strength and resilience of that interest even when public policy prefers fiscal constraint expressed in the form of tax and expenditure limitations, program retrenchment, reductions-in-force (RIFs) and other restrictive measures[9]

3. The presence of emergency, temporary or short-term jobs, public works or other public employment-generating programs including provisions for blacks and other groups disproportionately vulnerable to unemployment or underemployment

4. Black efforts to legitimate public employment through the political, administrative and judicial processes[10]

The Policy Context

Given these four issues, it is essential to examine the policy and administrative context of the public employment debate. According to the Bureau of the Census, civilian employment in federal, state and local governments was estimated to be 15,933,000 as of October 1982, a 0.2 percent decrease from the estimated number of civilian employees in October 1981. Changes in public employment during the period from 1981 to 1982 included a decrease of 3,000 civilian employees (down 0.1 percent) in the federal government, an increase

Figure 3.1
Public Employment, 1972–1982

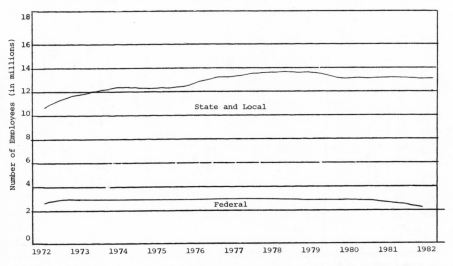

Source: Bureau of the Census, *Public Employment 1982* (Washington, D.C.: September 1982), p. 1.

of 21,000 state government employees (up 0.6 percent) and a decrease of 53,000 employees (down 0.6 percent) in local government (see Figure 3.1 and Table 3.1).

In a study sponsored by the Joint Center for Political Studies, Peter Eisinger indicated that from 1973 to 1980 the total number of city government jobs held by blacks in the forty cities studied increased from 100,796 to 110,207, or 9.3 percent. This increase occurred despite a 7.1 percent decrease in the overall number of city government jobs in these cities during the same period.[11] As a microcosm of overall municipal public employment trends, what is most interesting about the Eisinger study is the period between 1978 and 1980. Eisinger notes: "Black municipal employment peaked around 1978, when blacks held 124,840 city government jobs but between 1978 and 1980 the number of municipal jobs held by blacks dropped by more than 10,000."[12]

It is important to consider these trends in relation to overall increases in the U.S. and black populations. Given aggregate increases in the U.S. population of 229.3 million in 1981 to 235.7 million in 1982, regional distribution of population among states and localities and a comparative birthrate of 14.8 per 1,000 whites and 23.7 per 1,000 blacks and other nonwhites in the same period, declines in civilian public employment in relation to increasing public service needs of the U.S. population, and in particular the nonwhite population, are probably

Table 3.1
Changes in State and Local Government Employment, 1972–1982

Span of Full-time Equivalent Employment	Year-to-Year Change (percentage)		
	All Functions	Education	Other Functions
1981 to 1982	-0.8	-1.7	*
1980 to 1981	-1.2	-0.7	-1.6
1979 to 1980	0.9	0.9	0.9
1978 to 1979	2.1	1.7	2.4
1977 to 1978	1.3	1.3	1.2
1976 to 1977	3.8	2.6	4.9
1975 to 1976	1.1	1.0	1.2
1974 to 1975	2.5	1.0	4.0
1973 to 1974	3.2	3.8	2.5
1972 to 1973	3.7	3.6	3.8
Average, 1977 to 1982	0.4	-0.3	0.6
Average, 1972 to 1982	1.6	1.3	1.9
Average, 1962 to 1982	3.0	3.3	2.8

Source: Tabulated from Bureau of the Census, *Public Employment 1982* (Washington, D.C.: September, 1982), p. 2.

*Less than 0.05 percent.

understated. The result is a declining ratio of civilian employment to population between 1981 and 1982.

It is also important to emphasize that the decline of 35,000 civilian government employees in 1982 followed a decline of 245,000 in 1981, the first decline in civilian employment since World War II. The 1981 decline can be attributed primarily to elimination of the public service employment portions of the Comprehensive Employment and Training Act (CETA).[13] The CETA public service employment provisions employed a large number of blacks. These provisions drew more opposition from detractors of the CETA program in both the Carter and Reagan administrations than any other provisions of the statute. Thus, conflict between the policy preferences of those interests supporting job generation, affirmative action and other policies supportive of black public employment and the groundswell of interest groups and policymakers pursuing fiscal constraint sharpened in the 1970s and 1980s. Advocates of fiscal constraints on federal, state and local governmental spending almost universally opposed governmental intervention to generate or sustain jobs. The $3.8 billion eliminated for the CETA public service jobs program was but a small part of a sweeping reduction in unemployment insurance, housing assistance, energy assistance, food stamps, Aid to Families with Dependent Children and other goods and services provided by government to the needy. Piven and Cloward note: "The overall attack [of the Reagan administration program cuts] was limited, for a time, to cutting those programs that enjoy less popular support and whose constituencies are ineffectively organized."[14] Stated differently, collective actions to ensure public policies which constrained public spending, including spending for public employment, prevailed over actions to expand such spending. Definitions of "the public interest" by the White House and congressional leaders excluded the maintenance or expansion of government employment, of which blacks are major beneficiaries.

THE DISTRIBUTIVE IMPACT OF PUBLIC EMPLOYMENT RETRENCHMENT ON BLACKS

To comprehend the full implications of the policy of declining public employment for blacks, an examination of selected data on the distribution of black public employment is necessary. First, state and local data on the distribution of public employment in 1981 provides comparative data on whites, blacks, Hispanics (Spanish surname), Asians (including Pacific Islanders) and Native Americans. These data are generated by the Equal Employment Opportunity Commission (EEOC) from their EEO-4 files. These files are generated every two years. However, time-series analyses of these data are complicated because they vary in the number and type of reporting units from reporting period to reporting period. This inconsistency in reporting EEOC data understates the disparities in the overall minority picture. Nevertheless, Table 3.2 describes the distribution of state and local public employees by race, ethnicity and selected

Table 3.2

Distribution of State and Local Public Employees for 5,932 Reporting Units by Race, Ethnicity and Function, 1981 (number and percentage)

	Total	White	Black	Hispanic	Asian	Native American
Officials/Administrators	244,964 (100.0)	215,007 (87.8)	20,083 (8.2)	6,534 (2.7)	2,360 (1.0)	980 (0.4)
Professionals	891,388 (100.0)	748,132 (83.9)	90,079 (10.1)	25,727 (2.9)	23,194 (2.6)	4,206 (0.5)
Technicians	481,867 (100.0)	387,742 (80.5)	58,918 (12.2)	16,780 (3.5)	6,361 (1.3)	12,066 (2.5)
Protective Service	667,088 (100.0)	568,043 (85.2)	70,434 (10.6)	24,051 (3.6)	19,912 (0.3)	2,438 (0.4)
Para-Professionals	397,349 (100.0)	258,069 (64.9)	117,385 (29.7)	16,160 (4.1)	3,257 (0.8)	2,028 (0.5)
Office/Clerical	861,896 (100.0)	653,107 (75.8)	147,156 (17.1)	44,476 (5.2)	12,162 (1.4)	4,995 (0.6)
Skilled Craft	378,910 (100.0)	307,864 (81.2)	46,298 (12.2)	19,681 (5.2)	2,649 (0.7)	2,418 (0.6)
Service Maintenance	741,722 (100.0)	452,902 (61.1)	229,631 (31.0)	51,186 (6.9)	4,349 (0.6)	3,704 (0.5)

Source: Equal Employment Opportunity Commission, *EEO-4 Summary Report, 1981*, p. C-1.

job functions for 5,932 reporting units in 1981. These data cover 30.6 percent of the total number of federal, state and local government employees in 1981.[15]

Blacks are most represented in the functional categories of "service/maintenance," "paraprofessionals" and "office/clerical" employees and least represented in the functional categories of "officials/administrators," "professionals" and "protective service." Given pervasive concerns in what Eisinger calls a "fair share ratio," the percentage of blacks in the government work force compared to the percentage of blacks in the population, blacks remain behind parity in several critical functional categories. According to the Bureau of the Census, blacks were 11.8 percent of the U.S. population in 1981 (27,170,000).[16] The relationship of black representation in state and local em-

Figure 3.2
Percentage Distribution of Black Public Employees by Function in Relation to Population Parity, 1981

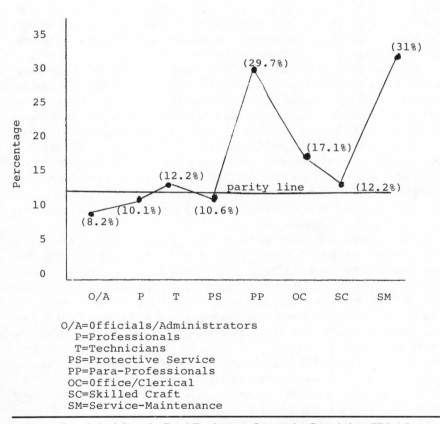

O/A=Officials/Administrators
P=Professionals
T=Technicians
PS=Protective Service
PP=Para-Professionals
OC=Office/Clerical
SC=Skilled Craft
SM=Service-Maintenance

Source: Data derived from the Equal Employment Opportunity Commission, *EEO-4 Summary Report, 1981;* and Bureau of the Census, *Statistical Abstract of the United States, 1982–83.*

ployment functions to the proportion of blacks in the U.S. population is best illustrated in Figure 3.2. The "parity line" represents the proportion of blacks in the U.S. population. It is essential to keep in mind two critical facts when reviewing the relationships of the parity line to black representation in state and local job functions. First, the 1981 EEO–4 data fail to reflect the elimination of the CETA public service employment program, a loss of nearly 200,000 jobs. Second, it is unclear whether additional reporting units would have appreciably altered these data.

Nevertheless, it is also useful to look at the distribution of blacks in full-time, part-time and "new hires" categories. Table 3.3 describes this distribution. What is important about these data is their relationship to affirmative action, particularly following the enactment of the 1972 Equal Employment Opportunity Act.[17] Although blacks are disproportionately represented among part-time public employees, they are even a larger proportion of the "new hires" in state and local government. This suggests that although affirmative-action policies at the state and local government levels appear to be efficacious in recruiting more blacks into public employment, the new hires may also be more vulnerable to the reduction of public employment as state and local governments yield to pressures for more fiscal control.

The underrepresentation of blacks in the category of officials/administrators represents a potent public policy challenge for emerging black political aspirations. Although black elected officials now number more than 5,000, including 230 black mayors, they are still less than 1 percent of the total number of elected officials in the United States.[18] And of the 4,285 city managers and chief administrative officers in local government in 1983, black city managers and chief administrative officers numbered only 44 (see Table 3.4).[19] Given the highly publicized elections of black mayors in Chicago, Philadelphia, Charlotte, North Carolina, and other cities, the recruitment of black administrative talent may be as critical as the election of black mayors if blacks are to realize appropriate benefits from the public policy process.[20]

As significant as the dilemmas facing blacks in state and local government employment is the decline of employment in the federal sector. President Reagan's determination to reduce the size of the federal government and to control federal spending has resulted in an unprecedented preoccupation with reductions-in-force (RIFs) and other adverse job actions among federal employees. Historically, federal employment has been perceived as the most stable and secure source of employment. However, President Jimmy Carter committed the federal government to an employment reduction of 23,000 annually and President Reagan committed his administration to a greater reduction of 75,000 employees annually until federal spending comes "within acceptable limits." Although a significant number of these reductions have been accomplished by natural work force attrition in the federal sector, many, particularly between 1981 and 1983, have been accomplished by reductions-in-force.

The Federal Government Service Task Force, a bipartisan organization chaired

Table 3.3

Distribution of Full-Time, Part-Time and Newly Hired Employees in 5,932 Reporting Units of State and Local Government by Race and Ethnicity, 1981 (number and percentage)

	White	Black	Hispanic	Asian	Native American
Total					
Full-Time					
4,665,184	3,590,866	780,434	204,595	56,454	32,835
(100.0)	(77.0)	(16.7)	(4.4)	(1.2)	(0.7)
Part-Time					
918,502	739,045	126,466	36,681	12,751	3,559
(100.O)	(80.5)	(13.8)	(4.0)	(1.4)	(0.4)
New Hires					
704,317	511,240	131,170	43,240	14,148	4,519
(100.0)	(72.6)	(18.6)	(6.1)	(2.0)	(0.6)

Source: Equal Employment Opportunity Commission, *EEO-4 Summary Report, 1981*, p. C-1.

Table 3.4
City Managers and Chief Administrative Officers, by Sex and Race, 1983

Sex	Total	White	Black	Hispanic
Male	3,968	3,884	40	44
Female	317	311	4	2
Total	4,285	4,195	44	46

Source: *Municipal Yearbook 1983*, International City Management Association, 1983, p. 247.

by Congressman Michael Barnes, a Democrat from Maryland, has assiduously monitored the impact of federal reductions-in-force, downgrades, lateral reassignments and other actions designed to control the growth of federal employment. In its first report on December 30, 1981, the task force indicated that between January and October 1981 "minorities were RIFed at $1^1/_2$ times the rate of non-minorities, or, simply stated, for every 2 non-minority employees RIFed, three minority employees were RIFed." In addition, the task force indicated that four minority employees were affected by an adverse personnel action such as a downgrade or a lateral reassignment for every three nonminority employees.[21] This represented the first substantial wave of reductions-in-force during the Reagan administration.

In its third-quarter fiscal year 1982 report, the task force indicated that within the quarter, minorities experienced 33.41 percent of the total reductions-in-force, although they are only 19.9 percent of the total federal work force. Minority women received a higher share of RIF-related actions (19.5 percent) than minority men (14 percent). Minority women experienced 26.48 percent of the lateral reassignments, compared to 8.43 percent for minority men. However, minority men were the victims of more downgrades and discontinued service retirements (two actions more severe than lateral reassignments). Minority men experienced 18.8 percent of the downgrades, compared to 12.9 percent for minority women. Similarly, 19.8 percent of the discontinued service retirements were minority men, while 9.38 percent were minority women.[22] Table 3.5 shows the impact of these adverse actions on minorities and nonminorities. The data illustrate, first, the vulnerability of black public employees to fiscal, personnel and other policies whose immediate impact is a reduction of employment opportunity and, second, the inadequacy of most public sector affirmative-action policies in the face of government retrenchment. Most of these policies were formulated in a period of relatively stable employment growth, particularly in the public sector.[23] Third, the data show that the Reagan administration has been pursuing a theory of the public interest which excludes public employment maintenance or expansion for blacks or other minorities.

Nevertheless, the federal government remains the largest employer in the na-

Table 3.5
Federal Reductions-in-Force, Laterals, Downgrades and Discontinued Service Retirements in the Third Quarter of Fiscal Year 1982 (number and percentage)

	RIFs	Laterals	Downgrades	DSRs	Total Actions
Total	1,393 (38.5)	1,155 (31.9)	881 (24.3)	192 (5.3)	3,621 (100)
Minority Women	283 (20.3)	179 (26.5)	87 (12.9)	18 (9.4)	567 (19.5)
Nonminority Women	415 (29.8)	193 (28.5)	132 (19.6)	36 (18.8)	776 (26.4)
Minority Men	191 (13.7)	57 (8.4)	128 (18.8)	38 (19.8)	414 (14.1)
Nonminority men	491 (35.2)	247 (36.6)	326 (48.4)	99 (51.6)	1163 (39.6)
Total Minority	474 (34.0)	236 (34.9)	215 (31.9)	56 (29.7)	981 (33.0)
Total Nonminority	906 (65.0)	440 (65.0)	458 (67.8)	135 (70.3)	1939 (66.0)

Source: Adapted from *Reduction in Force Survey, Third Quarter, Fiscal Year 1982*, Federal Government Service Task Force, 1983, p. 2.

tion. In 1978 it employed over 2.4 million full-time civilian workers, 22 percent of whom were classified as minority employees.[24] It is important not to lose sight of the economic impacts of federal, state and local black public employment. As George Borjas indicates, "The evidence in several recent studies suggests that the earnings of minorities and women employed by the federal government are substantially lower than the earnings of 'similar' white males."[25] Salary differentials are evident when one compares black state and local government employees to their white and Asian counterparts. For example, taking the functional categories indicated earlier, Table 3.6 describes median salaries for white, black, Hispanic, Asian and Native American employees. In every instance, black employees trailed white employees in median earnings. Most significant, blacks also trailed Hispanic, Asian and Native American employees in salaries for the same functional categories. These comparisons reflect the growing problem of interminority competition after equal employment opportunity and affirmative-action policies were expanded to include minorities other than blacks.[26]

IMPLICATIONS FOR PUBLIC POLICY AND THE PUBLIC INTEREST

The relationship of black public employment to current articulations of "the public interest" is problematical for the future of blacks in government. Fiscal and personnel retrenchment policies are reducing, if not eliminating, generation of public employment as a policy priority. Reductions in civilian employment at the federal, state and local levels reflect this trend. This freeze on public employment is coincident with the emergence of black electoral power, particularly in local government, with general economic malaise in the U.S. economy and with rising unemployment.

Although such legislation as the Surface and Mass Transportation Act of 1983 and the Emergency Jobs Act of 1983 have been signed by President Reagan, they seem to be designed less to provide permanent employment in the public sector and more (1) to promote a policy of revitalizing and repairing the crumbling and decaying infrastructure of U.S. cities and transportation networks, (2) to provide *temporary* recessionary relief, particularly for the unemployed, (3) to provide a modicum of assistance to the poor in such categories as food and shelter, child health and community and Native American health services (areas subject to budget reduction earlier in the Reagan administration), and (4) to assuage both opponents and supporters of the Reagan presidency and thereby avert severe political erosion.

Given the current state of affairs in the public employment arena it is essential for blacks to continue to insist on penetrating higher-paying and more permanent occupational categories in the public sector; continue advocating public employment development, particularly in local government, where myriad service needs are most felt; continue advocating reassessment of affirmative-action

Table 3.6
Median Salaries of Whites, Blacks, Hispanics, Asians and Native Americans in 5,932 Reporting Units of State and Local Governments, 1981

	Total	White	Black	Hispanic	Asian	Native American
Officials/Administrators	$24,399	$24,624	$21,186	$22,731	$29,865	$25,298
Professionals	$19,977	$20,137	$18,312	$20,441	$24,458	$20,183
Technicians	$16,216	$16,369	$14,394	$16,301	$19,492	$17,952
Protective Service	$18,168	$18,278	$16,885	$18,601	$21,866	$17,632
Para-Professionals	$11,831	$12,015	$11,396	$12,017	$13,874	$13,023
Office/Clerical	$11,979	$12,003	$11,722	$11,978	$15,086	$12,354
Skilled Craft	$16,679	$16,737	$15,825	$16,720	$22,432	$18,114
Service/Maintenance	$12,784	$13,094	$12,147	$12,763	$15,076	$13,590

Source: Equal Employment Opportunity Commission, *EEO-4 Survey*, 1981, pp. C-4–L-4.

policies to include governmental retrenchment as well as expansion; and continue efforts to penetrate the private sectors, particularly through local governmental contracts with corporate and nongovernmental entities.

NOTES

1. The Census Bureau defines *public employment* as "all persons gainfully employed by and performing services for a government." These include "all persons paid for personal services performed, including persons paid from federally-funded programs, paid elected officials, persons in paid leave status and persons paid on a 'per meeting' annual, semi-annual or quarterly basis." Employment created by government contracts with private industry, nonprofit or other nongovernmental organizations is excluded from this definition. See U.S. Department of Commerce, *Public Employment in 1982* (Washington, D.C.: Government Printing Office, 1982).

2. Federal labor relations are examined in Sar A. Levitan and Alexandra B. Noden, *Working for the Sovereign: Employee Relations in the Federal Government* (Baltimore: Johns Hopkins University Press, 1983).

3. See Warren Ilchman and Norman Uphoff, *The Political Economy of Change* (Berkeley, Calif.: University of California Press, 1971).

4. On black political participation, see Hanes Walton, *Black Politics: A Theoretical and Structural Analysis* (Philadelphia: J. B. Lippincott, 1972); Milton Morris, *The Politics of Black America* (New York: Harper & Row, 1975); and Michael B. Preston, Lenneal J. Henderson and Paul Puryear (eds.), *The New Black Politics: The Search for Political Power* (New York: Longman, 1982).

5. Rufus F. Browning, Dale Rogers Marshall, and Davis H. Tabb, "Minority Mobilization and Urban Political Change, 1960–1979," Paper delivered at the 1979 Annual Meeting of the American Political Science Association, September 3, 1979.

6. Peter O. Steiner, "The Public Sector and the Public Interest," in Robert H. Haveman and Julius Margolis (eds.), *Public Expenditure and Policy Analysis*, 2d ed. (Boston: Houghton Mifflin, 1977), pp. 28–29.

7. Ibid., p.29.

8. Edith Stokey and Richard Zeckhauser, *A Primer for Policy Analysis* (New York: W. W. Norton, 1978), p. 308.

9. See Richard A. Eribes and John S. Hall, "Revolt of the Affluent: Fiscal Controls in Three States," *Public Administration Review* 41 (January 1981): 107; Jerry McCaffery and John H. Bowman, "Participatory Democracy and Proposition 13," *Public Administration Review* 38 (November/December 1978): 531; and Lenneal J. Henderson, *Proposition 13: Managing the Income Security Impacts* (Washington, D.C.: National Institute for Public Management, 1979).

10. See Marguerite R. Barnett and James Hefner (eds.), *Public Policy for the Black Community* (Port Washington, N.Y.: Alfred, 1976); and Lawrence Howard, Lenneal J. Henderson and Deryl Hunt, *Public Administration and Public Policy: A Minority Perspective* (Pittsburgh: Public Policy Press, 1977).

11. Peter Eisinger, *Black Employment in City Government* (Washington, D.C.: Joint Center for Political Studies, 1983), chap. 1.

12. Ibid.

13. Department of Commerce, *Public Employment in 1982*, p. 2.

14. Frances Fox Piven and Richard A. Cloward, *The New Class War: Reagan's Attack on the Welfare State and Its Consequences* (New York: Pantheon, 1982), p. 7.

15. See U.S. Department of Commerce, *Governmental Organization, Volume I* (Washington, D.C.: Government Printing Office, 1982).

16. U.S. Bureau of the Census, *Statistical Abstract of the United States, 1982-83* (Washington, D.C.: Government Printing Office), p. 26.

17. See Grace Hall and Alan Saltzstein, "Equal Employment Opportunity for Minorities in Municipal Government," *Social Science Quarterly* 57 (March 1977): 864.

18. Joint Center for Political Studies, *National Roster of Black Elected Officials* (Washington, D.C., 1983).

19. *Municipal Yearbook, 1983* (Washington, D.C. International City Management Association, 1983), p. 247.

20. Mitchell F. Rice, "Support for Equal Employment Opportunity and Affirmative Action Among Municipal Administrators in Texas," *Public Affairs Comment* 26 (May 1981): 1–6; and Frank J. Thompson, "Types of Representative Bureaucracy and Their Linkages: The Case of Ethnicity," in Robert T. Golembiewski, Frank Gibson and Geoffrey Y. Cornog (eds.) *Public Administration: Readings in Institutions, Processes, Behavior and Policy* (Chicago: Rand McNally, 1976), p. 576.

21. *Impact of 1981 RIFs on Minorities and Women and Updated RIF Projections for Fiscal Year 1982* (Washington, D.C.: Government Printing Office, 1983).

22. Federal Government Service Task Force, *Reduction in Force Survey, Third Quarter, Fiscal 1982* (Washington D.C.: Government Printing Office, 1983).

23. On this point, see Lenneal J. Henderson, "The Impact of the Equal Employment Opportunity Act on Women and Minorities in Municipal Government," *Policy Studies Journal* 7 (Winter 1978): 234–239.

24. U.S. Office of Personnel Management, *Equal Employment Opportunity Statistics No. 2* (Washington, D.C.: Government Printing Office, 1978), p. 31.

25. George J. Borjas, "The Politics of Employment Discrimination in the Federal Bureaucracy," *Journal of Law and Economics* 25 (October 1982): 271.

26. For a discussion of interminority competition, see Mitchell F. Rice, "Personnel Attitudes, Interminority Competition and Affirmative Action," *Municipal Matrix* 15 (March 1983): 1–4; David H. Rosenbloom, "A Note on Interminority Group Competition for Federal Positions," *Public Personnel Management* 4 (November/December 1973): 43–48; and David H. Rosenbloom and Peter N. Grabosky, "Racial and Ethnic Competition for Federal Service Positions," *Midwest Review of Public Administration* 11 (December 1977): 281–290.

Black Business Enterprise and Public Policy

INTRODUCTION

The malaise afflicting the U.S. economy and the treatment prescribed by President Ronald Reagan for its recovery pose serious challenges to black business ownership and performance. Continued economic recession characterized by high interest rates, inflation, foreign competition, increased inventories and corporate retrenchment beleaguer the economy. The internationalization of American economic interdependency is illustrated daily by continued U.S. dependency on petroleum imports, competition from Japanese and European electronics, automobiles and steel and the disposition of American agricultural products on the world market. Balance-of-payments deficits symbolize the decline of the United States as a world economic power, and work force reductions, salary givebacks and bankruptcies symbolize the struggle of declining productivity and rising labor costs.[1]

Government response to and participation in this malaise is equally important. President Reagan's "supply-side economics" prescribes reduced government spending, particularly for social programs, individual and corporate income tax reductions and efforts to shield U.S. industry from foreign competition. Full but gradual economic recovery is the intended result, with all sectors of the economy, including black business, the supposed beneficiaries. But as Edward Gibbon observed in his *Decline and Fall of the Roman Empire*, "in the prosecution of a favorite scheme, the best of men satisfied with the rectitude of their intentions are subject to forget the bounds of moderation."[2] "Staying the course," the slogan of the Republican party during the 1982 midterm elections, apparently meant among other things a relentless determination to remove the federal dollar from as many minority-oriented programs as possible. Consequently, black businesses, historically dependent on both the vagaries of the

U.S. economy and the caprices of public policy rooted deeply in the lingering legacy of slavery and segregation, struggle valiantly to maintain as well as to expand economic opportunity. To steer a successful course through this storm of economic and governmental hardship, black businesses need a reassessment of their past, present and future relationship to the American and global economies. This reassessment revolves around the concepts of ownership, business performance and economic development. This chapter will explore these concepts within the framework of public policy.

BLACK BUSINESS IN A "BLACK ECONOMY"

Black-owned businesses are popularly defined as commercial organizations with at least 51 percent black ownership. Behind this purely numerical definition of ownership lie the agonies and ecstasies, the ambiguities and realities, of black economic, social and political power in the United States. Simply because blacks own 51 percent of a business does not mean that they totally control the business. To some degree they may be dependent on outside financing, whether private or public, or subject to the wishes of creditors. Thus, 51 percent ownership does not ensure control of the credit and capital flowing into the enterprise, the organizational and managerial dynamics of the enterprise or the quality and quantity of goods and services produced by the enterprise. "Ownership" of black business is related to black unemployment, income, occupational status, management skill, human resource deployment and the circulation of money and capital in black communities. Ownership ambiguity resulting from deliberate manipulation by outside economic interests, negative debt-equity ratios in the credit profile of the firm or excessive dependency on government financial assistance for business viability profoundly affects the already regressive "balance of payments" in the black community. This is especially true since at least part of the business receipts will flow out of the black community, and black businesses are the major circuits through which the wealth of the black community circulates.[3]

However, ownership is but one indispensable dimension of business. *Business performance* is business ownership at work and what it accomplishes. What is owned is animated and enhanced by actions and decisions that result in the profitable production of goods and services. How businesses ride the broncos of the business cycle, how they accumulate and deploy capital and how they sense and serve market demand are as critical to their survival as the characteristics of their ownership.[4] The irony of black business is that both ownership and performance have produced economic dependency instead of independence. There are more black business owners, but at the same time they exercise less control over their businesses. There is more public and private technical assistance available, but for a number of reasons there is less business performance.

A PROFILE OF BLACK BUSINESS TRENDS

In 1977 there were 14,731,000 firms in the United States with a net income of more than $4 trillion, an increase of more than 3 million firms since 1969.[5] In 1969, the first year that data on black-owned firms were compiled, the Census Bureau reported 163,073 black-owned firms. By 1972 the number of black-owned firms increased by more than 15 percent to 194,986,[6] and by 1977 the most recent available survey showed that black-owned firms increased by 24 percent to 231,203.[7] The survey reported that the majority of the black-owned firms in 1977 were concentrated in selected services and retail trade as opposed to manufacturing. These two categories of industries comprised 68 percent of all black-owned firms and 61 percent of their gross receipts.[8] The ten industry groups accounting for the largest dollar volume of receipts for black-owned firms in 1977 are described in Table 4.1.

Other key characteristics of black-owned firms in 1977 include:

1. Almost 95 percent of black-owned firms operated as sole proprietorships rather than partnerships or corporations.

2. Most black-owned businesses operated with no full-time paid employees other than the owner (see Table 4.2).

Table 4.1
Ten Largest Major Industry Groups of Black-Owned Firms, in Receipts, 1977

Industry Groups	Number of firms	Receipts (in $ millions)
Automotive dealers and service stations	5,002	1,108
Food stores	10,679	786
Miscellaneous retail	20,880	590
Eating and drinking places	13,008	572
Special trade contractors	17,126	497
Health services	14,560	433
Personal services	35,035	399
Business services	15,461	358
Trucking and warehousing	11,552	353
Wholesale trade - nondurable goods	1,250	333

Source: Bureau of the Census, *1977 Survey of Minority-Owned Business Enterprises, Blacks* (Washington, D.C., 1977), pp. 10–23.

Table 4.2
Number and Gross Receipts of Black-Owned Firms With and Without Paid Employees, 1977

	All Black Firms	With Paid Employees		Without Paid Employees	
		Number	Percent of total	Number	Percent of total
Number	231,203	39,968	17.1	191,235	82.9
Total gross receipts	$8,645,200	$6,396,850		$2,248,350	

Source: Bureau of the Census, *1977 Survey of Minority-Owned Business Enterprises, Blacks* (Washington, D.C., 1977), p. 172.

3. Less than 1 percent (0.3 percent) of all black-owned firms had gross receipts of more than $1 million, with an average of $37,392 in gross receipts.
4. The 231,203 black-owned firms accounted for over $8 million in gross receipts, a mere fraction of the more than $4 trillion generated by American business in the same year.
5. The largest increase in the number of black-owned firms between 1972 and 1977 occurred in the finance, insurance and real estate category (28 percent). The 54 percent in black bank ownership largely accounts for this increase (see Table 4.3).[9]

Table 4.3
Industries Reflecting Greatest Black Increases, 1972–1977

Industry	Number of black firms		Percent change
	1972	1977	
Manufacturing	3,664	4,243	16
Transportation and Public Utilities	21,356	23,061	8
Wholesale Trade	1,708	2,212	30
Retail Trade	53,924	55,428	3
Banking	99	152	54
Finance, Insurance and Real Estate	7,669	9,805	28

Source: Bureau of the Census, *1977 Survey of Minority-Owned Business Enterprises, Blacks* (Washington, D.C., 1977), pp. 10–11.

6. The geographical distribution of black-owned enterprises indicated that the South Atlantic states had the largest number of firms and the states of California, Illinois, Texas, New York and Ohio accounted for more than 30 percent of all black-owned firms in the United States. Like the black population, black-owned firms continued to urbanize. Twenty-six cities had more than 1,000 black-owned enterprises in their jurisdictions in 1977 (see Table 4.4).

7. The top one hundred black industrial firms accounted for some $1.5 billion in sales and employed 17,827 persons. When related to aggregate employment, black-owned firms are labor-intensive without being employment-intensive; that is, black-owned firms employ a tiny portion of the total number of blacks in the work force, but their industries tend to require more labor than automated processes.

8. As Robert Hill points out, "black businesses have been lagging behind the U.S. businesses over the past decade . . . because they have been disproportionately impacted by periodic recessions and soaring interest rates . . . . [T]he devastating ef-

Table 4.4
Major Cities for Black Business Enterprise by Number and Receipts, 1977

Cities with at Least 1,000 Firms	Number of Firms		Receipts	
	Total	With Paid Employees	Total Gross	Average Per Firm
Chicago	7,353	1,511	$665,257	$90,474
New York	11,714	1,323	431,919	36,872
Los Angeles	7,325	1,094	268,446	36,648
Detroit	4,500	979	233,029	51,784
Washington, D.C.	7.339	833	212,750	28,988
Philadelphia	4,418	653	172,273	38,993
Memphis	1,905	403	149,973	78,725
Houston	5,104	862	141,435	27,710
Atlanta	2,244	467	129,012	57,492
Blatimore	3,093	553	122,944	39,749
Cleveland	2,365	403	119,377	50,476
Oakland	1,758	304	89,022	50,638
Dallas	2,353	373	81,048	34,444
St. Louis	1,994	422	75,656	37,942
New Orleans	2,319	395	68,485	29,532
Indianapolis	1,774	322	67,971	38,315
San Francisco	1,547	282	62,451	40,368
Alsip, Ill.	1,066	191	48,585	45,576
Milwaukee	1,207	210	40,995	33,964
East Los Angeles	1,186	172	39,778	33,539
Nashville	1,220	203	37,957	31,112
Kansas City	1,327	230	37,354	28,149
Jacksonville	1,031	276	36,289	35,198
Richmond	1,054	243	35,636	33,810
Columbus	1,358	186	33,709	24,822
Cincinnati	1,200	198	32,701	27,250
Total	79,754	13,138	$3,434,052	$43,058

Source: Bureau of the Census, *1977 Survey of Minority-Owned Business Enterprises, Blacks* (Washington, D.C., 1977), pp. 122–168.

fect of the 1974–75 recession on black businesses is reflected in the sharp declines in the following businesses between 1972 and 1977:

a. The number of auto dealerships and service stations fell by 24%—from 6,597 to 5,002.

b. The number of hotel and other lodging facilities declined by 21%—from 2,196 to 1,733.

c. The number of food and eating establishments fell by 10%—from 26,000 to 24,000.

d. The number of intercity transporting firms fell by 9%—from 8,881 to 8,088." [10]

Hill's data reflect the structural consolidation of some industries into chain and franchise operations, as well as recession-induced reduction. Some black-owned businesses were bought out by incoming hotel, fast-food and other chains. Other reductions, such as in the service station business, reflect realignments by major oil companies during the energy crisis. Conversion of full-service stations to self-service stations and precipitous increases in the operating costs of service stations induced the closing of many black-owned service stations. [11] Finally, the absorption of some black-owned intercity transporting firms by city and county transit systems accounted as much for black business decline in this category as the ravages of an ailing economy. Living at bare margin, struggling against market erosion, unable to adjust to large-scale demographic, technological and regulatory events, some black businesses were consumed by the juggernaut of encroaching majority businesses or sprawling governmental agencies that under the right of eminent domain took over their business sites.

THE DECLINE OF BLACK COMMUNITIES AS EXCLUSIVE MARKETS

This profile of black business points up the changing role of black consumers and workers. For the proper perspective, it is important to recall that in the nineteenth century, following the Civil War, the corporation struggled to become the dominant American economic institution, just as blacks struggled to become individual entrepreneurs or find the wherewithal to form partnerships. As Daniel Boorstin observes,

The corporation had many advantages over the enterprising individual. A creature of the law, it was immortal, and therefore its contracts and leases [and] had a longevity which no natural person could provide . . . . Pieces of ownership, in the form of shares and stocks, could be offered to thousands of small investors, who (as "limited liability" became common) could be confident that they would not be liable for the debts of the company. [12]

Through a myriad of federal, state and local legislative enactments, grants of monopoly, land grants, permits, licenses, loans and favorable judicial opinions, government has always been prominent in the American business success story. Historians agree that the swift and mercurial rise of the U.S. economy to its premier global position was borne on the wings of government.[13] But blacks were excluded from the corporate scene, and those blacks who did enter business had few resources to call on. Historically, however, black businesses, being geographically and racially localized, depended almost exclusively on black patronage and labor for survival. For example,

By 1914, approximately 55 Negro banks had been organized. Most of them were closely connected with [black] fraternal or insurance organizations or churches or both. Most of the banks were short-lived, however, for the reason that its Negro depositors and borrowers did not engage in trade, industry and commerce in sufficient volume to support them satisfactorily.[14]

Black businesses and consumers, workers and institutions, were confined by racial segregation to transact with each other. Blacks were seldom allowed to shop "downtown" at white department stores and haberdashers, to see shows or movies in white theaters or to board at white hotels and inns. Black retail stores, theaters, inns, newspapers and banks served black customers, managed the circulation of the meager black cash flow and thereby became the economic infrastructure of small and large Southern and Northern black communities.

With urbanization, black businesses proliferated in new segregated markets in Chicago, New York, Philadelphia, Washington, D.C., and other cities. Harold Rose observes, "Black business development is essentially contingent upon the territorial expansion of the black population."[15] As the ghetto expanded from the 1950s on, potential for black business expanded, but dispersal of ghetto residents to other urban sites and their diffusion to suburban areas were seldom followed by black business relocation to the new sites. Whether to follow fleeing black customers into new neighborhoods or to savor the safety of remaining in place became a recurring problem for small black businesses.[16] When black businesses did make forays into markets outside black communities, they were met by larger, better financed, more diverse and racially restrictive white businesses. Defended by federal, state and local governments, these businesses enjoyed favorable tax, regulatory and competitive positions vis-à-vis black businesses. Larger white businesses accumulate sufficient land, work force, capital and political influence to greet black business with almost silent indifference. Smaller white businesses thrived on ethnic markets and on networks that overlapped but transcended black communities. Meanwhile, government encouraged black businesses to focus on "community" and "economic development"—a euphemism for concentrating on the black market—while it (the government) became the largest customer in the U.S. economy. As government anchored the position of multinational and large-scale products and systems, black businesses steadily lost traditional black customers to larger white businesses and increasingly to unemployment.

Paradoxically, the civil rights movement and resulting civil rights laws contributed to black business erosion. The laws opened up new positions for blacks in terms of where they could buy and where they could work. As a result, what remained of traditionally black patronage was the residue of black residential segregation and the provision of goods and services that white businesses had not found profitable to deliver to blacks. The civil rights movement of the 1950s and 1960s shattered many barriers to black employment, education, politics and economic advancement, but it also released many black consumers and workers from captive black business markets into the general marketplace.

PUBLIC POLICY AND THE EMERGENCE OF "BLACK CAPITALISM"

It is ironic that public policy objectives of the "Great Society" programs during the John Kennedy and Lyndon Johnson administrations focused on "maximum feasible participation" of the poor in neighborhoods and communities just as blacks began to move into the general marketplace. Manpower development and training, antipoverty community action agencies and "model cities" assumed that black communities would be the citadels of economic development.[17] Interaction between community economic institutions and the larger community was aimed at empowering the community, not just individuals seeking to escape from the community. It is not being argued that attention should not have been paid to economic development within the community, but what is being questioned is whether total emphasis should have been placed on this type of development when the principal economic growth was occurring in other areas.

Public policies for minority businesses between 1964 and 1968 consisted primarily of the 6 x 6 program, designed to assist disadvantaged owners of very small retail and service enterprises, and its successor, the Economic Opportunity Loan (EOL) program authorized under Title IV of the Economic Opportunity Act. Between 1964 and 1966, some 794 6 x 6 loans were approved and minority businesses in five cities received 393 loans. The average loan amount was $4,500. Most loans were awarded to minority businesses "in the community." Between 1966 and 1968, some 7,628 EOL loans were approved, totaling over $80 million. Minorities received about 40 percent of these loans (in both number and dollar amounts).[18] Frequently, political considerations came into play, the concern being primarily to increase the number of black businesses without regard for the performance of the business. Ownership maintenance and expansion were the objectives of these loan policies, not economic performance. Little technical and professional assistance accompanied small black, minority and white businesses.

In contrast, 1968 was a momentous year for black business policy. First Richard Nixon promoted "Black Capitalism" as the anchor of his civil rights policy while campaigning for the presidency. "By early 1968 a handful of prominent individuals and groups of diverse attitudes were beginning to embrace terms like 'compensatory capitalism,' 'green power,' 'minority entrepreneurship,' 'economic self-help,' 'ghetto self-determination,' and 'community economic development.' " [19] To woo political support, Nixon capitalized on these slogans and criticisms of the social-welfare orientation of "Great Society" programs. Second, Project OWN was initiated by the new Small Business Administration (SBA). Project OWN sought to narrow the ownership gap between the proportion of minority business owners and white business owners by stimulating enormous increases in private-sector lending to minority entrepreneurs.[20] Once elected, President Nixon renamed this program Operation Business Mainstream, simplified loan approval procedures, lowered the proportion of equity financing required for these loans and relaxed rules prohibiting loans to finance a change in ownership of a business.[21] The result was increased bank participation in programs for lending to blacks, minorities and whites owning small businesses. Third, amendments to the Small Business Act of 1958 resulted in the development of the SBA's 8(a) Contracting and Business Development Program. Through the 8(a) program, small companies owned by socially and economically disadvantaged persons could obtain federal government contracts. The SBA acted as a prime contractor for selected federal government contracts and then awarded the contracts to small companies in the 8(a) program.[22] "Socially and economically disadvantaged" applicants included blacks, Hispanic Americans, Native Americans and Asian Pacific Americans. Other groups were obliged to demonstrate that they were sufficiently disadvantaged to warrant participation in the program.

The ascent of Richard Nixon to the presidency enveloped these occurrences into fateful twists of economic and political history. Operation Business Mainstream, loans and loan guarantees for minority businesses, Minority Enterprise Small Business Investment Corporations (MESBICs) and the 8(a) program—the progeny of Nixon's "Black Capitalism"—encountered competition for the available dollars from white small business. Between 1970 and 1973, distribution of loans and loan guarantees enhanced white and nonblack minority firms more than black firms. Timothy Bates' survey of approved SBA direct and guaranteed loans in five major cities (see Table 4.5) portrays clearly the dwindling benefit of SBA assistance to black business. Although SBA guaranteed bank loans increased from 396 to 547 during the period 1970 to 1973, loans to black businesses increased a mere 8 percent, loans to other minorities increased 73.3 percent and loans to whites increased 234.3 percent in the same period.[23] Submerged in the generic designation "minority," the reduction of black business participation in loan guarantee programs was less conspicuous. SBA data portrayed 1970 as the year "minorities" enjoyed the largest percentage of federal government loans (see Table 4.6), but the failure to separate black from minority loan beneficiaries conceals the decline of black business participation in the program. The volume of loans to minorities increased until 1973, when

Table 4.5
Number of Approved SBA Direct and Guaranteed Loans in Five Major Cities, by Race of Borrower, 1970–1973

Year	Blacks	Other Minorities	Whites	Total
1970	685	205	201	1,091
1971	697	269	345	1,311
1972	715	345	463	1,523
1973	740	357	672	1,769
Total	2,837	1,176	1,681	5,694
Percent Increase From 1970-1973	8.0	73.3	234.3	62.1

Source: Timothy Bates, "Trends in Government Promotion of Black Entrepreneurship," *Review of Black Political Economy* (Winter 1975), p. 179. Published by permission of Transaction, Inc. from the *Review of Black Political Economy*, Vol. 5, No. 2. Copyright © 1975 by Black Economic Research Center.

it declined for three years and then began to increase again in 1977, reaching a new peak of $470 million in 1980, but black business participation in the loan program had sunk to its lowest point in 1973.[24]

The most novel and perhaps most controversial of the black capitalism programs, the 8(*a*) program, steadily increased its member firms from 1970 to 1982 (see Table 4.7). Unlike the other minority enterprise programs, the 8(*a*) program was designed to enhance business performance by subcontracting government work to minority businesses. Participating firms were to graduate from the program after a specified period of time or as they attained a predetermined volume of business. These firms were eligible to receive a wide range of assistance in management through counseling, seminars and professional guidance.[25] The combination of loans, loan guarantees and subcontracts through the 8(*a*) program diversified federal minority business policy and polarized its participants. As Hispanics and Asians became more politically visible, they implicitly challenged the preeminent position of blacks as the most visible and active minority in the United States. Native Americans, although traditionally caught between the vacillations of separatist and assimilationist federal policies, had also received "protected status" from the federal government. Interminority competition became as solid a reality as minority-white competition. The distribution of meager public policy rewards within the minority designation became as delicate an item of negotiation as formal and informal efforts to mediate between minority and majority businesses.

The internal struggle of competing minorities to prevail as beneficiaries of

Table 4.6
Federal Government Loans to Minority-Owned Businesses, 1970–1980

	1970	1972	1973	1974	1975	1976	1977	1978	1979	1980
Loans to all businesses (unit equals 1,000)	15.1	28.0	33.9	27.5	22.3	26.1	31.8	31.7	30.2	31.7
Minority-owned businesses (unit equals 1,000)	6.3	9.0	9.1	6.9	5.4	5.5	6.2	6.1	5.5	6.0
Percentage of all Businesses	41	32	27	25	24	21	19	19	18	19
Value of total loans ($ millions)	710	1,574	2,196	1,948	1,594	2,071	3,049	3,314	3,407	3,858
Loans to minority-owned businesses ($ millions)	160	258	334	289	229	262	352	402	428	470
Percentage of all loans	23	16	15	15	14	13	12	12	13	12

Source: Unpublished data, U.S. Small Business Administration.

Table 4.7
Number of Firms in the 8(a) Program by Fiscal Years Ending 1968–1982

Fiscal Year	Number
1968	9
1969	33
1970	405
1971	1,095
1972	1,477
1973	1,397
1974	1,336
1975	1,892
1976	1,605
1976A	1,632
1977	1,497
1978	1,634
1979	1,819
1980	2,111
1981	2,276
1982	2,225

Source: Unpublished data, U.S. Small Business Administration.

federal minority business policy paled in significance beside the series of economic and political traumas which gripped the United States between 1973 and 1982. The Arab petroleum embargo of 1973–1974 jolted the American consciousness as to the meaning of economic vulnerability, and the Watergate crisis shocked Americans, disemboweled the office of the President and absorbed the energies of Congress and the courts. In the tumultuous fray, the tiny vessel of black capitalism was cast adrift while the nation stumbled through domestic and international convulsions.[26] The oil crisis became "the energy crisis," boosting fuel prices more than 800 percent in less than eight years, igniting an economic recession that cast thousands out of jobs, closed factories, fueled inflation and overturned a favorable U.S. balance-of-trade posture.[27] Blacks, particularly those with low and fixed incomes, suffered disproportionately from rapidly rising fuel costs and uncertain oil, coal, wood and natural gas supplies.

The relative prosperity in which black capitalism had been born disintegrated into the economic trauma besieging the United States. The regressive interdependency of the black economy and the U.S. economy is now manifested in the disproportionately higher rates of unemployment, poverty, business failure, foreclosure and bankruptcy in black communities. As these failures reverberate through black households, institutions and neighborhoods, and as the fervor that animated the civil rights movement dissipates, even as blacks become more "politically sophisticated," many black businesses must overcome an enfeebling of racial pride as well as challenges to business confidence. Further, blacks must endure eroding support from federal policymakers while transcending dwindling support from black customers and patrons, prepare for more rigorous competition, and perhaps combat, with former "minority" allies, small majority businesses, women-owned businesses and foreign firms[28] as well as with the behemoths that have traditionally dominated the U.S. and global marketplace.

What characteristics of black businesses require retooling, retrofitting and revitalization to confront such a set of challenges? What combination of psychological, financial, managerial, marketing, industrial and human resources is required to increase the chances of black business during the last two decades of the twentieth century? What policy, educational and institutional resources now existing inside and outside the black community can be used to rearm black businesses for these profound challenges? Aside from the tangibles of manpower, money, and materials, what intellectual, intuitive and psychic intangibles are required to sustain and expand black business motivation? What is at stake for blacks, other minorities, whites and the global community in the survival and growth of black business? Working answers to these questions go to the heart of black business development strategies. Beginning with what is known about black businesses, what needs to be known can be ferreted out. The search for existing working models can trigger a technology transfer process to businesses in need of guidance. Where no working model exists, new models must be designed and tested.

STRATEGIC CHARACTERISTICS OF BLACK BUSINESSES

Key characteristics of black businesses are rooted in the relationship of American and Afro-American society. Austerity restrains black consumption, savings, investments, assets and risk-taking, particularly as disposable income—severely battered by unemployment, underemployment, poor consumer habits, taxation and poor household management—declines. Essentials such as housing,[29] fuel,[30] health care,[31] food and education[32] all but destroy discretionary income in most black households. Recreation—records, tapes, stereos, concerts, gambling, movies—takes whatever discretionary income remains and often invades budgets for essentials. The économics of black consumer choice motivate and are motivated by the socio-psychological dynamics of race and class in the United States. Although blacks are no longer captives of black business, black business remains captive to blacks. Recreation-oriented black businesses, both small and large, continue to appeal to black consumers. Motown Records in 1981 was top black business in the nation with sales of $91.7 million. Smaller entertainment firms appeal directly to black, particularly young black, consumers. Conversely, black management consulting firms, more dependent on public policy and a few majority firms than directly on the patronage of black communities, suffer dozens of casualties daily as federal, state and local governments reduce spending and procurement to majority firms with which some black firms co-ventured or subcontracted. Black firms deeply rooted in black fraternal, church or social organizations, particularly insurance companies, credit unions and banks, have fared better.[33]

Therefore, specific business characteristics deserving priority strategic consideration by the makers of public policy and by black business include:

Business liquidity—Cash and accounts receivable minus current liabilities

Business net worth—Total assets minus total liabilities

Cash flow—Net profits plus depreciation

Collateral—Assets pledged as security for loan repayment

Outside new worth—Owner's assets and liabilities that are not related to the business

Labor/capital ratio—Number of business employees divided by fixed assets

Experience—Years of managerial experience of owners and/or senior management

Credit rating—Extent to which recorded credit standing of business is attractive to investors and lendors[34]

Debt/capital ratio—Relation of liquidatable assets to outstanding debt

Labor profile—Number and type of personnel; distribution by occupation, training and skill; relative labor vs. capital intensity of firm

Technological intensity—Degree of computerization, word processing, and automation of production and distribution processes in the firm; degree of dependability of dependence on technology; technology costs

Business specialties—Product focus of the firm; major markets and clients; potential clients

Marketing capability—Marketing behavior of firm; percentage of budget, personnel and level of effort devoted to marketing[35]

Government support—Percentage of capitalization, direct or indirect, supplied by government; percentage of government business; nature, types, levels and duration of government support[36]

Market characteristics—Nature, geography, demography, diversity and behavior of major clients and customers of the firm

Although far from exhaustive and clearly overlapping, these characteristics and their particular configuration within and among black business in various industries constitute a checklist on which a diagnosis of black business needs and performance, resources and potentialities, can be conducted. However, these characteristics are animated only in the subtleties and dynamics of transaction and exchange with black, white, governmental and international parties. Both the absolute and relative *performance* of these businesses, beyond more descriptors of ownership, are suggested only partially by available statistical detail. Thus, in addition to these characteristics of black businesses, we must identify those interactions with the larger economy that relate to the success of black business. These include:

Business retention—The proportion of repeat customers, clients, lenders and investors

Negotiation skill—Internally, the success of labor relations with the firm's employees, both unionized and nonunionized; externally, the ability of firm management to negotiate favorable contract and award terms

Market diversification—The extent to which the firm transacts with blacks, other minorities, whites, government and big and small businesses and thereby reduces dependency on single or narrow markets

Business expansion—The extent to which the firm generates more business as manifested in production, distribution and sales volume; capital expansion; and growth in assets

These four criteria are among those that constitute business success. Internally, the ability to meet these criteria is related to the quality, deployment and productivity of those employed by black businesses. Externally, the ability to meet these criteria determines the marketability, resource acquisition and utilization of black business, both within industries in which black business is active and within industries that attract the aspirations of black business. Thus, to overcome the lack of resources which Welsh and White argue is innate to small business and the stigma of race,[37] four additional strategic issues that face black business must be dealt with: (1) maintenance of public policy support, (2) the need to penetrate key industries, (3) resource utilization and (4) internationalization.

Maintenance of Public Policy Support

Historically, government support has been an indispensable, though meager, stimulant of black business. From the fledgling efforts of the Freedmen's Bank in the 1870s,[38] to the creation of the Division of Negro Economics during World War I,[39] and from "Great Society" economics to Nixonian "Black Capitalism," governnment has sought in vain to compensate for minimal black business transactions with the American corporate sector. The United States is now strewn wiith business casualties, large and small, of every kind and nature. This situation is more pronounced in the older industrial areas of New England and the Midwest and is overrun by cost rather than driven by profit. Thus, much of the business community is seeking a wide variety of public policy supports. Automobile, steel, rubber, electronics, real estate, banking, agriculture and other megaindustries, traditionally stellar examples of American capitalism, now struggle to avoid embarrassing failures. Black businesses associated with the most ailing of these megaindustries reflect worsening declines.

There are several programs—frequently unrelated subsets of other policies and almost always undersubsidized—which have been generated in the last ten years aimed at "small and disadvantaged" "minority," "women-owned" and, less frequently, black-owned businesses. These programs have certain key characteristics:

1. Origins in intensive lobbying by minority interest groups, who were outmaneuvered by larger, better-financed, more conservative interests

2. An association with a curious coalition of liberal Democrats and liberal-to-moderate Republicans in Congress, including vigorous and consistent advocacy by the Congressional Black Caucus[40]

3. Regulatory redirection of the statutory base of these programs, particularly in federal agencies

4. Weak funding and staffing of agencies that provide capital and/or assistance to minority business

5. Poor administrative coordination among federal agencies and agency subunits involved with minority firms

6. Inadequate updating of useful bases on minority business *ownership* and *performance*

7. Policy discontinuity, from each new administration's reorganizing minority business programs in the imasge of its own policy preferences

8. Imbalance in policy emphases on minority business, for example, direct loans vs. loan guarantees, procurement vs. tax incentives, financial vs. technical assistance

9. Minimal policy pressure on majority businesses, both large and small, to transact with minority business, thereby accenting the "minorityness" of public policy

In addition, minority business programs are currently being reorganized and affected by restrictive requirements for participation in the 8(a) program, elimination of direct SBA loans, sharp retrenchment of federal procurement dollars, reduced budgetary and staff support to minority business agencies inside and outside the federal government and tax policies aimed less at small and minority businesses and more at large businesses.[41] The tax side of the Reagan administration's business policy is far less ominous to black business than the expenditure side. Efforts of the administration to reorganize the 8(a) program include a reduction of procurements that the SBA can purchase on behalf of minority business, acceleration of the graduation of participating firms from the program without compensating recruitment of new eligible firms and overall retrenchment of federal effort in agencies most susceptible to involvement through the SBA in the program. Although staff reductions in the Minority Business Development Agnecy (MBDA), a part of the Department of Commerce, have been less severe, sharp reductions in loan and loan guarantees through the SBA threaten the viability of federal support of minority firms.[42]

In addition, financial support for the Minority Resource Center in the Department of Transportation[43] and the Public Works Act of 1977 and its requirement for 10 percent minority business set aside has expired.[44] Offices of Small and Disadvantaged Business Utilization, established in most cabinet-level federal agencies to assist minority procurement efforts, languish from budget cuts. The Office of Minority Economic Impact (OMEI), established by the National Energy Conservation Policy Act of 1978[45] and responsible for brokering more than $400 million of procurements, grants, loans and other financial assistance to minorities,[46] is threatened with budgetary extinction (perhaps along with the Department of Energy, which houses it). The fiscal extinction of these programs simultaneously terminates the troubled history of federal support for black business while impeding industry-specific as well as general efforts to expand minority business opportunities.

The Need to Penetrate Key Industries

Despite substantial dependence on business with government, industry groups still account for the majority of gross receipts of black businesses. Services, retail trade, construction, transportation and communications, finance, real estate, insurance and manufacturing and wholesale trade are the major industry groups in which there is a significant black business presence. However, the pruning of federal support for minority businesses discourages advances in industries in which they are presently least active and which offer the greatest potential. For example, some significant industries, particularly petroleum, synthetic fuels and solar energy, require high capitalization and high-level government support for penetration by small and minority business. Other growth industries include defense work, electronics, computer capability (both hardware and software) and telecommunications. The vast and complex telecommunications industry, including activities ranging from postal service to communications satellites, from mass electronic media to telephones and from computers to CBs, continues to be among the most challenging growth industries. As of 1981, more than one hundred black-owned radio stations, a dozen black-owned television stations and ten black-owned cable television franchises existed, with applications for additional television, cable television and radio stations pending.[47] But as Herbert Wilkins observes,

The recent and rapid development of new communications technologies parallels the development at the turn of the century of American railroads and the electric utilities. These changes have been so rapid and so pervasive . . . that few of us have taken time to consider their cumulative impact on the country or, for that matter, on our individual lives.[48]

Nor has the black business community been able to gauge advances in telecommunications technology. Broadcast pay television (STV), multipoint distribution systems (MDS), low power television, satellite-to-home broadcast television and a plethora of other telecommunications systems and technological innovations have made varied inroads into the national communications infrastructure. Their penetrability by black business is an uncertain as their eventual impact. But beyond the obvious financial and economic implications they hold for blacks, they also represent a formidable image-, value- and language-projecting technology capable of bolstering or destroying black perceptions of whites, white perceptions of blacks and global regard for black aspirations.

These limited examples of desirable industries for penetration by black businesses highlight the problems of understanding the industry, affecting interaction with its influential institutions and individuals, finding capital to pursue the industry and mobilizing public policy support for black business penetration of and expansion in the industry.[49] Although successful black business firms in growth industries provide models for aspiring black firms that should be emulated, the rapid, multidimensional and frequently indiscernible changes in these industries, and the financial and technological contexts in which they operate, require continuous surveillance. This surveillance should be conducted by trade associations, majority and minority universities and business development centers rather than by prospective black businesses preoccupied with daily chores.

Resource Utilization

Policy monitoring and industry penetration require a nose for strategic resources as well as the assistance of black business allies. Stagnation in the economy and insensitivity in the White House cannot overrule the many national and local bastions of black business support that persist. Maintaining advocacy, technical assistance, information and sensitive personnel are the National Business League (NBL), the Opportunity Funding Corporation (OFC), the Booker T. Washington Foundation and less well known national organizations.[50] Howard University, Atlanta University, Alabama A & M, Tuskegee Institute and more than twenty-five other historically black colleges and universities enjoy vibrant business administration enrollments as other disciplines languish. For example, Howard's Small Business Development Center offers regular and substantive courses and training in accounting, procurement, marketing and other business skills for participating small and minority businesses. Joining national and educational resource institutions are smaller but equally resilient regional, state and local black business development centers, clearinghouses and consulting resources. This plethora of external resources combine with the financial, managerial, organizational, marketing and human resources that are animating black business. Beyond these more tangible resources are the intangible but invaluable resources of the legitimacy of the business, the credibility of its products and leadership, the adequacy and reliability of its information and the suppleness of its organizational design.[51]

Failure to employ tangible and intangible resources capable of motivating and enlivening the basic operations of the firm is matched only by failure to secure capitalization to underwrite the cost of new business initiatives. Thus, more and better utilization of outside and inside resources available to black firms precedes the unending search for resources now less likely to be forthcoming from the treasuries of government and the boardrooms of business.[52]

Internationalization

Internationalization of business transactions promises new resources as well as new challenges to black business and assumes several forms relevant to black business development and public policy. Despite chronic global recession, the Third World enjoys unprecedented economic influence. Petroleum, rubber, bauxite, uranium and key agricultural products needed by United States, Europe and Canada have and are increasing the economic bargaining power of the nonwhite world in the postcolonial era. At the same time, the United States' position of economic superiority in the world is yielding to the economic influence of Japan, Europe and the Middle East. Increased penetration of the U.S. market by foreign business is resulting in added competition for small and minority businesses,[53] and nonblack minority U.S. businesses offer increasingly rigorous competition for black businesses. In addition, U.S. multinational corporations continue to expand their overseas markets in search of cheaper labor, land, materials, capital and better profit margins, while continued and often bitter trade skirmishes and wars within and outside the U.S./Atlantic alliance leave a strained trading context in which black business transactions with the former colonies of Europe, as well as with Europe itself, must struggle.[54]

Unprecedented black business activity exists in Africa, Asia, the Middle East and the Caribbean. Even against the adamancy of world recession, the persistence of depressed commodity and tourist markets and the volatility of political systems, a sufficiently strong and durable anchor of black trade secures a modicum of business with Pan-Africa. From this base must come the ventures and forays of black business into markets not only in the Third World but also into the walled markets of Europe and North and South America. These globalized transactions enforce and are enforced by the identity of the black community.

CONCLUSION AND POLICY IMPLICATIONS

Government policies, in their zeal for economic recovery, in their desire to restore the economic position of the United States in the global economy and in their efforts to stimulate black business, raise as many problems for black business as they solve. They have traditionally focused more on increasing the number of black business owners than on improving the business performance of black business owners. Not only is the federal government reducing direct loans and loan guarantees through the Small Business Administration and pursuing new regulations for the 8(*a*) program, but it is also reducing the number of participating minority firms without any direct incentives to private firms to compensate for loss of public sector opportunities.

Eroding government support for black business is coincident with rising energy, labor, real estate and other business costs, greater interminority business competition and serious reduction of the traditional consumer and labor markets of black business. Although the Economic Recovery Act of 1981 offers some relief to black business, it is not sufficient to stimulate black business activity. Thus, public policy strategies must understand the strategic characteristics of black businesses while enhancing the capacity of black business to transact with public, private and international markets as well as with minority markets. A new black business policy must focus on maintaining remaining public policy supports, efforts at penetrating energy, telecommunications, defense and other growing industries, recognizing and mobilizing all tangible and intangible black business resources and developing offensive and defensive capability to transact in an increasingly international business market.

Bold but pragmatic, multidimensional but focused, zealous but clever, this new black business public policy orientation should focus on the global market as well as the neighborhood market, should resolve to advocate as well as advise black business and should never sacrifice the community roots of black businesses as they seek the most from regional, public, private and international business networks. Should present federal policy continue the relentless march away from the comfort of black business support to the chill of indifference, blacks, though beaten and weary from current and past assaults of the economy, should be sufficiently aroused to spend money, political support and other resources to back up the courageous advocates of black business. Only the financial, political and social abandonment of the black community can complete the erosion of the National Business Leagues, the Booker T. Washington Foundations, the Howard Universities and other sources of black business support the federal government has allowed. Like the Congressional Black Caucus in 1982, the network of black sororities and fraternities, historically black educational institutions, professional and occupational organizations, churches, fraternal organizations and ultimately the black consumer must seize the reins of black business survival as insurance against fluctuations of government policy.

NOTES

The author wishes to thank Milton Wilson of Howard University, Reginald Dunn of the Booker T. Washington Foundation, David Rice of the National Business League and Chester Banks for their generous assistance in the preparation of this chapter.

1. See Walter Adams (ed.), *The Structure of American Industry*, 5th ed. (New York: Macmillan, 1977), pp. 5–10.

2. Edward Gibbon, *The Decline and Fall of the Roman Empire* (New York: Dell, 1963), p. 177.

3. See Robert B. Hill, *Economic Policies and Black Progress: Myths and Realities* (Washington, D.C.: National Urban League, 1981), chap. 1.

4. See Paul A. Samuelson, *Economics*, 11th ed. (New York: McGraw-Hill, 1980), chaps. 1 and 2.

5. U.S. Bureau of the Census, *Statistical Abstract of the United States, 1981* (Washington, D.C.: Government Printing Office, 1982), p. 534, table 896.

6. A major flaw in the 1972 survey of black-owned businesses was the exclusion of health and legal firms from the survey. The increase in the number of black-owned firms between 1972 and 1977 is therefore exaggerated.

7. U.S. Bureau of the Census, *1977 Survey of Minority-Owned Business Enterprises (Black)* (Washington, D.C.: Government Printing Office, 1977), p. 5.

8. Ibid. Updating of the 1977 survey is in progress. Once published, these data should be correlated with adjusted 1980 demographic data to relate and interrelate black income, occupations status, educational attainment and other variables with the incidence and status of black business ownership and performance. The impact of sales reductions in the auto, rubber, glass and steel industries, proliferating energy business and other developments reflective of general economic trends are related to the distribution, growth and decline of black-owned businesses.

9. However, the recent economic recession has closed several black banks and savings and loan companies. See William D. Bradford, Alfred E. Osborne and Lewis J. Spellman, "The Efficiency and Profitability of Minority-Controlled Savings and Loan Associations," *Journal of Money, Credit and Banking* 10 (February 1978): 65–74; and Andrew F. Brimmer, "The Black Banks: An Assessment of Performance and Prospects," *Journal of Finance* 26 (May 1971): 379–406.

10. Robert B. Hill, "The Economic Status of Black Americans," *The State of Black America 1981* (New York: National Urban League, 1981), pp. 38–39.

11. For a discussion on this point, see Lenneal J. Henderson, "Energy Policy and Socioeconomic Growth in Low-Income Communities," *Review of Black Political Economy* 8 (Fall 1977): 87–103.

12. Daniel J. Boorstin, *The Americans: The Democratic Experience* (New York: Vintage, 1974), p. 415.

13. See, e.g., Thomas C. Cochran and William Miller, *The Age of Enterprise* (New York: Harper Torchbooks, 1961), pp. 77–81.

14. John Hope Franklin, *From Slavery to Freedom: A History of Negro Americans* (New York: Vintage, 1969), p. 404.

15. Harold M. Rose, *The Black Ghetto: A Spatial Behavioral Perspective* (New York: McGraw-Hill, 1971), p. 76.

16. See Robert T. Ernst and Lawrence Hugg (eds.), *Black America: Geographical Perspectives* (New York: Anchor, 1976).

17. See G. Douglas Pugh and William F. Haddad (eds.), *Black Economic Development* (Englewood Cliffs, N.J.: Prentice-Hall, 1969).

18. On these points, see Timothy Bates, "Trends in Government Promotion of Black Entrepreneurship," *Review of Black Political Economy* 5 (1) (Winter 1975): 176; and "Government as Financial Intermediary for Minority Entrepreneurs: An Evaluation," *Journal of Business* 48 (October 1975): 541–557.

19. Arthur I. Blaustein and Geoffrey Faux, *The Star-Spangled Hustle: The Story of a Nixon Promise* (New York: Doubleday, 1973), p. 12.

20. See U.S. General Accounting Office, *Limited Success of Federally-Financed Mi-*

nority Businesses in Three Cities (Washington, D.C.: Government Printing Office, 1973).

21. Bates, "Trends in Government Promotion of Black Entrepreneurship," p. 179.

22. Small Business Administration (SBA), *Fact Sheet No. 36* (Washington, D.C., June 1982), p. 1.

23. Bates, "Trends in Government Promotion of Black Entrepreneurship," p. 179.

24. See *Black Enterprise*, "The Top 100 Black Businesses," 10th Anniversary Issue (June 1982): 71.

25. SBA, *Fact Sheet No. 36*, p. 2.

26. See Kenneth Knith and Terry Dorsey, "Capital Problems in Minority Business Development: A Critical Analysis," *American Economic Review* 66 (May 1976): 328–331.

27. For detailed discussion of these points, see Lenneal J. Henderson, "Energy, Urban Policy and Socioeconomic Development," *Urban League Review* (Winter 1978): 9.

28. Direct investment by foreign films in the American economy increases. Smaller investors are as critical as large investors. See, e.g., U.S. Department of Commerce, *OPEC Direct Investment in the United States* (Washington, D.C.: Government Printing Office, November 1981).

29. See Wilhelmina A. Leigh, *Housing and Black Affordability* (Washington, D.C.: National Urban League, 1982).

30. See Ellis Cose (ed.), *Energy and Equity: Some Social Concerns* (Washington, D.C.: Joint Center for Political Studies, 1978).

31. See Bernadette P. Chachere, "The Medicaid Program: The Low-Income Health Care Subsidy," *Review of Black Political Economy* 11 (Fall 1980): 80.

32. See Faustine Childress Jones, *The Changing Mood in America: Eroding Commitment* (Washington, D.C.: Howard University Press, 1977).

33. See David Abner, "Negro Life Insurer: An Historical Perspective, 1883–1930," *Asa T. Spaulding Insurance Journal* 1 (1) (1981–1982): 1–2.

34. Most of these variables were developed by Timothy Bates in his study of credit availability for black business. See Timothy Bates, "Financing Black Enterprise," *Journal of Finance* 29 (June 1974): 747–748.

35. See Richard F. America, "What Do You People Want?" *Harvard Business Review* (March/April 1969): 25.

36. See Bates, "Trends in Government Promotion of Black Entrepreneurship." Tax liability is also an essential dimension of government support. Knowledge and utilization of tax laws and opportunities and skillful management of burdensome tax liability depends both on business acumen and on effective accounting support.

37. John A. Welsh and Jerry F. White, "A Small Business Is Not a Little Big Business," *Harvard Business Review* 59 (July/August 1981): 18–32.

38. See Franklin, *From Slavery to Freedom*, p. 314.

39. See Henry P. Guzda, "Labor Department's First Program to Assist Black Workers," *Monthly Labor Review* 105 (June 1982): 39–44.

40. See Marguerite Ross Barnett, "The Congressional Black Caucus: Illusions and Realities of Power," in Michael B. Preston, Lenneal J. Henderson and Paul Puryear (eds.), *The New Black Politics: The Search for Political Power* (New York: Longman, 1982), pp. 28–54.

41. Although implementation of tax reductions scheduled for 1983 and 1984 has faced and continues to face serious congressional opposition, black businesses can benefit from tax reduction and cost recovery provisions, particularly if they pursue research and de-

velopment, construction and more capital-intensive business. Few provisions seem to favor more labor-intensive firms.

42. Isaiah J. Poole, "Black Business: A Negative View of Washington," *Black Enterprise* 12 (June 1982): 57.

43. 49 U.S.C. 1657a (1976 ed.).

44. 91 Stat. 116, sec. 103f2, 1977; see also, Leslie W. Dunbar, "Toward Equality, Toward a More Perfect Union," *The State of Black America—1982* (New York: National Urban League, 1982).

45. Public Law 95–619, 1978.

46. Lenneal J. Henderson, "Energy Policy and Public Administration: A Social Systems Perspective," *Howard Law Journal* 24 (November 1981): 211–233.

47. See "Appendix: Minority-Owned Broadcast Properties," *Journal of Minority Business Finance*, Summer 1980, pp. 38–50.

48. Herbert P. Wilkins, "Technology and Investment in the Communications Industry," ibid., p. 5.

49. See Tyrone Brown, "The Federal Communications Commission and Minority Radio Ownership: Evolving Opportunities," ibid., pp. 23–28.

50. Through a skillfully coordinated and effectively managed "portfolio" system, the Booker T. Washington Foundation has brokered defense awards to more than sixty black firms with an average dollar value of more than $400,000. One firm in the network received a $9.1 million award, another a $4.5 million award. More vigorous efforts are under way at the foundation to expand black business participation in contracting and subcontracting in advanced weapons systems, installation development and management, construction and electronics.

51. See Warren Ilchman and Norman Uphoff, *The Political Economy of Change* (Berkeley: University of California Press, 1971).

52. See Ivan H. Light, *Ethnic Enterprise in America: Business and Welfare Among Chinese, Japanese and Blacks* (Berkeley: University of California Press, 1972).

53. See Joint Center for Political Studies, *Foreign Trade Policy and Black Economic Advancement* (Washington, D.C., May 1980).

54. See Werner Feld, *The European Community in World Affairs: Economic Power and Political Influence* (New York: Alfred, 1976).

5

Huey L. Perry

Black Participation and Representation in National Energy Policy

---

The energy problem is one of the most important public policy issues the United States has faced in the postwar era. Until the Arab oil embargo during the winter of 1973–1974, the United States comfortably depended on foreign oil, much of it from Arab nations in the politically unstable Middle East, to meet increasing proportions of its energy needs. The nation's vulnerability in this regard was dramatically exposed when the Arab-dominated Organization of Petroleum Exporting Countries (OPEC) ordered a halt to the sale of oil to the United States because of the latter's support for Israel in the Arab-Israeli War. This action resulted in widespread inconvenience to Americans, principally in the form of long waits in line to purchase gasoline. For most Americans this was the beginning of "the energy crisis," although technically the nation's energy problem had begun a few years earlier with the decline in domestic production of oil and gas.

The U.S. energy problem was increasingly exacerbated in the postembargo period by a series of OPEC increases in the price of crude oil. In the five-year period between 1972 and 1977, these increases amounted to a quadrupling of the price of OPEC oil. The price increases by OPEC, coupled with declining production of domestic oil and gas, caused the cost of energy in the United States to rise dramatically in the 1970s. Compared with a 46 percent increase in the consumer price index from 1972 through 1977, energy prices over the same period rose about 37 percent in real (constant dollar) terms and about 83 percent in current dollar terms.[1] This increase occurred even though price controls had been in effect for oil and natural gas.[2] Not only was this a very large increase in energy costs, but it was also the first increase in real terms in the cost of energy since the end of World War II.[3]

One consequence of the nation's energy problem has been that energy production and development matters have been thrust more deeply into the public policy arena. In terms of how to address the energy problem, it was widely felt that the federal government should develop a comprehensive approach to energy policy making rather than continue with the disaggregate, incremental style that had historically characterized both federal and state energy policy making.[4] President Jimmy Carter, a strong advocate of the comprehensive approach to energy policy making, set in motion a process designed to produce the blueprint for a comprehensive energy policy. In early 1977 the Carter administration submitted to Congress its National Energy Plan, a comprehensive and complex package of regulatory and tax proposals emphasizing conservation and a shift from oil and natural gas to coal.[5]

Another issue of national importance, which also emerged in the 1970s principally as a progression of the civil rights movement of the 1950s and 1960s, centers on the question of increasing minority input into policy process. The emphasis of the civil rights movement was on legitimizing black participation in the political process primarily as voters. By the turn of the 1970s, owing in no small measure to national government policy, this objective had been realized and blacks were participating in the electoral process in record numbers. Having become recognized as legitimate and active participants in the electoral process, blacks and their supporters shifted their emphasis toward increasing black input into the policy process. The rationale for this emphasis was the desire to participate at a level that would provide greater opportunities to exert more direct and substantive influences on policy outputs. It is now widely accepted that demands by blacks and other minority groups for an increased presence in the policy process are proper and legitimate. In fact, in some instances increased minority participation in the policy process has been made a formal objective, with provisions designed to accomplish this end having been incorporated into legislation and/or administrative regulations.[6] This chapter fuses these two policy-centered goals, resolving the energy problem and increasing minority input into the policy process, by examining the extent of input by blacks in the formulation and administration of national energy policy during the Carter administration.

REVIEW OF THE LITERATURE AND CONCEPTUAL FRAMEWORK

There has been a considerable increase in the amount of scholarly attention being devoted to the subject of energy in recent years. These activities, along with a similar heightening of scholarly interest in the effort to increase minority input in the policy-making process, has resulted in a small but growing body of literature that examines the interface between minorities and energy policy. The major thrust of this corpus has been an attempt to assess the impact of energy policies on blacks, other minority groups and the poor. Lenneal Henderson[7] is one of several energy policy analysts to argue that the current energy policy matrix, which purposely results in rising energy costs, disproportionately puts minorities and other low-income people at a disadvantage because they can least afford to absorb these increased costs.[8]

The impact of energy policy on blacks and other minority groups is an important consideration. Since energy policy is a recent development, questions of how minority and other disadvantaged groups are being affected are not resolved and therefore should continue to be rigorously examined. A related issue, also deserving of careful examination but not yet addressed in the scholarly community, involves the question of how much input blacks and other minority groups have in shaping the nation's developing energy policy. This issue is growing in importance in the policy community, especially among minority legislative and administrative officials, and can be linked to the general question of impact. George Brown, former lieutenant governor of energy-rich Colorado and one of the few minority public officials to express an early interest in energy policy, states the position in operational terms:

Unless we aggressively address national energy policy, and see to it that the . . . administration and Congress consider our interest in this area, we will undoubtedly find that federal solutions will not at all be tailored to our needs and particular problems.[9]

Brown's observation leads to a critical question: Are blacks addressing national energy policy issues and seeing to it that the legislative and executive branches of government consider their interests in formulating and administering energy policy? Vernon Jordan, former executive director of the National Urban League, offers one answer:

Black and poor people have seen their fuel costs rise, their jobs endangered, and their interest ignored. To date, black people and low-income families have been allowed to participate to the extent of bearing the burdens of energy prices. It is time now for these groups to participate in framing the policies as well, so that their interests, their concerns, and their needs may be honored.[10]

Jordan's observation is supported by others. Brown, for example, contends that the Carter administration National Energy Plan was developed "without even a modicum of involvement from the Black community." Brown attributes this to the traditional disinclination of black leaders to be interested in technical subjects such as energy as well as to "insensitivity on . . . the part of the federal government as to the impact of energy choices and energy problems on the minorities in this country."[11] Congressman Mickey Leland, a Texas Democrat and member of the House Energy and Power Subcommittee, also feels that blacks and other minorities have had little input in the formulation and administration of the nation's energy policy.[12]

The assertion that blacks have had little or no input in the formulation and administration of the nation's energy policy has not yet been subjected to empirical examination, either in the academic community or the policy community. This important issue must be empirically analyzed if reliable conclusions are to be drawn. By assessing the character and magnitude of black input into the formulation and administration of national energy policy during the Carter administration, this chapter represents a beginning effort toward filling. this void.

The notion of "input" is central to this chapter's analysis. As employed in this analysis and consistent with its standard usage, the term refers to any communications with government officials designed to influence the decision-making process. Inputs originate from the environment of the political or decision-making system as well as from within the system itself. Examples of the former are the efforts undertaken by interest groups to influence public policy. Examples of the latter are efforts made by government officials to influence other government officials to undertake a certain action or not to undertake a certain action, as the case may be. Three concepts that cover the range of political behavior connoted in the notion of political inputs are *representation, representative bureaucracy*, and *participation*. These concepts are salient to an analysis of input because they form the conceptual underpinnings of the interrelationships that exist between government and political groups in our democratic political system. Their instrumental value to this analysis is that they are the dimensions by which black input in energy policy matters will be assessed.

Representation is an important component of democratic decision-making, especially with regard to input into the policy process by political groups. John Stuart Mill referred to representation as "the first principle of democracy."[13] Hanna Pitkin defines representation as "the making present *in some sense* of something which is nevertheless not present literally or in fact."[14] Pitkin distinguishes between representation as "standing for" others and representation as "acting for" or on the behalf of others.[15] This chapter examines black participation in the formulation of national energy policy for evidence of both forms of representation, although the latter is a more significant source of input.

In terms of black representation in the administrative component of the policy process, the operative concept, derived from the general concept of representation, is representative bureaucracy. Simply put, representative bureaucracy postulates that the administrative apparatus of a political system should reflect the composition of the general population. The primary benefit of representative bureaucracy is presumed to be increased bureaucratic responsiveness to the entire society.[16] Paul Van Riper posits that in addition to increasing responsiveness, representative bureaucracy promotes upward mobility on the part of minorities.[17]

Like Pitkin, Frederick Mosher distinguishes between two forms of representation. Mosher's active and passive forms of representation appear to be the same as Pitkin's "acting for" and "standing for" distinction.[18] Active representation occurs when bureaucrats advocate their constituents' interests, or as James Thompson puts it, when the administrator "presses for the interests and the desires of those whom he or she is presumed to represent."[19] Mosher's passive representation is demographic representation. It refers to the degree to which the socioeconomic backgrounds of administrative personnel reflect those of the general population.

Borrowing from Pitkin's and Mosher's concept of active representation, Lenneal Henderson presents the concept of administrative advocacy in his analysis of the representative role of black administrators. Administrative advocacy, conceptually the same as active representation, occurs when specific actions are taken by an administrator "to pursue or to implement policy references articulated by persons or groups on whose behalf" the administrator acts. Administrative advocacy transcends a concern about the extent to which the number of black administrators reflect the proportion of blacks in the general population. What is more critical, Henderson argues, is whether and to what extent black administrators can and do advocate the interests of blacks.[20]

If representation is the first principle of democracy, as John Stuart Mill declared, then participation is a very close second. This analysis is not concerned with the more basic forms of electoral participation such as voting and campaign activities, although their importance cannot be overlooked. Rather, participation as employed here refers primarily to lobbying activities and participation in congressional hearings.[21] The lobbying activities include contacting individual legislative and administrative officials in order to inform them of policy preferences and goals. The primary asset of these more specialized forms of political participation is that they generally are very good avenues for providing input into the policy process. This chapter examines the extent to which blacks used these participatory forms as sources of input into the energy policy during the Carter administration.

THE RESEARCH DESIGN

The principal research techniques used to collect data for this study were the interview and the survey. Also utilized were content analysis of documentary resources and secondary data analysis. The collection of data was done in four phases, coinciding with the four research techniques used. In the first phase, both telephone and personal interviews were conducted. Telephone interviews were conducted with policy specialists in selected black organizations and with selected legislative and Department of Energy staff and assistants. These were followed by personal interviews with selected House and Senate members active in and presumably influential in energy policy making and selected high-level officials in the Department of Energy. The objective of the telephone interviews was to obtain information on the energy policy–related activities of these black organizations and energy policy developments in Congress and the Department of Energy in relationship to blacks, respectively. The objective of the personal interviews was to obtain the opinions and assessments of some key actors in the energy policy arena regarding the nature and extent of input by blacks into the formulation and administration of national energy policy. A related additional purpose of the interviews—both telephone and personal—was to obtain information on whether black congresspersons had actively participated in energy policy making during the time under study. Attention was focused on the Congressional Black Caucus, the organization of black Democratic members of the House of Representatives. The largest and most visible minority caucus in Congress, the Congressional Black Caucus has identified itself to be a national body that seeks to represent and advance the interests of blacks and other minorities at the national level of government.[22]

In the second phase of data collection, a mail survey was conducted in order to obtain additional and comprehensive information on the extent to which minority organizations provided input into energy policy formulation and administration during the Carter presidency. The questionnaire used in the survey was designed to obtain information on four specific questions: (1) whether these organizations had adopted a position in national energy policy, (2) whether these organizations had participated in congressional hearings on national energy policy, (3) whether these organizations had communicated their position on national energy policy to individual members of Congress active in energy policy making and (4) whether these organizations had communicated their position on national energy policy to high-level officials in the Department of Energy. The questionnaire was sent to thirteen black organizations; eleven responded, making for a very good response rate of 85 percent. These organizations are listed in Table 5.1.

The third phase of data collection, which involved an analysis of documentary resources, consisted of two parts: (1) The published proceedings of hearings of all energy and energy-related congressional committees and subcommittees held between May 1977 and December 1979 were examined for evidence of minority participation. (2) Department of Energy data were examined for purposes of identifying the black composition of its personnel force. The personnel makeup of bureaucracy is important principally because of its considerable capacity to shape policy[23] and to a lesser extent because of its role as a source of employment.[24] This component of the analysis is especially salient because the federal government has committed itself to the policy objective of representative bureaucracy.[25]

The fourth and final phase of the data-gathering process took the form of secondary-data analysis. The guiding objective of this phase of the research, as is standard in academic research, was to cull any additional data, information and insights from the works of others that seemed likely to illuminate the analysis and application of the primary data and in general to contribute to accomplishing the overall purposes of the research. The approach utilized in this phase proved valuable in providing additional information on the energy policy–related activities of black organizations, especially the role of the Congressional Black Caucus in black representation and participation in the drawing up of the National Energy Plan by the team of Carter energy planners in early 1977. Considering the latter, the operationally relevant questions are whether blacks were represented on this planning task force, and if so, what was the extent of their participation.

Table 5.1
Black Organizations Surveyed on Energy Policy Input

Organization	Office Location Surveyed
American Association of Blacks in Energy**	Denver, Co.
*American Association of Minority Enterprise Small Business Investment Corporation**	Washington, D.C.
Center for Urban Environmental Studies**	Washington, D.C.
Joint Center for Political Studies**	Washington, D.C.
*Minorities Organized for Renewable Energy**	Washington, D.C.
National Association for the Advancement of Colored People**	New York City
National Urban Coalition**	Washington, D.C.
National Urban League**	New York City
People United to Save Humanity	Chicago
San Bernardino West Side Community Development Corporation**	San Bernardino, Calif.
Southern Christian Leadership Conference	Atlanta
South End Solar, Inc.**	Albany, N.Y.
*Urban Environmental Conference**	Washington, D.C.

*Although membership in these organizations includes all minorities, they have a strong black focus.
**Organizations responding to the survey.

Implicit in the structure of this analysis is the premise that group input into the national policy process can take several forms: (1) participation in the initial formulation of the policy, (2) participation in relevant public hearings, (3) lobbying members of Congress and (4) lobbying administrative officials. A fifth way a group can participate in the national policy process is by having members of the group gain formal positions in government. Especially relevant are gaining representation in Congress and gaining representation in bureaucratic departments and agencies. Implicit in this observation is the assumption that a group's ability to provide input into the policy process is enhanced if some members of the group hold formal positions or responsibilities in government. This assumption is fully consonant with democratic theories of participation and representation and with the concept of representative bureaucracy, the three conceptual guideposts of this analysis.

RESULTS AND ANALYSIS

The foundation for the national debate over the composition of U.S. energy policy during the Carter administration was laid with the development of the National Energy Plan (NEP) by the small task force of energy planners during the first three months of the new administration. The assessment of black input into the national energy policy process begins at this point. Operationally, the concepts of representation and participation are used to guide the assessment of black input into the development of the NEP.

Black Input into the Development of the National Energy Plan

The team of energy planners which developed the NEP was comprised of fifteen economists, public administrators and lawyers.[26] There were no blacks on this team of planners.[27] In fact, there was not any minority representation on the task force.[28] The lack of black participation in the development of the Carter administration's energy proposals is the principal factor accounting for the impression among some black public officials and interest group leaders that blacks had little or no input into the energy policy process during the Carter presidency.

Black Input into Congressional Energy Policy Making

Three categories of congressional activity are relevant to an overall assessment of the extent of black input into congressional energy policy making: hearings, lobbying and the role of the Congressional Black Caucus. The principal concept used to operationalize input in the hearings and lobbying categories is participation, and in the category examining the role of the Congressional Black Caucus the operational concepts are representation and participation. With respect to hearings and lobbying, interest groups first must develop positions on policy questions before these two participatorial structures can be used as serious avenues of input into the policy process. On this very basic dimension the data from the mail survey show that black organizations fared quite well. Eight of the eleven organizations responding to the survey (73 percent) reported that they had adopted formal positions on national energy issues, and two others reported that they had formulated informal positions on issues of national energy policy. Thus ten of the black organizations responding (91 percent) considered energy policy important enough to develop a formal or informal policy stance. One responding organization reported no formal or informal position on issues of national energy policy.

Hearings

Data from the survey show that five organizations (45 percent) presented testimony at six different congressional hearings. Among those organizations presenting testimony were three major black civil rights organizations—the National Association for the Advancement of Colored People (NAACP), the National Urban League (whose representative presented testimony at two different congressional hearings) and the National Urban Coalition—and one new black organization formed exclusively for the purpose of advancing minority interests in the energy sector—the American Association of Blacks in Energy. The hearings in which these organizations presented testimony included the Senate Oversight Committee for the Nuclear Regulatory Commission, the House Subcommittee on Domestic Monetary Policy, the House Subcommittee on Energy and Power and the Joint Energy Subcommittee.

In an effort to corroborate the above information on participation in congressional energy hearings, the published proceedings of all congressional energy policy hearings held between May 1977 and December 1979 were examined for evidence of participation by black interest groups. Not only did this examination confirm the participation of the black organizations in the indicated congressional hearings, it also revealed that three of these organizations—the NAACP, the National Urban League and the American Association of Blacks in Energy—had presented written testimony to the hearings of several other important energy and energy-related committees and subcommittees. In sum, black organizations actively participated in congressional energy policy hearings.

Lobbying

Ten organizations (91 percent) reported that a member of the organization had presented the organization's position on energy policy to a member of Congress active in energy policy making. It is significant that included in this number are the six organizations that participated in the congressional energy hearings. In addition to presenting their positions on energy policy issues to congressional hearings, these organizations also communicated their positions to selected individual congressional energy policy makers. Equally as significant is the fact that five of the six black organizations which did not present testimony before congressional energy policy hearings did communicate their energy policy positions to selected individual congressional energy policy makers. These data indicate an impressive rate of participation by minority organizations in the lobbying component of the policy process.

The Congressional Black Caucus

The most basic point that can be made in assessing the extent of input by the Congressional Black Caucus in energy policy making is that the seventeen Democratic members of the House who comprised the caucus during the congressional debate on the Carter administration's National Energy Plan automatically enjoyed certain policy-relevant participatory opportunities. In addition to the general policy input opportunities available to all legislators, the Congressional Black Caucus enjoyed additional opportunities to provide input

into congressional energy policy making in the form of three of their members
who sat on an important energy committee and two important energy subcommittees. Probably most important is the caucus member who sat on the forty-
member Ad Hoc Select Committee on Energy,[29] a special committee created
by Speaker of the House Thomas P. "Tip" O'Neill for the exclusive purpose
of guiding the House's deliberations on the NEP in an attempt to ensure its
passage.[30] In the end, this committee was the committee most responsible for
passage of the NEP in the House of Representatives. A second member of the
Congressional Black Caucus sat on the House Subcommittee on Energy and
Power, and a third member sat on the House Subcommittee on Energy and Water
Development.

The formal position of members of the Congressional Black Caucus as members of the House of Representatives, in addition to the formal position of the
three caucus members who sat on the important energy committee and the two
important energy subcommittees, guaranteed *ipso facto* a measure of formal
minority representational and participatory opportunities in the area of congressional energy policy making. This view of representation is fully consistent with
Pitkin's "standing for" representation and Mosher's passive representation.

Members of the Congressional Black Caucus also provided active representation of minority interests during congressional deliberations on the National
Energy Plan. This was done in two ways: (1) members of the caucus themselves presenting testimony at hearings of energy and energy-related committees and subcommittees on which there was no formal minority representation
and (2) publicly criticizing the President when they felt that his proposals were
insensitive to the needs of minorities and other low-income groups. An example of the latter occurred when the caucus criticized President Carter's decision
to decontrol crude oil prices because he did not accept its advice to link decontrol with the passage of a windfall profits tax. Caucus members sought this linkage
in order to provide a source of financial assistance to the poor to help offset the
negative impact of the increased energy costs that would ensue from decontrol.

Although our analysis is principally concerned with an assessment of inputs,
two instances where input by the Congressional Black Caucus resulted in a more
or less direct impact on policy outputs are worthy of mention. One involved
the decontrol policy discussed above. Although President Carter rejected the
advice of the caucus to link decontrol with passage of the windfall profits tax,
he did go along with an alternative caucus proposal to recommend to Congress
an emergency financial assistance plan to help the poor pay fuel bills during the
winter months. The rationale of this plan was to provide financial relief for the
poor until the windfall profits tax could be acted on by Congress. In Congress,
members of the Black Caucus lobbied strongly for passage of this measure and
presented testimony before relevant congressional hearings. Ultimately the bill
was passed and signed into law by President Carter, and it was generally acknowledged that the caucus contributed significantly to the realization of this
policy output.

Another example of influential input by the Congressional Black Caucus involves congressional creation of the Office of Minority Economic Impact (OMEI)[31] within the Department of Energy in 1978. The purpose of the OMEI is to advise the Secretary of the Department of Energy (DOE) on the effects of national energy policies, programs, and regulations on minorities and to recommend policies to increase participation of minority educational institutions and businesses in DOE programs.[32] The two legislators most responsible for OMEI's creation are Congressman Charles B. Rangel (D–New York), a member of the Black Caucus, and Senator Birch Bayh (D–Indiana).[33] Rangel's efforts in this regard were supported by the other members of the caucus. Subsequent input by caucus members in the appropriations process contributed to the office being funded to set up operation.

The above discussion suggests a favorable assessment of the extent of input by the Congressional Black Caucus in congressional energy policy making during the Carter administration. Members of the Congressional Black Caucus publicly and vigorously represented black interests during the national debate on energy policy issues, served on an important energy committee and two important energy subcommittees, testified at energy hearings held by committees and subcommittees on which there was no black representation and at least in a few instances demonstrated the capacity to shape policy outputs directly. In sum, the Congressional Black Caucus was an active and visible component of the interface between black interests and the energy policy process during the Carter administration.

Thus in all three categories of congressional activity, hearings, lobbying and the role of the Congressional Black Caucus, blacks fared quite well in congressional energy policy making during the Carter presidency. Black organizations were active in terms of participation in congressional energy hearings and very active in the lobbying of policy and high-level officials in the Department of Energy. In addition, the Congressional Black Caucus actively represented black interests by participating in several dimensions of the energy policy process. These conclusions are at variance with the view that black organizations and political leaders had little or no input in the formulation and administration of national energy policy during the Carter administration. With respect to the formulative phase of the energy policy process, there was a black presence, which at least in a few instances translated itself into a discernible impact on policy output. Although assessment of the extent of black input in the administrative component of the energy policy process is the subject of the following section, it must be noted at this point that the influential role played by Congressman Rangel, with support from other members of the Congressional Black Caucus, in the creation of the Office of Minority Economic Impact within the Department of Energy, is of obvious relevance to an assessment of black input in the energy bureaucracy. By successfully assuming a lead role in the creation of the OMEI, the Congressional Black Caucus extended its influence into the administrative realm of the energy policy process.

BLACK INPUT IN THE DEPARTMENT OF ENERGY

Two categories are relevant in assessing the extent of black input in the Department of Energy: lobbying and personnel composition. The principal concepts used to operationalize input in these categories are participation and representative bureaucracy.

Lobbying

The survey data showed that black organizations actively communicated their position on energy policy issues to senior DOE officials. Eight of the eleven organizations that responded to the survey (73 percent) said that someone from their organization had presented the organization's position to a high-level official in the Department of Energy. It is significant that the same five minority organizations that presented testimony before congressional energy hearings and lobbied selected congressional energy policy makers are included among these organizations that lobbied high-level DOE officials. Thus 45 percent of the black organizations surveyed were active across a range of political activity in terms of providing input in the energy policy process. That these five organizations, in addition to three others, participated in the lobbying of high-level DOE officials is a telling statistic because it reflects the growing political sophistication of black organizations in recognizing the ability of bureaucratic structures to shape policy outcomes in the contemporary policy process.

Personnel Composition

The concept of representative bureaucracy suggests that black penetration of the bureaucracy is important in terms of making the bureaucracy more accountable to interests of blacks as well as constituting a source of employment. As David Rosenbloom notes, there are several ways of assessing the racial composition of a public bureaucracy.[34] The first step in analyzing available data on black composition of the energy bureaucracy consists of an examination of the data presented in Table 5.2. The data show the number and percentage of employees in the different general schedule (GS) grades for blacks and three other standard census minority groups (Hispanics, Native Americans and Asian Americans). The data reveal a familiar pattern in terms of the racial composition of the federal government's work force.[35] Although blacks constitute a significant portion (9.7 percent) of the total Department of Energy work force (the comparable figure for GS employees only is 10.3 percent), they are heavily concentrated in the lower levels. A comparison of the lowest and highest GS grade groups clearly illustrates this point. Whereas GS 1–4 is 21.4 percent black, GS 16–18 (the policymaking level) is only 3 percent black. The data also collapse all grade groups into two categories, GS 1–8 and GS 9 and above. The

Racial Composition of the U.S. Department of Energy, 1980

Grade Group	Total	Minority Total Number	%	Black Total Number	%	Hispanic Total Number	%	Native American Total Number	%	Asian Total Number	%	All Other Employees Total Number	%
GS1-4	1,588	476	30.0	340	21.4	96	6.0	17	1.1	23	1.4	1,112	70.0
GS5-8	4,559	1,284	28.2	828	18.2	349	7.7	44	1.0	63	1.4	3,275	71.8
GS1-8	6,147	1,760	28.6	1,168	19.0	445	7.2	61	1.0	86	1.4	4,387	71.4
GS9-12	5,010	688	13.7	676	13.5	138	2.8	33	0.7	101	2.0	4,322	86.3
GS13-15	6,198	464	7.5	238	3.8	107	1.7	11	0.2	106	1.7	5,734	92.5
GS16-18*	564	28	5.0	17	3.0	4	0.7	3	0.5	4	0.7	536	95.0
Executive and Statutory 12		3	25.0	2	16.7	1	8.3	0	0.0	0	0.0	9	75.0
GS9-above	11,784	1,183	10.0	673	5.7	250	2.1	47	0.4	213	1.8	10,601	90.0
Total GS	17,931	2,943	16.4	1,841	10.3	695	3.8	108	0.6	317	1.8	14,988	83.6
Wage Board	1,943	193	9.9	86	4.4	52	2.7	49	2.5	6	0.3	1,750	90.1
Total of all classifications	19,874	3,136	15.8	1,927	9.7	747	3.8	157	0.8	305	1.5	16,738	84.2

Source: Unpublished data, U.S. Department of Energy, Equal Opportunity Programs Division.

Note: This Table excludes employees of the Federal Energy Regulatory Commission as well as ungraded experts and consultants and stay-in-school employees.

*This entry should actually read SES, AD and GS16–18.

respective black percentages in these two categories, 19.0 percent and 5.7 percent, also show a clear pattern of significantly less black representation in the higher-grade groups.

Another standard way of assessing the racial composition of a public bureaucracy is to examine the extent to which the racial composition of the bureaucracy reflects that of society as a whole. This is done by computing the ratio of the percentage of racial group members in the bureaucracy to the percentage of the group in the total population. Arithmetically, this ratio, called the index of representation, is obtained from the following operation:

$$\frac{\text{percentage of racial group members in the bureaucracy}}{\text{percentage of racial group members in the total population}}$$

Using this index, a value of 1.0 indicates perfect proportional representation, values less than 1.0 indicate underrepresentation and values greater than 1.0 indicate overrepresentation. Table 5.3 presents the indexes of representation for blacks and the three other minority groups for all pay classifications in 1980. The data show that blacks and Hispanics are underrepresented in the DOE work force, the latter group more so than the former; that Asians are perfectly represented; and that Native Americans are overrepresented, even more so than whites, who comprise the "all others" category. Thus, relative to whites and the other three minority groups, blacks fare next to last in terms of personnel composition of the Department of Energy.

Table 5.3
Racial Representation in the U.S. Department of Energy, 1980

Groups	Percent of all pay classifications*	Percent of total U.S. population, 1970	Index representation
Blacks	9.70	11.70	0.80
Hispanics	3.80	6.50	0.58
Native Americans	0.80	0.62	1.30
Asians	1.50	1.50	1.00
Total	15.80	20.32	0.78
All others	84.20	80.00	1.05

*Source: Data from Table 5.2.

BLACK PARTICIPATION AND REPRESENTATION IN ENERGY POLICY FORMULATION AND ADMINISTRATION: BENEFITS AND BURDENS

The degree of black participation in the formulation and administration of the nation's energy policy had some important implications for the character of national energy policy and the impact of national energy policy on black Americans. Henderson, among others, observes that energy policy strategies generally bear disproportionately heavily on minority and low-income populations because the limited financial resources of these populations make them acutely vulnerable to the rising costs that tend to accompany the energy policies of recent years.[36] The Carter administration energy policies, which remain the central component of the nation's energy policy, definitely fall in that category.

The Carter administration's decontrol policy is a good example of a policy that results in rising energy costs, which in turn results in a disproportionately heavy impact on minority and low-income populations. Because the Carter decontrol policies removed the government price ceilings on crude oil and put in their place a phased-in removal of the ceilings on the various categories of natural gas prices, the costs of both these natural resources have escalated. Because low-income groups have less discretionary income than other income groups, people in this economic stratum, which is disproportionately comprised of blacks and other minorities, are least able to make the adjustment necessary to absorb increased energy costs. It would not be unreasonable to argue that one reason blacks and other low-income groups are further disadvantaged in the distribution of burdens associated with the oil and gas decontrol policies has to do with the absence of black and minority participation in the executive formulation of the National Energy Plan.

But this example is also a tribute to the influence of black participation in policy formulation. While the decontrol policies did result in rising costs, which have a disproportionate impact on minority and other low-income groups, it was the participation of the Congressional Black Caucus which stimulated President Carter to earmark some of the windfall profits tax money to provide financial assistance to the poor to help them bear the increased cost of energy caused by decontrol. Having persuaded the President to do this, the members of the caucus worked hard to get the measure through Congress. The legislative influence of the Congressional Black Caucus manifested itself in the deliberations surrounding the creation of the Office of Minority Economic Impact within the Department of Energy. The caucus, led by Congressman Charles Rangel, played an important role in the authorization and appropriation phases associated with making the OMEI a functioning reality in the executive bureaucracy.

The above consideration suggests that where black participation and interest were present they had a favorable influence on the character of the policy inputs, and where black participation was absent, black interest representation presumably suffered, the outcome being that the policy outputs did not serve black interests well. Thus one might argue that black participation in the energy policy arena distributed some benefits to blacks, while minimizing burdens and the absence of black participation resulted in the distribution of some burdens to the black population. But there appears to be an even larger point that derives from the lack of minority participation in the formulation of the National Energy Plan by the Carter planners, and that point has to do with public perception and policy legitimation. While black interest groups and the Congressional Black Caucus did participate actively in the formulation and administration of national energy policy during the Carter years and did have some influence, the general public perception, which is shared by some black interest group leaders and public officials, is that blacks were without influence in the energy policy arena during the Carter years. This paradox can be attributed greatly to the widely known fact that the National Energy Plan was devised without minority participation. It thus seems that one significant implication of this analysis is that the perception by the public or a group that its opinions were not consulted in the policy formulation phase creates a legitimacy problem for the policy. And it is well documented in the study of political systems and public policies that public perception of a policy as being legitimate is an important ingredient to the overall success of the policy. The Carter administration could have endeared the black community to its energy policy by including black representation on the planning team that formulated the National Energy Plan.

CONCLUSION

The data consulted in this study do not offer an unequivocal answer regarding the extent of black input in the formulation and administration of national energy policy during the Carter presidency. On some dimensions of the policy input process, blacks fared well; on other dimensions blacks fared poorly. Black organizations and political leaders did quite well in the congressional phase of energy policy making. On the three indicators utilized to assess input in that phase of the policy process, black input was rated favorably. Black organizations participated in important congressional energy policy hearings and actively lobbied selected congresspersons active in the area of energy policy. Also, within Congress itself, the Congressional Black Caucus actively participated, and represented black interests, in congressional energy policy making, even to the point of substantively influencing policy outputs at least on a few occasions.

Black input is judged to be null in terms of participation in the initial formulation of national energy policy by the team of Carter energy planners and uneven in the administrative phase of the energy policy process. There was no black representation on the task force of energy planners that formulated the National Energy Plan, the foundation of the nation's energy policy during the Carter years. The assessment of black input in the energy bureaucracy, based on the two indicators utilized, returned a mixed evaluation. On the dimension of lobbying high-level officials in the Department of Energy, black organizations fared well. However, it was found that blacks are poorly represented on the DOE's personnel force, and that is especially the case at the policymaking level. Overall the data seem to suggest that black input into the administrative phase of the national energy policy during the time under study was minimal.

The lack of black participation in the formulation of the National Energy Plan, combined with minimal black representation on the Department of Energy's work force, is primarily accountable for the view held by some black policymakers and interest group leaders that blacks had little or no input in the national energy policy process during the Carter administration. The relevant empirical data do not support that conclusion, however. As this study shows, there was considerable black input in the congressional phase of the energy policy process. What this observation suggests, probably more than anything else, is the important policy-relevant implication to be attached to having blacks in formal governmental positions. The visible presence of the Congressional Black Caucus encouraged, aided and furthered black input in the energy policy process. The lack of such a presence in the Department of Energy, especially in the higher reaches of the bureaucracy, had a general retardative effect regarding black input in that phase of the national energy policy process. Those black policymakers, interest group leaders and academics who have been asserting that blacks have little representation in the Department of Energy will find empirical support in this study. But equally important, these individuals should not generalize the lack of black input in the Department of Energy to apply to the entire national energy policy process. Such a generalization would be at considerable variance with the relevant empirical data.

NOTES

1. Robert S. Pindyck, "The Characteristics of the Demand for Energy," in John C. Sawhill (ed.), *Energy: Conservation and Public Policy* (Englewood Cliffs, N.J.: Prentice-Hall, 1979), p. 23.

2. Until the decision by Congress and the Carter administration to phase in decontrol of oil and natural gas in 1979, controls had been on oil since 1971 and on the well head price of natural gas sold on the interstate market since 1954.

3. In fact, between the end of World War II and the early 1970s the price of energy fell in real terms, owing to technological advances and new discoveries of oil and gas deposits. Between 1950 and 1970 the price of energy in real terms fell by 1.8 percent each year, with the result that in 1970 energy was about 30 percent cheaper in real terms than in 1950. See Pindyck, *Energy*, p. 22.

4. For a brief but thorough description of the highly fragmentized federal administrative energy policy process prior to the creation of the Department of Energy in 1977, see John E. Chubb, *Interest Groups and the Bureaucracy: The Politics of Energy* (Ph.D. diss., University of Minnesota, 1979), pp. 29–30. Congress' approach to energy policy making during this time was also very fragmented. See Charles O. Jones, *An Introduc-*

tion to the Study of Public Policy, 2d ed. (North Scituate, Mass.: Duxbury, 1977); and *Congressional Quarterly Weekly Report*, November 3, 1979, p. 2486. Both the House and the Senate have subsequently undertaken reforms to reduce fragmentation in the area of energy.

5. Michael E. Kraft, "Congress and National Energy Policy: Assessing the Policy-making Process," in Regina S. Axelrod (ed.), *Environment, Energy, Public Policy: Toward a Rational Future* (Lexington, Mass.: D. C. Heath, 1981), p. 40.

6. The antipoverty program of the 1960s and recent policies encouraging the full participation of Native Americans in matters pertaining to Indian land policy provide the best illustration of this trend.

7. Lenneal J. Henderson, "Energy Policy and Socioeconomic Growth in Low-Income Communities," *Review of Black Political Economy* 8 (1) (Fall 1977); "Public Utility Regulations: The Socioeconomic Dimension of Reform," *Review of Black Political Economy* 9 (3) (Spring 1979); and "Energy Policy and Social Equity," in Robert Lawrence (ed.), *New Dimensions to Energy Policy* (Lexington, Mass.: D. C. Heath, 1979).

8. See also Ellis Cose and Milton Morris, *Energy Policy and the Poor* (Washington, D.C.: Joint Center for Political Studies, 1977); Ellis Cose, *Energy and the Urban Crisis and Energy and Equity: Some Social Concerns* (Washington, D.C.: Joint Center for Political Studies, 1978); and John M. Brazzel and Leon J. Hunter, "Trends in Energy Expenditures by Black Households," *Review of Black Political Economy* 9 (3) (Spring 1979). This point is also made by several observers in Rocky Mountain Region State Advisory Committee to the U.S. Commission on Civil Rights, *Energy Resource Development: Implications for Women and Minorities in the Intermountain West* (Washington, D.C.: Government Printing Office, 1979); and by Eunice S. Grier, *Colder . . . Darker: The Energy Crisis and Low Income Americans—An Analysis of Impact and Options* (Washington, D.C.: Community Services Administration, 1977).

9. George L. Brown, "Invisible Again: Blacks and the Energy Crisis," *Social Policy* 7 (4) (January/February 1977): 40.

10. Quoted in Richard Pollock, "Black America Speaks Out on Energy," *Critical Mass Journal* 3 (12) (March 1978): 13.

11. Brown, "Invisible Again," p. 39.

12. Personal interview, August 21, 1980.

13. John Stuart Mill, *Utilitarianism, Liberty and Representative Government* (London: J. M. Dent, 1974), p. 260.

14. Hanna F. Pitkin, *The Concept of Representation* (Berkeley: University of California Press, 1967), pp. 8–9. An analysis that reviews pluralist theory using the National Energy Plan as a test case is David Howard Davis, "Pluralism and Energy: Carter's National Energy Plan," in Lawrence, *New Dimensions*.

15. Pitkin in *The Concept of Representation* discusses this at length in chapters 4, 5 and 6.

16. For a brief but excellent discussion of this point, see Kenneth John Meier, "Representative Bureaucracy: An Empirical Analysis," *American Political Science Review* 69 (2) (June 1975): 527–528. For a comprehensive delineation of the meanings and assumptions of the representative bureaucracy concept as distilled from a review of the literature, see Samuel Krislov, *The Negro in Federal Employment: The Quest for Equal Opportunity* (Minneapolis: University of Minnesota Press, 1976), p. 64.

17. Paul P. Van Riper, *History of the United States Civil Service* (White Plains, N.Y.: Row Peterson, 1958).

18. Frederick C. Mosher, *Democracy and the Public Service* (New York: Oxford University Press, 1968), pp. 12–13.

19. James Thompson, *Organizations in Action* (New York: McGraw-Hill, 1967).

20. Lenneal J. Henderson, "Administrative Advocacy and Black Urban Administrators," *Annals of the American Academy of Political and Social Sciences* 439 (September 1978): 71. Henderson presents an expanded discussion of administrative advocacy in *Administrative Advocacy: Black Administrators in Urban Bureaucracy* (Palo Alto, Calif.: R & E Research Associates. 1979), chap. 2.

21. For an excellent discussion of the functions of public hearings in the policy process, see Thomas A. Heberlein, "Some Observations on Alternative Mechanisms for Public Involvement: The Hearing, Public Opinion Poll, the Workshop and Quasi-Experiment," in Albert E. Utton, W. R. Sewell and Timothy O'Riordan (eds.), *Natural Resources for a Democratic Society: Public Participation in Decision Making* (Boulder, Colo.: Westview, 1976), pp. 199–204.

22. The self-described purpose of the Congressional Black Caucus is to "introduce and press for legislative, administrative and judicial remedies that would benefit black and other similarly situated people throughout the United States." Quoted in Bruce W. Robeck, "The Congressional Black Caucus and Black Representation," unpublished manuscript, Texas A & M University.

23. This point has become well established in the public administration literature. See, e.g., Wallace S. Sayre, "Introduction: Dilemmas and Prospects of the Federal Government Service," in Wallace S. Sayre (ed.), *The Federal Government Service* (Englewood Cliffs, N.J.: Prentice-Hall, 1965), p. 2; and David Rosenbloom, *Federal Service and the Constitution: The Development of the Public Employment Relationship* (Ithaca, N.Y.: Cornell University Press, 1971), pp. 12–13. For a comprehensive discussion of this point, including a review of the literature, see Harry Kranz, *A More Representative Bureaucracy: The Adequacy and Desirability of Minority and Female Population Parity in Public Employment* (Ph.D. diss., American University, 1974), pp. 99–118.

24. David H. Rosenbloom and Douglas Kinnard, "Bureaucratic Representation and Bureaucrats' Behavior: An Exploratory Analysis," *Midwest Review of Public Administration* 11 (1) (March 1977): 36.

25. See David H. Rosenbloom, "The Civil Service Commission's Decision to Authorize the Use of Goals and Timetables in the Federal Equal Employment Opportunity Program," *Western Political Quarterly* 26 (2) (June 1973): 236–251; and "Implementing Equal Employment Opportunity Goals and Timetables in the Federal Service," *Midwest Review of Public Administration* 9 (2–3) (April/July 1975): 107–120.

26. Kraft, "Congress and National Energy Policy," p. 40.

27. Brown, "Invisible Again," p. 39.

28. *New York Times*, April 10, 1977.

29. Congressional Black Caucus Press Release, April 12, 1979.

30. There are several good descriptions of the function of this committee in the energy policy literature. Two of the best are Charles O. Jones, "Congress and the Making of Energy Policy," in Lawrence, *New Dimensions*, 168–172; and Kraft, "Congress and National Energy Policy," pp. 42–44.

31. The Office of Minority Economic Impact was established pursuant to Section 641 (Title VI, Part 3) of the National Energy Conservation Policy Act (Public Law 95–619, dated November 9, 1978). Department of Energy document, "Office of Minority Economic Impact (OMEI)."

32. Ibid.

33. Personal interviews with Louis Moret, director of the Office of Minority Economic Impact, Department of Energy, August 20, 1980, and with Marion Bowden, former director of the Equal Opportunity Office, Department of Energy, August 20, 1980.

34. The following discussion of the statistical techniques employed in this chapter borrows heavily from David H. Rosenbloom, *Federal Equal Employment Opportunity: Politics and Public Personnel Administration* (New York: Praeger, 1977), pp. 5–11 and 28n.

35. See ibid., pp. 5–11.

36. Henderson, "Energy Policy and Socioeconomic Growth in Low Income Communities," "Public Utility Regulations: The Socioeconomic Dimension of Reform," and "Energy Policy and Social Equity."

The Influence of Military Policy on Black Men

INTRODUCTION

Today as never before, blacks are serving their nation in uniform. At the end of 1981 almost one out of every five black males born between 1957 and 1962 had entered military service.[1] The armed forces offers its soldiers an uncommon blend of benefits and burdens. First, as the nation's largest employer and trainer it supplies much-needed jobs. The military also prepares men to compete in the civilian labor market. Research has shown that black veterans score higher than black nonveterans on measures of labor market success.[2] Also, in the field of race relations the military is considered a progressive institution.[3] Yet service in the armed forces brings with it risks to life and limb. For this reason, special attention should be given to norms of fairness and equity when evaluating armed forces policy.

The military is unlike other governmental agencies in that it creates a microcosm of larger society. The armed forces has separate health, housing and criminal justice systems. In addition, both in the United States and abroad, members of the armed forces segregate themselves from the larger society by wearing uniforms and living in military installations.

Most policy research explores outputs. For example, when studying blacks and health policy one might compare a health output measure such as infant mortality. The armed forces is unique in that its output, "defense," is shared equally by all regardless of race. Hence, this chapter will focus on how military policy affects black men who serve. Specifically, the chapter will examine the military recruitment process and blacks and the effects of such internal policies as promotion and occupational assignment on black servicemen.[4]

HISTORICAL SETTING

Revolution to Korea

Blacks have served ably and with honor in each of America's conflicts.[5] During the American Revolution, however, a pattern of sanctioned institutional racism was established, and it remained until the Korean War.[6] Prior to and during World War II the military was strictly segregated and employed racial quotas to limit black participation.[7] In addition, blacks were usually excluded from such benefits of military service as officer status and skilled occupations. Instead, they were often relegated to kitchen/servant work, backbreaking labor or, when needed, combat. Further, their effectiveness, ability and patriotism were often questioned.

Shortly before World War II, segregationist policies began to change slowly. The growing political power of Northern blacks made President Franklin D. Roosevelt sensitive to the demands of their leadership. By pressuring chief executives and monitoring policy implementation, the black press also helped initiate change.[8]

During the transition process (1940–1955) the military bureaucracy fought integration through the twin dictates of tradition and efficiency. Those who favored the status quo argued that neither military mission nor efficiency was served by mixing the races. The military was not and never could be an institution of social reform. They maintained that military policies should mirror local tradition, usually Southern local tradition. Poor performance among the all-black divisions of World War II was used as evidence to support segregation. Reformers, on the other hand, maintained that segregation was inefficient. The dual facilities of segregation created logistic problems and increased expenses. They believed that the poor performance of black divisions was caused by segregation and that blacks generally entered the military with an inferior education. As a result, a large proportion of blacks were clustered at the bottom end of the achievement scale. Whites who scored poorly on aptitude tests were scattered evenly throughout the numerous white units. These men were absorbed and had little influence on military effectiveness. In black divisions, performance was affected because the relatively few black divisions were unable to absorb the large numbers of men who had low scores on military aptitude tests. At the same time the limited availability of challenging positions wasted superior black talent. The reformers also argued that segregation hurt black morale and thus hurt efficiency.[9]

Ironically, proof of the success of integration existed. Toward the close of World War II, (summer and fall of 1944) in Germany, blacks were given the opportunity to serve alongside whites. The army carefully reviewed this experiment (over 3,500 white officers and enlisted men received questionnaires).[10] The results of the survey showed that most whites got along "very well" with blacks. "Nearly all of the officers questioned admitted camaraderie between whites and blacks was far better than expected . . . . Not a single [enlisted man] stated that [he] developed a less favorable attitude [toward blacks]."[11] As was often the case, the results did not reach key decision makers. Rather, they were channeled into bureaucratic limbo.

President Harry Truman is justly credited with eliminating segregation within the military (Executive Order 9981). This order declared "equality of treatment and opportunity for all persons in the armed services without regard to race, color, religion or national origin."[12] But the military was slow to implement the order. For example, at the dawn of the Korean War the Twenty-fourth Infantry Division remained all black.[13] The military finally integrated for pragmatic reasons. Shortages of whites during the Korean War made black replacements a necessity. Blacks and whites fought well together, proving that those who pushed for integration were correct.[14] This has been referred to as the "unbunching" of black troops.[15]

Throughout the 1940s and 1950s, when the military was inching toward integration, blacks were confronted with inconsistent or illogical bureaucratic blindspots. For example, during World War II officers from the South were often assigned to black units because Southern officers were believed to be "generally more competent to exercise command over Negroes."[16] Not only was this policy bad for black morale, but the officers resented being placed in dead-end commands. The case of black officers is another example. Top officials believed that whites should not take orders from blacks,[17] so the number and responsibilities of black officers were severely limited. In another instance, after the Navy began full integration of the general services it continued to employ a fully black or brown "Steward's Branch." Somehow policymakers failed to understand that true integration moved both ways.[18]

After Korea, the military quickly desegregated and became a recognized leader in racial reform among institutions. It even stepped outside traditional boundaries and tried to alter local civilian customs. For example, the Department of Defense took steps to topple segregationist education, housing and entertainment policies of communities located near military bases.[19] Army posts at this time have been described as "islands of integration in a sea of Jim Crow."[20]

Vietnam to the All-Volunteer Force

As the Vietnam conflict began to unfold, the military was recognized as one of the most progressive institutions in the United States. For example, after a 1966 visit to Vietnam, Whitney Young, Jr., declared, "In this war there is a degree of integration among black and white Americans far exceeding that of any other war in our history as well as any other time or place in our domestic life."[21] By the war's end, however, the picture had changed radically. Racial strife was surfacing.[22] Blacks were voluntarily resegregated during off-duty hours.[23] They also questioned the Communist threat,[24] showed a new "sense of racial pride and solidarity" and expressed anger with "fighting and dying for a racist America."[25]

This change occurred in part because the civil rights movement within the

United States helped create a new militant black soldier.[26] Further, Vietnam
was a prolonged, unpopular war. Much of the unrest, however, occurred because blacks felt that military policy exposed them to greater risks.[27]

Subsequent research has confirmed that blacks bore a disproportionate burden. The baby boom provided the military planners of the Vietnam era with a
manpower surplus.[28] To deal with this, the predominantly white Selective Service devised a system that excluded men at both ends of the socioeconomic
scale.[29] College students were deferred, and significant numbers of low-income
men failed to meet minimum mental requirements. Approximately 30 percent
of both whites and blacks entered the military,[30] but whites tended to enlist,
and this gave them some occupational choice as well as opportunities for technical training. Blacks were more likely to be drafted. The draft is unlike most
policy tools. It eliminates choice and requires those selected to risk life and
limb. Clearly, it is essential to formulate and implement draft policy in an equitable manner.

The draft failed to achieve equity. And healthy black high school graduates
were among the most draft vulnerable.[31] In addition, draftees were more likely
to enter the combat arms of military service. Paradoxically, past generations of
black soldiers had fought for the right to bear arms. Years later, during Vietnam, their sons were disproportionately fighting and dying.[32] Finally, there is
evidence that the draft was used as a "weapon to intimidate and imprison civil
rights leaders."[33]

During the 1960s the United States also fought a "war on poverty." The
military was criticized because large numbers of disadvantaged men were unable to meet minimum entrance requirements. The ineligibility rate was particularly high among blacks. In some Southern states, over 70 percent of all blacks
were rejected.[34] Hence, these men were denied the benefits of military service,
such as steady employment and technical training.[35]

In 1966 the armed forces joined the nation's "war on poverty" with Project
100,000.[36] Under this program, men who were formerly unacceptable entered
the military. As often happens in the policy implementation process, however,
there was a wide gap between policy intention and implementation. A disproportionate number received little transferable training. Instead, they entered the
combat arms of the military. Approximately 40 percent of the "new standards"
men were black.[37]

THE ALL-VOLUNTEER FORCE

President Richard Nixon compaigned on a promise to end the draft and received broad-based support. Liberals, antiwar activists and many conservatives
all held strong antidraft positions. However, critics of a volunteer system argued that the draft would be replaced by "economic conscription," which would
draw heavily from the disadvantaged and minorities.[38] But, the President's
Commission on the All-Volunteer Force dismissed this concern, arguing that
"the composition of the military will not be fundamentally changed by the end

of conscription." [39] This prediction proved to be wrong. Throughout its brief history (1973 to the present), the All-Volunteer Force has drawn heavily from minorities, particularly blacks. The Army has attracted more blacks than any other branch; in 1981 one-third of all Army soldiers were black. [40] Overall, close to 20 percent of all active duty personnel are black. [41]

The large concentration of blacks in the military has been a continuing and controversial issue. A separate but related issue is the quality of recruits. [42] The representation debate is remarkably varied. Some scholars have argued that a nonrepresentative force is inconsistent with democracy. [43] There is also speculation about lasting institutional change. They express apprehension over a possible "tipping" or "threshold effect." The "tipping" hypothesis maintains that as black participation grows, whites will be reluctant to join a "black" organization. There exists a threshold, or point of no return, where the Army will become all black. [44] A "Black Army" might experience withdrawal of public support and present national security problems. Charles Moskos is concerned about the prospect of the military being labeled a minority institution. Traditionally, minorities have used the military as a bridge that facilitated successful transition to the civilian labor market, [45] but as a "black" organization, the armed forces would lose its ability to aid in the transition. [46]

Some military manpower scholars maintain that the representation issue is more aptly described as nonparticipation among middle-class whites. The military is attracting the best of the blacks. For example, both parental education and occupation of black soldiers is higher than that of employed black civilians. [47] This phenomenon is particularly evident in the Army. Moskos points out:

Today's Army enlisted ranks are the only major arena in American society where black educational levels surpass those of whites, and by a significant degree. Whereas the black soldier seems fairly representative of the black community in terms of education and social background, white entrants in the all-volunteer Army have been coming from the least educated sectors of the community. The Army has been attracting . . . an unrepresentative segment of white youth, who are more uncharacteristic of the broader social mix than are our minority soldiers. [48]

A. J. Schexnider and John Butler, two prominent black scholars, suggest that the representation issue is nothing more than the age-old quota question in new clothes. They note that this is the first time a volunteer system has not had quotas to moderate black participation. [49] They also discuss the unspoken fear that a "Black Army" would turn on white society or that the black soldier would put race over nation and be unreliable in a conflict with Africa. [50]

The Cause of Disproportionate Black Participation

There are several reasons that the racial composition of the armed forces does not reflect that of society as a whole. First, white enlistment is more heavily draft-motivated, and a key white enlistment incentive was removed with the end of the draft.[51] Second, market signals suggest greater black participation. Relatively high levels of unemployment and low civilian wages attract young blacks to the military.[52] The armed forces also offers job security. Further, John White and James Hosek estimate that black average military pay was 106 percent of civilian pay. In the critical eighteen-to-twenty-year-old age-group they found military pay to be 132 percent of civilian pay. For whites, on the other hand, military wages average 86 percent of civilian pay.[53]

Aside from the market forces, demographic trends suggest that black military participation would grow in the 1970s and 1980s. The proportion of blacks ages seventeen to twenty-one is greater than the percentage of blacks in the population. In addition, today's black youth scores higher on military achievement tests and is more likely to be a high school graduate than in years past.[54] Finally, blacks are attracted to the military because it has a reputation and tradition of being a progressive institution. It should be noted that black participation may have peaked. For example, in 1979 the proportion of new black Army entrants was at an all-time high (36.7 percent). By 1981 this proportion had dropped to 27.4 percent.[55] An increase in entry-level pay, increased benefits, intensified suburban recruiting and the recession are credited with the change.[56]

Inside the Institution

The military has long recognized the importance of racial harmony. Educational programs on race relations are well developed. For example, a Defense Race Relations Institute was conducted to train instructors in race relations and to develop curricula, conduct research and perform program evaluations.[57] John Butler maintains that the race relations programs of the Army are "the greatest effort of any institution to deal with the race problem."[58] Despite this effort, it is difficult to assess race relations in the armed forces accurately. First, race relations are hard to measure and subject to quick change, and society at large can influence attitudes. Studies have found race relations in the military to be generally positive, but tension tends to be high in units that are predominantly black.[59] One source of racial tension stems from the previous lack of contact new enlistees have had with individuals of other races. James Fallows characterizes the situation as country whites meeting city blacks.[60] An increase in Ku Klux Klan types of activities is attributed to the background disparities.[61] All in all, however, military personnel of either race view themselves primarily as soldiers or members of a particular branch of the service, not as whites or blacks.[62]

Inside the institution blacks and whites differ in their ability to reap its benefits. First, blacks are less likely to meet the standards of the armed forces. Fewer than half the blacks who attempt to enlist qualify.[63] Once accepted, blacks are disproportionately clustered in combat arms and are thus more apt to be among the casualties of war. In addition, skills acquired in combat specialities are the hardest to translate to civilian skills.[64] This may be particularly disillusioning to black youths, most of whom enter to "better themselves in life" or get training for civilian jobs.[65] Moskos criticizes early All-Volunteer Force policies, maintaining that these policies actually accentuate the tracking of poor and minority youths into the combat arms of the military.[66]

Blacks are also not evenly distributed across occupational categories. They are more likely to serve in nontechnical jobs, where advancement is slow and training limited.[67] Performance on entry exams is used as the basis for occupational assignment, and blacks are apt to do relatively poorly on these tests.

Another problem that plagues black soldiers is their slower promotion rate. Some scholars claim that whites are promoted more quickly than blacks because they do better on such universalistic criteria as education and testing.[68] Butler tested this hypothesis using the Army's entire 1973 enlisted force. He controlled for such criteria as achievement exam scores, occupation and education and found that black promotions lagged behind promotions of comparable whites (see Table 6.1). For example, blacks who score in the highest cate-

Table 6.1
Mean Months in Army to Make Enlisted Grades E4, E5-E6, E7-E9, by Race and Selected Controls

Grade	TOTAL ARMY Black	White
E4	19 (18,673)	15 (107,949)
E5-E6	68 (30,046)	59 (112,212)
E7-E9	173 (11,152)	169 (47,179)

	SELECTED CONTROLS					
	High AFQT [a]		High Education		Technical	
Grade	Black	White	Black	White	Black	White
E4	23 (1,657)	14 (44,368)	15 (2,199)	12 (18,695)	17 (5,388)	14 (36,047)
E5-E6	93 (7,096)	62 (52,164)	56 (2,742)	41 (15,069)	66 (9,735)	56 (45,946)
E7-E9	181 (5,311)	173 (30,448)	173 (1,477)	173 (6,120)	165 (4,033)	165 (18,756)

Source: Data derived from John S. Butler, "Inequality in the Military: An Examination of Promotion Time for Black and White Enlisted Men," *American Sociological Review* 41 (October 1976): 810–818.

[a] Armed Forces Qualification Test.

gory of the Army's standardized achievement test (AFQT) take over two and a half years longer to be promoted to the rank of E5 or E6. He also found that blacks in technical occupational specialities are, on average, promoted to E5 or E6 ten months later than similar whites. He concludes: "The black enlisted man in the U.S. Army is subject to inequality which is not the result of failure to meet universalistic criteria, i.e., indirect impersonal institutions, but rather a result of the direct racist actions of real-life people."[69]

There is a serious underrepresentation of black officers in all four branches. Only 4.9 percent of all male officers are black (see Table 6.2). Although the Army's enlisted personnel are almost one-third black, only 7 percent of its male officer corps is black. The most serious underrepresentation is in the Navy (2.6 percent black male). In addition, black officers are found most often in such non-mainstream jobs as supply, procurement and administration.[70] It should be noted that the proportion of officers is roughly equivalent to that of black college graduates in the relevant age category. Further, the percentage of blacks in the officer corps has risen steadily. And civilian competition has made recruitment of qualified blacks difficult.[71]

Blacks do not fare well within the armed forces criminal justice system. The most obvious place is the area of serious crimes. Between 1977 and 1979, over 51 percent of the military prison population was black.[72] Even though the proportion of blacks in the military prison system is less than that of civilian society, the high proportion of blacks in prison is surprising in light of the tighter screens that are applied to blacks as opposed to whites.[73] There could be many reasons for this disparity. Within the armed forces, officers have great discretion in initiating corrective action. Only 4.9 percent of male officers are black. Further, blacks are underrepresented within the entire criminal justice system. In the Army, for example, blacks made up only 4 percent of the lawyers, 13 percent of the police officers and 2 percent of the judges during 1978.[74]

CONCLUSIONS AND POLICY IMPLICATIONS

Perhaps more than any policy change of the 1970s, the move from a draft to an all-volunteer system has touched the lives of black men. Without the draft to stimulate white enlistment or quotas to moderate black enlistment, blacks have entered the armed forces in unparalleled numbers. The effect of these men on military institutions and the effect of the military on the black family, lifestyle and culture will take decades to assess. In addition, those who eventually enter military service are among the black community's best and brightest.[75]

Some fear that if this trend continues the military's enlisted force will be so black that whites will no longer enter. A closer look suggests that concerns over a "Black Army" are premature. The lifting of the draft did lead to an overall increase in black participation, but minority participation also depends on larger economic cycles. For example, during downswings (such as the recession of the early 1980s) whites find military life more attractive. Increased competition

Table 6.2
Black Males as a Percentage of Officers Assigned to Major Occupational Categories, by Service, September 1981

Occupational Category[a]	Army	Navy	Marine Corps	Air Force	All Services
General Officers and executives	5.0	1.1	0.2	1.9	1.5
Technical Operations Officers	5.2	2.4	2.6	2.6	3.4
Intelligence Officers	4.4	1.6	3.0	3.4	3.5
Engineering and Maintenance Officers	9.3	2.6	7.0	4.8	5.7
Scientists and Professionals	6.0	2.6	5.0	4.3	4.2
Medical Officers	5.3	2.4	b	3.4	4.0
Administrators	9.4	2.5	7.6	8.2	6.8
Supply Procurement and Allied Officers	11.8	3.6	8.7	7.9	7.7
Black Officers as Percentage of all Officers	7.2	2.6	4.0	4.2	4.9

Source: Based on data from Defense Manpower Center.

[a] Approximately 25 percent of all Army officers and 12 percent of all Navy officers could not be identified by major occupational category.
[b] The Navy provides the Marine Corps with medical support.

leads to fewer minority soldiers. On the other hand, upswings seem to provide more civilian jobs for whites and open military slots for blacks. The military is not designed to be an employer of last resort, but it does seem to take on that roll. In doing so, it masks the problem that the civilian labor market has absorbing young semi-skilled blacks. Policymakers should be aware of this process. Ironically, the shortage of black officers may be reduced by economic downturns. During the 1970s many potential black officers found attractive civilian positions. As the economy weakens, black college graduates view a career in the military more positively.

The military has been characterized as "an institution that has gone further than any other to attack racism."[76] Nevertheless, when evaluating its policies using equity norms, it falls short. Compared with whites, blacks are promoted more slowly and receive poor occupational and training assignments. Also, the proportion of blacks in the officer corps and criminal justice system is out of balance.

NOTES

1. Martin Binkin and Mark Etelberg with Alvin Schexnider and Marvin Smith, *Blacks and the Military* (Washington, D.C.: The Brookings Institution, 1982), p. 65.

2. H. L. Browning, S. C. Lopreato and D. L. Poston, Jr., "Income and Veteran Status: Variations Among Mexican Americans, Blacks and Anglos." *American Sociological Review* 38 (February 1973): 73–85.

3. John S. Butler, *Inequality in the Military: The Black Experience* (Saratoga, Calif.: Century Twenty One, 1980), p. 35.

4. This chapter limits itself to an examination of black men and the military. For much of our history, women were ineligible to serve or made up less than 2 percent of the force. While women currently make up a larger component of our military, data on black women is limited.

5. See, e.g., Jack D. Foner, *Blacks and the Military in American History: A New Perspective* (New York: Praeger, 1974); and Marvin Fletcher, *The Black Soldier and Officer in the United States Army, 1881–1917* (Columbia: University of Missouri Press, 1974).

6. Butler, *Inequality in the Military*, pp. 19–22.

7. Alvin J. Schexnider and John S. Butler, "Race and the All-Volunteer System: A Reply to Janowitz and Moskos," *Armed Forces and Society* 2 (May 1976): 421.

8. For a successful discussion on how the black leadership and press helped shape policy, see Morris J. MacGregor, Jr., *Integration of the Armed Forces, 1940–1965* (Washington, D.C.: U.S. Army Center of Military History, 1981).

9. Ibid., pp. 17–44.

10. Ibid., p. 54.

11. Ibid.

12. Executive Order 9981, *Federal Register* 13 (July 28, 1948): 4313.

13. Binkin et al., *Blacks and the Military*, p. 28.

14. MacGregor, *Integration of the Armed Forces*, pp. 428–459.

15. Butler, *Inequality in the Military*, p. 29.

16. MacGregor, *Integration of the Armed Forces*, p. 37.

17. Of course blacks could take orders from whites.

18. For an interesting discussion of Navy policy on this matter, see MacGregor, *Integration of the Armed Forces*, chaps. 3, 9, 13 and 16.

19. MacGregor, *Integration of the Armed Forces*, pp. 581–608.

20. Charles C. Moskos, "Has the Army Killed Jim Crow?" *Negro History Bulletin*, November 1957, p. 29.

21. Whitney Young, Jr., "When the Negroes in Vietnam Come Home," *Harper's Magazine*, June 1967; reprinted in U.S. Congress, Senate, Committee on Veterans' Affairs, *Source Material on the Vietnam Era Veteran*, S. Committee Print No. 26, 93rd Cong., 2d sess., 1974, p. 173.

22. Binkin et al., *Blacks and the Military*, p. 36.

23. Butler, *Inequality in the Military*, p. 29.

24. Wallace Terry II, "Bringing the War Home," *Black Scholar*, November 1970; reprinted in Committee on Veterans' Affairs, *Source Material on the Vietnam Era Veteran*, p. 204.

25. Butler, *Inequality in the Military*, p. 30.

26. Terry, "Bringing the War Home," p. 201.

27. Ibid., p. 208.

28. Patricia M. Shields, "The Burden of the Draft: The Vietnam Years," *Journal of Political and Military Sociology* 9 (Fall 1981): 215.

29. James W. Davis and Kenneth Dolbare, *Little Groups of Neighbors: The Selective Service System* (Chicago: Markham, 1968), p. 57.

30. Patricia M. Shields, *The Determinants of Service in the Armed Forces During the Vietnam Era* (Columbus, Ohio: Center for Human Resource Research, 1977), p. 84.

31. Shields, *The Burden of the Draft*, p. 221.

32. Butler, *Inequality in the Military*, p. 30.

33. Lawrence Baskir and William Strauss, *Chance and Circumstance: The Draft, the War and the Vietnam Generation* (New York: Knopf, 1978), p. 99.

34. During the mid–1960s some 59.3 percent of all black men failed to meet the minimum score on the mental achievement portion of the entrance exam. States such as Louisiana (74%), Alabama (73%), Mississippi (84%), North Carolina (79%) and South Carolina (81%) are among states with particularly high ineligibility rates. See B. D. Karpinos, "The Mental Qualification of American Youth for Military Service and Its Relationship to Educational Attainment," *Proceedings of the American Statistical Association: Social Statistics Section* (1966), pp. 101–102.

35. Daniel P. Moynihan, "Who Gets in the Army?" *New Republic*, November 5, 1966, p. 22.

36. Before Project 100,000, young men were not eligible to serve in the military if (1) they scored below the 10th percentile on the Armed Forces Qualification Test (AFQT) or (2) they scored between the 10th and 30th percentiles and failed the minimum requirements on the Army Classification Battery or the Army Qualification Battery. See Karpinos, "The Mental Qualification of American Youths for Military Service and Its Relationship to Educational Attainment," p. 97. Under Project 100,000, minimum mental test scores were lowered. Under the new minimum standard, a youth could score as low as the 10th percentile on the AFQT if he was a high school graduate or received a minimum score on one of seven aptitude tests. See Harold Wool and E. S. Flyer, "Project 100,000," in P. B. Doeringer (ed.), *Programs to Employ the Disadvantaged* (Engle-

wood Cliffs, N.J.: Prentice-Hall, 1969). It is important to note that while the minimum requirements were lowered, they were not abolished. These "new standards" men comprised 9 percent of the military's entrants between 1966 and 1968. See Shields, *Determinants of Service in the Armed Forces During the Vietnam Era*, pp. 9–10.

37. Approximately 37 percent of the new standards men received combat-type skills. Over half the Army and Marine recruits went to Vietnam. Some 47 percent were drafted. See Binkin et al., *Blacks and the Military*, p. 34.

38. For an excellent discussion of the policy process surrounding the end of the draft, see Gus Lee and Geoffrey Parker, *Ending the Draft: The Story of the All-Volunteer Force* (Washington, D.C.: Human Resource Research Organization, 1977).

39. *The Report of the President's Commission on an All-Volunteer Force* (New York: Macmillan, 1970), p. i.

40. Binkin et al., *Blacks and the Military*, p. 43.

41. Ibid.

42. When quality is measured by performance on aptitude tests, 58 percent of the blacks in 1980 were classified as below average. See ibid., p. 47.

43. Morris Janowitz and Charles Moskos, "Racial Composition in the All-Volunteer Force," *Armed Forces and Society* 1 (November 1974): 110.

44. For a discussion of the "tipping" effect, see Kenneth J. Coffey, *Strategic Implications of the All-Volunteer Force: The Conventional Defense of Central Europe* (Chapel Hill: University of North Carolina Press, 1979), p. 68; Janowitz and Moskos, "Racial Composition in the All-Volunteer Force," p. 113; and Charles C. Moskos, J. S. Butler, A. N. Sabrosky and A. J. Schexnider, "Symposium: Race and the United States Military," *Armed Forces and Society* 6 (Summer 1980); see contributions by Moskos (p. 592) and Schexnider (p. 609).

45. Browning et al., "Income and Veteran Status."

46. Charles Moskos, "The Enlisted Ranks in the All-Volunteer Army," in John B. Keeky (ed.), *The All-Volunteer Force and American Society* (Charlottesville: University Press of Virginia, 1978), p. 73.

47. Choongsoo Kim et al., *The All-Volunteer Force: An Analysis of Youth Participation, Attraction and Reenlistment*, prepared for the Employment and Training Administration, Department of Labor (Columbus: Ohio State University, Center for Human Resource Research, 1980), p. 12. It should be noted, however, that overall socioeconomic status is higher among whites than blacks. See Binkin et al., *Blacks and the Military*, p. 49.

48. Charles C. Moskos, "Social Considerations of the All-Volunteer Force," in Brent Scowcroft (ed.), *Military Service in the United States* (Englewood Cliffs, N.J.: Prentice-Hall, 1982), p. 132.

49. Schexnider and Butler, "Race and the All-Volunteer System," p. 421.

50. Ibid., p. 425.

51. Patricia M. Shields, "Enlistment During the Vietnam Era and the 'Representation' Issue of the All-Volunteer Force," *Armed Forces and Society* 7 (Fall 1980): 221.

52. Richard V. L. Cooper, *Military Manpower and the All-Volunteer Force* (Santa Monica, Calif.: Rand Corporation, 1977), p. 218.

53. John P. White and James R. Hosek, "The Analysis of Military Manpower Issues," in Scowcroft, *Military Service in the United States*, pp. 63–64.

54. Cooper, *Military Manpower and the All-Volunteer Force*, p. 213.

55. Binkin et al., *Blacks and the Military*, p. 45.

56. Ibid., p. 44.

57. Guy R. Marbury et al., *Race Relations in the Army: Policies, Problems and Programs* (McLean, Va.: Champion, 1972), pp. 28–29.

58. Butler, *Inequality in the Military*, p. 35.

59. Binkin et al., *Blacks and the Military*, pp. 104, 105.

60. James Fallows, *National Defense* (New York: Random House, 1981), p. 127.

61. Binkin et al., *Blacks and the Military*, p. 107.

62. Charles Moskos, "The Changing Composition of the AVF," in Kenneth J. Coffey (ed.), *Strategic Implications of the All-Volunteer Force: The Conventional Defense of Central Europe* (Chapel Hill: University of North Carolina Press, 1979), p. 68.

63. Binkin et al., *Blacks and the Military*, p. 96.

64. Ibid., p. 73.

65. Ibid., p. 67.

66. Moskos et al, "Symposium: Race and the United States Military," p. 594.

67. Binkin et al., *Blacks and the Military*, p. 55.

68. For further discussion on this point, see Nijole Benokraitis and Joe Fagin, "Institutional Racism: A Critical Assessment of the Literature," in C. V. Willie (ed.), *Institutional Racism: In Search of a Perspective* (Chicago: Transaction, 1974); and James Jones, *Prejudice and Racism* (Reading, Mass.: Addison-Wesley, 1972).

69. John Butler, "Inequality in the Military: An Examination of Promotion Time for Black and White Enlisted Men," *American Sociological Review* 41 (October 1976): 817.

70. Binkin et al., *Blacks and the Military*, pp. 59–60.

71. Ibid., p. 61.

72. Ibid., p. 53.

73. Ibid., p. 55.

74. Ibid., p. 54.

75. Ibid., p. 96.

76. Moskos et al., "Symposium: Race and the United States Military," p. 588.

Mark S. Rosentraub
Karen Harlow

Police Policies and the Black Community: Attitudes Toward the Police

Few issues are as important to urban communities as the relationship between its citizens and the police. The importance of this relationship may not be related solely to the issue of crime. The police play an important role in the fight against crime, but their true importance to an urban community may be the image they project of a local government and its policies toward particular racial groups in the urban community. While city governments provide numerous services for citizens, the highly visible actions of the police department can represent, for many citizens, a statement by local government officials of their concern or lack of concern for a particular racial group.

Many studies of police-community relations recognize the years 1964 through 1967 as a critical period. If the civil unrest that began in Watts and continued in other urban areas had a unifying theme, it was the dissatisfaction with police officers expressed by black communities from Los Angeles to Detroit to New York. The Kerner Commission, which investigated the urban unrest of the 1960s, noted that dissatisfaction with police practices ranked first in a list of twelve major grievances identified by riot-area residents.[1]

The tension between the black community and the police was not solely the result of black residents' attitudes toward the police. If black citizens were dissatisfied with urban police departments, some officers were also extremely critical of the black community. Indeed, police officers held views of black citizens which contributed to the explosive situation. Clarence Stone and his colleagues highlighted the tendency of white police officers to consider black citizens as lazy, violence prone, disrespectful, irresponsible and from unstable families.[2]

Discussions for improving relations between the police and black communities have included numerous proposals, the more radical of which called for the removal of white police officers from black communities. These recommendations were tied to the view that the police were the occupation army of a

middle-class society. It was argued that black officers would be more qualified
to deal with black citizens and would be more sensitive to the values and needs
of the black community. Taking a less radical position, many police departments responded with programs that emphasized recruitment and employment
of blacks as police officers, rap sessions between police department officials
and neighborhood organizations, and new training programs for all police officers designed to sensitize officers to the needs and concerns of the black community.[3]

In the twenty years since these policies have been implemented, social scientists have studied the relationship between police departments and the citizens they serve. These studies relied largely on surveys of random samples of
citizens which question victimization patterns, fear of crime, satisfaction with
the police, and other issues. The largest surveys, conducted for the Department
of Justice, interviewed more than 200,000 Americans in fifteen cities.[4] This
large data base has been amplified by many other studies conducted by and for
individual police departments interested in attitudes in their own communities.[5]
In this chapter we will look at the attitudes of black citizens toward urban police departments from 1967 through 1981, using survey data collected for the
federal government and various police departments since 1967, involving interviews with more than 230,000 people.[6]

A study of this nature is important for two reasons. First, in the two decades
since the first urban riots, police departments have instituted a number of new
policies and programs designed to improve police relations with the black community and to distribute to the black community some of the benefits of a highly
professional and efficient police force. Given the importance of this objective
and the resources that have already been committed, it is appropriate to assess
whether the new policies have changed attitudes in the black community toward
the police. It is important to remember, however, that while data from more
than 200,000 people is reported here, this study is not a study of any particular
policy or set of changes. Instead, respondents' attitudes are analyzed in light of
the broad range of changing urban policies designed to improve the quality of
police services in the black community.

Second, this study is important in that it centers on the notion of crime-fighting. There is today substantial concern for the level of crime in the black community. It is now believed that the responses to this crime problem should involve both collective and individual actions on the part of citizens and the police.[7]
If police-community cooperation is necessary to reduce the level of crime in
the black community, it is important to determine whether there is within the
black community the level of support needed for cooperation with the police.

RESEARCH ON POLICE AND THE BLACK COMMUNITY, 1960–1982

With so many different surveys being used, it is easiest to review the research in terms of the three decades being studied. It is impossible to discuss

here all the studies performed in each decade, so representative selections were made.

The 1960s

Joel Aberbach and Jack Walker surveyed 855 residents of the city of Detroit in the fall of 1967. "A total of 855 respondents were interviewed (394 whites and 461 blacks). In all cases, whites were interviewed by whites and blacks were interviewed by blacks. The total *N* came from a community random sample . . . and a special random sample from areas where rioting took place in July, 1967."[8]

Five separate questions in the Aberbach and Walker study focused on respondents' evaluations of police services. In all instances, blacks gave the police a far more severe evaluation than whites did. More than one-third of the black respondents believed police officers did not respect blacks and were insulting; only 10 percent of the whites in Detroit gave a similar evaluation. Black respondents also complained about illegal searches and frisks by the police (38 percent, as opposed to 1 percent of whites) and the police department's unnecessary use of force, and less than one-third of the black respondents thought the police were doing as well as they could. In contrast, almost two-thirds of the whites believed the police were doing as well as they could. Finally, almost half the black respondents thought the police definitely treated black suspects with less respect and with more violence than white suspects; only 11 percent of the whites agreed with that position (see Table 7.1).

The data reported by the Kerner Commission for cities other than Detroit conform to the patterns observed in Detroit. In discussing the police and the black community, the Kerner Commission noted:

Negroes firmly believe that police brutality in Negro harassment occurs repeatedly in Negro neighborhoods. This belief is unquestionably one of the major reasons for intense Negro resentment against the police.

The extent of this belief is suggested by attitude surveys. In 1964, a *New York Times* study of Harlem showed that 43 percent of those questioned believed in the existence of police "brutality." In 1965, a nationwide Gallup Poll found that 35% of all Negroes now believe there is police brutality in their areas; 7% of the white men thought so . . . . A University of California at Los Angeles study of the Watts area found that 79% of the Negro males believed police lack respect or use insulting language to Negroes and 74% believed police use unnecessary force.[9]

The negative attitudes in the 1960s also involved the way police officers viewed black citizens. Many officers believed that individual and family problems were responsible for the urban unrest of the 1960s. Jerome Skolnick's work on police officers suggests that the views of officers toward protestors would minimize the opportunities for building relationships between certain segments of the urban population and the police. Skolnick observed that, viewing certain

Table 7.1
Evaluation of Police Services in Detroit, 1967

Some people say policemen lack respect or use insulting language. Others disagree. Do you think this happens in this neighborhood?

	Yes	No	Don't Know
Whites	10%	89%	1%
Blacks	34	62	4

Some people say policemen search and frisk people without good reason. Others disagree. Do you think this happens to people in this neighborhood?

	Yes	No	Don't Know
Whites	1%	90%	9%
Blacks	38	56	6

Some people say policemen use unnecessary force in making arrests. Others disagree. Do you think this happens to people in this neighborhood?

	Yes	No	Don't Know
Whites	7%	91%	2%
Blacks	34	60	6

Some people say the police in Detroit do not do as good a job as they could in protecting people from burglars, purse snatchers, and other law breakers. Others disagree. What do you think?

	Do as Good as They Can	Do Not Do as Good as They Could	Don't Know or No Answer
Whites	64%	33%	3%
Blacks	32	57	11

Source: Joel D. Aberbach and Jack L. Walker, "Attitudes of Blacks and Whites Toward City Services: Implications for Public Policy," pp. 519–538 in *Financing the Metropolis*, edited by J. P. Crecine. Copyright © 1970 by Sage Publications. Reprinted by permission of Sage Publications, Inc. and authors.

people as simply bad, many police officers looked at protestors as "rotten apples."

The "rotten apple" view of human nature puts the policeman at odds with the goals and aspirations of many of the groups he is called upon to police. For example, police often relegate social reforms to the category of coddling criminals or, in the case of recent ghetto programs, to "selling out" to troublemakers . . . [and] denounce welfare programs not as irrelevant *but as harmful* because they destroy human initiative. This negative view of the goals of policed communities can only make the situation of both police and policed more difficult and explosive. Thus, the black community sees the police not only as representing an alien white society but also advocating positions fundamentally at odds with its own aspirations.[10]

Therefore, research exploring the views of the police and the black community in the 1960s does establish a conflictual environment. More so than whites, blacks viewed the police as unfair and not doing their job as they should. The police viewed the black community as lazy and disrespectful. The 1970s, then, begin with a potentially explosive situation marked with little trust on either side.

The 1970s

The attitudes of black citizens toward the police can be considered a "baseline" view of sentiments in the black community. As a result of these opinions, virtually all cities in the United States made the hiring of black officers a priority in the 1970s. In addition to various employment programs, numerous studies of police departments by the Department of Justice indicated a plethora of community-involvement programs ranging from a civilian review board in New York to a police advisory board in several midwestern cities to a police-community coordinator. With these policy shifts, it is possible to view the data for the 1970s and the 1980s as the reactions to these virtually national responses to the crises in the black community's relations with the police in the 1960s.

In the 1970s the number of surveys to determine opinions and attitudes increased dramatically. Many urban managers realized the value of surveys of randomly selected residents and began to use the surveys as part of their planning processes.[11] Probably the largest group of surveys on the subject of police-community relations during this period were done for the National Criminal Justice Information and Statistics Service of the Law Enforcement Assistance Administration (LEAA). The cities used for these surveys were located in all regions. As a result, the data closely approximate a view of national sentiment on police-community relations.

National Surveys of Citizens' Attitudes Toward the Police

Race was clearly a factor in evaluating the performance of the police departments in each of the cities studied. In the eight largest, or impact, cities (Atlanta, Baltimore, Cleveland, Dallas, Denver, Newark, Portland and St. Louis), 54 percent of the white respondents gave the police a "good" grade, and 25 percent of the black respondents gave the police the highest grade of "good." Black respondents were also three times more likely to give the police the lowest evaluation—"poor." Slightly less than one-quarter of the black respondents believed the police were doing a "poor" job (see Table 7.2). In none of these cities was the differential between the evaluations given by whites and blacks less than 20 percent. In other words, in each city whites were at least 20 percent more likely to give higher evaluations than blacks. Only in Portland did more than a third of the black respondents give the police a "good" evaluation. By contrast, in five of the eight cities, at least half the whites interviewed believed the police were doing a "good" job (see Table 7.2).

Examining race by itself can sometimes hide the impact of other variables on the evaluation of police performance. Controlling for the effects of income, blacks

Table 7.2
Evaluation of Police Services, by Race, 1972 National Crime Survey

| | EVALUATION OF POLICE PERFORMANCE | | | | |
	Good	Average	Poor	Don't Know	No Answer
RACE (Total Sample)					
White	54%	34%	8%	5%	6%
Black/Other	25	47	22	6	1
Atlanta					
White	45	40	9	6	1
Black/Other	24	50	20	6	1
Baltimore					
White	57	32	6	4	1
Black/Other	32	48	15	5	1
Cleveland					
White	40	41	14	5	1
Black/Other	16	47	32	5	1
Dallas					
White	62	30	4	4	1
Black/Other	33	47	15	6	1
Denver					
White	56	33	7	4	1
Black/Other	32	47	16	4	1
Newark					
White	34	39	15	11	1
Black/Other	13	40	37	9	1
Portland					
White	54	34	7	5	1
Black/Other	38	36	19	7	1
St. Louis					
White	60	30	7	3	0.5
Black/Other	25	50	19	5	0.5

Source: James Garofalo, *Public Opinion About Crime: The Attitudes of Victims and Nonvictims in Selected Cities* (Albany, N.Y.: Criminal Justice Research Center, 1977), pp. 87–88.

still rated the police lower than whites did. For no income category was the difference in "good" evaluations less than 25 percent when comparing white and black citizens. At the highest level, 57 percent of the white respondents gave the police a "good" rating; 25 percent of the black respondents with incomes above $25,000 gave the police a "good" rating. At the lowest income level, more than half the white respondents gave the police a "good" rating; less than a third of the black respondents in this income range gave the police this evaluation (see Table 7.3).

The possible impact of age on the evaluation of the police is described in Table 7.4. Similar to the data comparing different racial groups by income, regardless of age, black respondents were less likely to give the police a rating of "good" within each age category. A total of 40 percent of the youngest

Table 7.3
Evaluation of Police Services, by Race and Income, 1972 Sample

| | EVALUATION OF POLICE PERFORMANCE | | | | |
	Good	Average	Poor	Don't Know	No Answer
Family Income of Whites					
Less than $3,000	53%	29%	10%	8%	1%
$3,000-$4,999	53	31	9	6	1
$5,000-$7,499	51	35	9	4	1
$7,500-$9,999	53	36	8	3	1
$10,000-$11,999	53	36	7	3	1
$12,000-$14,999	53	36	8	3	1
$15,000-$19,999	54	35	6	3	1
$20,000-$24,999	59	35	5	3	1
$25,000 or more	57	33	6	4	1
Family Income of Blacks/Others					
Less than $3,000	31	40	21	7	1
$3,000-$4,999	24	46	24	6	1
$5,000-$7,499	25	47	22	5	1
$7,500-$9,999	25	50	20	4	1
$10,000-$11,999	23	51	21	4	1
$12,000-$14,999	24	42	20	3	1
$15,000-$19,999	23	53	20	4	1
$20,000-$24,999	20	51	25	3	1
$25,000 or more	25	52	18	4	5

Source: James Garofalo, *Public Opinion About Crime: The Attitudes of Victims and Nonvictims in Selected Cities* (Albany, N.Y.: Criminal Justice Research Center, 1977), p. 89.

white respondents gave the police a "good" evaluation; 15 percent of the youngest black respondents gave the police this rating. While almost two-thirds of the oldest white respondents gave the police the highest evaluation, less than half of the oldest black respondents gave the police the highest evaluation. In the 25–34 and 35–49 age categories, the differential between white and black respondents was at least 20 percent, with whites more likely to give the highest ratings.

Two additional sets of control variables were used in the LEAA studies to

Table 7.4
Evaluation of Police Performance, by Age and Race

	Good	Average	Poor	Don't Know	No Answer	Total
Age of Whites						
16-19	40%	45%	11%	4%	0%	100%
20-24	40	44	12	4	0	100
25-34	46	39	10	4	0	100
35-49	55	34	8	3	0	100
50-64	61	28	6	4	0	100
65 or older	65	23	5	7	1	100
Age of Blacks/Others						
16-19	15	53	26	4	1	100
20-24	17	53	26	4	1	100
25-34	21	50	24	5	0	100
35-49	26	48	21	5	1	100
50-64	34	43	16	7	0	100
65 or older	43	33	13	11	1	100

Source: James Garofalo, *Public Opinion About Crime: The Attitudes of Victims and Nonvictims in Selected Cities* (Albany, N.Y.: Criminal Justice Research Center, 1977), p. 91.

analyze the impact of race on evaluation of the police: (1) controlling for race and victimization, and (2) race and a variety of forms of interaction with the police. Black respondents within each category consistently gave the police lower ratings. In sum, the principal finding of the data from the national crime surveys was that black respondents gave police officers a lower evaluation than white respondents did. The impact of race was evident when other factors were analyzed together with the race of the respondents.

Case Studies of Citizens' Attitudes Toward the Police in Southwestern Cities

The information generated by the national studies of citizen attitudes by the federal government convinced many cities to analyze the feelings and impressions of their own residents. The city of Dallas, for example, began a biannual survey of its residents in 1974 which offers an important data set on citizen impressions of the performance of the police. Surveys were conducted every other year from 1974 to 1978. The city of Fort Worth also conducted studies of citizen impressions of the police. These case studies do not provide the same national picture of citizen views, yet the data bases are large enough to offer an important insight into changes in attitudes toward the police in areas that did not suffer the violence of other communities but still have important racial issues dividing them.

The patterns observed in the national data with regard to the evaluation of police officers are also evident in the surveys in the cities of Dallas and Fort Worth. Table 7.5 reports the results from the 1974, 1976 and 1978 surveys in Dallas. In each year, black respondents gave the police department lower evaluations than white respondents when the "fairness" of police officers was evaluated and when the quality of the police officers' job performance was evaluated. It is interesting to note that in 1978 the police received their highest evaluations from black respondents. These higher ratings, compared to 1974 and 1976, were still below the evaluations given the police by white respondents in 1978.

In the 1978 Fort Worth survey, more than 20 percent of the white respondents considered the performance of the police to be excellent; 11.7 percent of the black respondents gave the police this high evaluation. Three-quarters of the white respondents in the Fort Worth survey considered the performance of

Table 7.5
Police Evaluation in Dallas, by Race, 1974, 1976, 1978

Year	Question	Black Respondents	White Respondents
1974	Are police fair?		
	Yes	49.0%	82.9%
	Depends	26.3	9.0
	No	24.8	8.1
	Rate performance of police 1 equals worst; 6 equals best	4.4	5.1
1976	Are police fair?		
	Yes	32.7%	75.7%
	Depends	45.5	17.2
	No	21.8	7.1
	Rate performance of police 1 equals worst; 6 equals best	4.2	4.6
1978	Are police fair?		
	Yes	64.6%	86.7%
	Depends	21.7	8.0
	No	13.7	5.3
	Rate performance of police* 1 equals worst; 10 equals best	6.5	7.4

Source: City of Dallas, *City Profile Surveys,* 1974, 1976 and 1978.

*Differences significant at .001 level.

the police either "excellent" or "good"; less than half the black respondents gave the Fort Worth police these ratings.[12]

As with the national samples, it is important to see whether any other demographic characteristics (e.g., income or age) influenced evaluations of the police. For purposes of illustration, one of these breakdowns is presented in Table 7.6 for the city of Dallas. Controlling for income, black respondents rated the police "fairness" lower. In no income category for any of the years studied did any group of black respondents give the police a higher rating with regard to "fairness" than did white respondents. The patterns were the same with regard to the other control variables in the city of Fort Worth.

In sum, the studies reviewed indicate that the 1970s were a period when the police were viewed with great suspicion by the black community. In national and local surveys, black respondents consistently gave police officers and police departments lower evaluations than white respondents did. Despite many programs designed to improve relations between the police department and black communities in different areas, black respondents were not nearly as satisfied with the police as white respondents were.

Table 7.6
Are Police Fair: Controlling for Income, City of Dallas

| | ARE POLICE FAIR? | | | | | |
| | Yes | | Depends | | No | |
	Blacks	Whites	Blacks	Whites	Blacks	Whites
1974						
Less than $3,000	46.2%	86.2%	28.8%	6.2%	25.0%	7.6%
$3,000-$4,999	45.0	78.7	17.5	9.8	35.5	11.5
$5,000-$7,999	49.6	83.3	26.4	8.4	24.0	8.4
$8,000-$9,999	45.0	78.7	30.0	11.8	25.0	9.6
$10,000-$14,999	46.1	82.2	31.5	9.0	22.5	8.7
$15,000 or more	52.8	86.1	28.3	7.1	18.9	6.8
1976						
Less than $5,000	30.2	62.0	45.5	17.8	18.0	8.5
$5,000-$7,999	30.9	74.0	42.0	11.9	18.5	7.3
$8,000-$9,999	31.8	68.3	37.9	17.7	24.2	5.5
$10,000-$11,999	25.5	63.4	40.0	22.1	29.1	4.1
$12,000-$14,999	33.9	68.9	39.0	19.3	22.0	7.1
$15,000-$24,999	32.8	62.6	37.9	10.6	20.7	8.8
$25,000 or more	25.0	74.4	37.5	13.5	18.8	4.1
1978						
Less than $5,000	61.7	85.9	22.9	6.3	15.3	7.7
$5,000-$9,999	60.0	82.9	22.9	10.0	17.2	7.1
$10,000-$11,999	68.2	87.8	21.3	10.3	10.5	1.9
$12,000-$14,999	63.8	85.8	25.2	7.3	11.0	6.9
$15,000-$24,999	78.9	86.8	17.1	9.8	4.0	3.3
$25,000-$49,000	53.0	86.5	23.4	8.0	23.5	5.5
$50,000 or more	39.5	88.6	60.5	6.0	-	5.4

Source: City of Dallas, *City Profile Surveys,* 1974, 1976, 1978.

The 1980s

Changing national priorities with regard to support for certain kinds of research has reduced the role of the federal government in surveys of citizens. Research involving citizens' views of the police performance, if performed at all, has been sponsored by local and state governments. Two of these surveys were performed for cities that were part of the data base for the analysis of the 1970s. In 1980 the city of Dallas performed what may have been its last survey of citizens; to date, it has not had the resources to complete another survey. In 1981 the city of Fort Worth performed the second survey of its citizens focusing specifically on the performance of the police and crime issues. Again, studies from these two cities cannot be interpreted as representative of national attitudes, but comparing these data with the other data sets does permit a continuation of the analysis of the relationship between the black community and the police. It should also be remembered that the results for Dallas and Fort Worth did not differ substantially from patterns recognized within the national data analyzed for the 1970s.

Despite a lack of civil conflict in these two cities in the past, a substantial difference in attitudes between white and black citizens in both cities can be identified. In 1980 some 63 percent of the white respondents considered the police in the city of Dallas to be doing an excellent job, and 78.4 percent believed the police were fair. In contrast, 57.5 percent of the black respondents believed the police were fair, but almost half the black respondents thought the performance of the police rated a "fair" or "poor" evaluation (see Table 7.7).

As with the other data sets, separate analyses were performed to determine if income, age or victimization changed the evaluation of police services for black or white respondents. Regardless of age, income or victimization status (whether a person had been a victim of crime), black respondents in both Dallas and Fort Worth gave lower evaluations to the police and believed the police were less fair than did white respondents. A few tendencies emerging from these two large surveys are still worth noting. First, the difference in evaluations and impressions between white and black respondents are still evident. Black respondents are more critical of the police than white respondents. Second, and perhaps more important, there does seem to be a larger percentage of black respondents who feel more satisfied with police services. For example, in Fort Worth in 1981, some 44.5 percent of the black respondents did consider the performance of the police to be either "excellent" or "good." This was a decline since the city's first survey in 1978, but it still indicates a level of support for the police not evident in other communities. In Dallas in 1980, more than half the black respondents gave the police an "excellent" or "good" evaluation. This was a considerable increase since the first survey was performed in Dallas for the LEAA. Last, in both cities, blacks were still more likely than whites to consider the police "unfair," but in both cities a majority of the black respondents did consider the police to be "fair."

The data from the 1980s, then, present a more hopeful tone. Although it is

Table 7.7
Evaluation of Police Services, Dallas 1980 and Fort Worth 1981

PERFORMANCE OF POLICE	Whites	Blacks
Dallas 1980		
Excellent	12.7%	5.9%
Good	60.3	45.5
Fair	21.4	28.7
Poor	5.6	18.9
Ft. Worth 1981		
Excellent	13.3	10.7
Good	51.7	33.8
Fair	29.0	42.2
Poor	5.9	13.3
ARE THE POLICE FAIR?		
Dallas 1980		
Fair	78.4	57.5
Depends	7.8	16.3
Unfair	4.0	15.0
Ft. Worth 1981		
Yes	81.5	69.4
No	18.5	30.6

Source: City of Dallas, *City Profile Survey*, 1980; and Mark Rosentraub and Karen Harlow, "Public/Private Relations and Service Delivery: The Coproduction of Personal Safety," *Policy Studies Journal*, 11 (3) (March 1983): pp. 445–457.

incomplete and from only two cities, there is some indication that problem relationships between the police and the black community may be less severe than at any other time in recent history. Before conclusions of this nature can be verified and supported, however, additional surveys of other cities and for the remaining years of the decade are needed.

CONCLUSION AND POLICY IMPLICATIONS

Given the critical nature of relations between black communities and police departments in the 1960s, it was not surprising the urban governments would issue new policy directives designed to change existing policies and programs. Two general approaches were attempted by most cities. An increased number of black police officers was one goal; the second goal was improved police-community relations through new outreach programs. The objectives of these programs were to reduce tensions between the black community and the police and to improve black citizens' views of the police. The data reported here suggest that these policies may have reduced some of the tension between the police and the black community. There have been few riots on the scale of the unrest of the 1960s, but there has been little change in the attitudes of blacks toward the police, especially when the attitudes of black respondents are compared to those of white respondents.

Our conclusions are not surprising. By the end of the Carter administration, data describing the employment patterns of many police departments indicated that the hiring of blacks as police had increased modestly at best. Surveying twenty-two cities in 1972, Terry Jones found the percentage of the population that was black was at least twice the percentage of the police officers who were black in nineteen of the cities. In more than half the cities, the ratio between citizens and officers was 3 to 1, and in 27 percent of the cities the ratio was more than 6 to 1.[13] The Equal Employment Opportunity Commission, looking at all police departments through their weighting formulas, reported that the percentage of police officers who were black had increased only from 1.8 percent to 7.9 percent between 1973 and 1980. Black police administrators accounted for 3.5 percent of all police administrators in 1980, representing an increase of 1.3 percent since 1973.[14]

As recently as 1980, while some cities police departments had been successful in hiring more minorities (40 percent of Detroit's police force, for example, is now black), other cities (for example, Los Angeles, Fort Worth and Dallas) have not only failed to hire or promote minorities in the police department,[15] but have been sued and fined because of their failure to do so. The police-community relations programs of the 1960s and 1970s seem to have disappeared behind a concern for tax levels and a maintenance of barely acceptable service levels. There are still police-community relations programs in some cities, but there are few working advisory boards or civilian review boards.

Given the small impact of the policy changes in the 1960s and 1970s, it is not surprising to find that attitudes of black respondents toward the police remain largely unchanged since the 1960s. Black citizens still give the police lower ratings than white respondents. The harsh views of the 1960s and early 1970s seem to have continued through the late 1970s, and while some of this has subsided, there is still a considerable difference between the evaluations by white respondents and those of blacks.

This continuing negative relationship between black citizens and the police remains an important policy issue in many black communities. Increasing unemployment and other social problems have again focused crime activities on the black community. Victimization among black citizens has increased dramatically, and the elderly have been singled out for particularly harsh treatment. Indeed, in some communities "black on black" crime has become one of the most important issues. For the police to work with these black communities in their fight against crime, it is necessary for the black community to have faith in the ability of their "partner" to work with them effectively and fairly, but the data are not optimistic for the future.

What policy approaches should be followed now? We seem to be in the uncomfortable position of maintaining that what needs to be done in the 1980s are the same things that were noted in the 1960s and the 1970s and that remain undone today. Police departments need to hire and promote black officers. An increase of 1 percent or 2 percent over an entire decade is not sufficient. Largely white police departments do not enjoy the confidence or support of black communities. Police departments must also negotiate directly with black communities concerning their needs. Advisory committees are needed, with a commitment from the police that they will listen to the needs and concerns of black citizens. It appears these policy proposals have gone unheeded for fifteen years. Before the urban unrest of the 1960s repeats itself, and before more black communities suffer from more crime, urban administrators and police officials must heed these recommendations. If they do not, the black community will suffer higher crime rates, be unable to work with the police on joint crime-fighting programs, and fear the police. If there is no resolve to implement new policies, the benefits of a highly professional police department may be absent in the black community.

NOTES

1. National Advisory Commission on Civil Disorders, *Report of the National Advisory Commission on Civil Disorders* (New York: New York Times Co., 1968).

2. Clarence N. Stone, Robert K. Whelan and William Murin, *Urban Policy and Politics in a Bureaucratic Age* (Englewood Cliffs, N.J.: Prentice-Hall, 1979); National Advisory Commission on Civil Disorders, *Supplemental Studies* (Washington, D.C.: Government Printing Office, 1969).

3. Armando Morales, "Police Deployment Theories and the Mexican American," in J. H. Skolnick and T. C. Gray (eds.), *Police in America* (Boston: Little, Brown, 1975), pp. 118–125.

4. James Garofalo, *Public Opinion About Crime: The Attitudes of Victims and Nonvictims in Selected Cities* (Albany, N.Y.: Criminal Justice Research Center, 1977).

5. Mark Rosentraub and Karen Harlow, "Public/Private Relations and Service Delivery: The Co-Production of Personal Safety," *Policy Studies Journal*, 11 (3) (March 1983), pp. 445–457.

6. Several limitations exist for the use of these data. First, while the survey instruments were generally similar, the surveys were performed by many different organizations, so some differences may have existed in survey techniques. Second, the vast majority of interviews were performed in face-to-face situations. More recent surveys relied on increasingly reliable and cost-efficient telephone interviews. These methods have usually been found to be as reliable as any other form of data collection. For further discussion of this point, see Alfred J. Tuchfarber and William R. Klecka, *Random-Digit Dialing:*

Lowering the Costs of Victimization Surveys (Washington, D.C.: Police Foundation, 1976). Readers should keep in mind, however, that the data were collected using two very different techniques. Finally, most of the data were collected without reference to any specific policy change or program and cannot be used to evaluate the success or failure of specific activities.

7. For further discussion on this point, see Richard Rich, "The Roles of Neighborhood Organizations in Urban Service Delivery," *Urban Affairs Papers* 1 (1979): 81–93; and Robert Warren, Mark Rosentraub and Karen Harlow, "Citizen Participation in the Production of Services: Methodological and Policy Issues in Co-Production Research," *Southwestern Review of Management and Economics*, forthcoming.

8. Joel D. Aberbach and Jack L. Walker, "The Provision of Services and the Perceptions of System Responsiveness: Do Public Dollars Matter," in J. P. Crecine (ed.), *Financing the Metropolis* (Beverly Hills, Calif.: Sage, 1970).

9. *Report of the National Advisory Commission on Civil Disorders, p. 302.*

10. *Jerome H. Skolnick, "The Police View of Protestors," in Skolnick and Gray, Police in America*, pp. 203–209. Emphasis in the original.

11. Mark S. Rosentraub and Lyke Thompson, "Bureaucratic Discretion and Surveys of Citizen Satisfaction," in Richard Rich (ed.), *Analyzing Urban Service Distributions* (Lexington, Mass.: Lexington Books, 1982), pp. 171–184.

12. Karen Harlow and Mark Rosentraub, *Crime Victimization and Citizens' Perceptions of Safety and Police Services in Fort Worth* (Fort Worth, Tex.: City of Fort Worth, 1978).

13. Terry Jones, "The Police in America: A Black Viewpoint," *Black Scholar*, October 1977, pp. 22–39.

14. The statistics on racial employment in police departments were taken from the Equal Employment Opportunity Commission's 1973, 1975, 1978, and 1980 publications entitled *Minorities and Women in State and Local Government*. These figures are based on their representative sample of all units of local government and not just cities with concentrations of black citizens.

15. There are few current estimates of the number of black police officers. The data cited here are from various newspaper accounts and B. Cory, "Minority Police: Tramping Through a Racial Minefield," *Police Magazine*, March 1977, pp. 4–14.

Affirmative Action, Reverse Discrimination and the Courts: Implications for Blacks

The contemporary public policy that may significantly affect the progress of blacks in the next twenty years is the sanctioning of the "double standard of judicial review" by the courts in the area of affirmative action. This double standard of judicial review rests on the premise that government benefits should be allocated to the individual on the basis of merit, or rights and privileges by law, instead of population needs.[1] According to critics, allocating benefits on the latter basis constitutes reverse discrimination. These critics have been successful in persuading the courts to sanction this argument on the basis that affirmative action constitutes racial discrimination against whites because it requires hiring a less-qualified black who may be well qualified for the benefit in question, but less qualified than some whites. It must be noted that the same whites who can successfully pursue their claim of reverse discrimination in court on the basis of merit cannot do the same if a less-qualified white, or even a marginally qualified white, is selected for a benefit over them. Judicial sanctioning of the claim of reverse discrimination constitutes a double standard of judicial review. The operative effect of such public policy is to deprive blacks of their liberty interest rights to acquire a just share of government supported benefits, that is, jobs, education and fringe benefits.[2]

Opponents of affirmative action launched a negative propaganda campaign designed to convince the "intellectual, judicial, and political institutions of the country" (1) that rights were attached to the individual and not to groups[3] and (2) that affirmative action disadvantages some whites who themselves are innocent of any wrongdoing.[4] They succeeded in persuading state and federal courts to reiterate the precedents that the U.S. Supreme Court had established, that equal protection is a personal rights.[5] The critics, led by Nathan Glazer, have proliferated the literature with articles and books claiming, among other things, that affirmative action "threatens the abandonment of our concern for individ-

ual claims to consideration on the basis of justice and equity, now to be replaced with a concern of rights for publicly determined and delimited racial and
ethnic groups."[6]

This chapter examines the critics' arguments within the framework of jurisprudence to determine whether affirmative action operates to disadvantage whites
or to deprive them of any rights that qualify for protection under the Fourteenth
Amendment, hereinafter referred to as "protected rights." It also looks at the
legal and policy questions that the reverse discrimination argument has raised,
such as (1) Does meritocracy confer protected rights on individuals? (2) Does
meritocracy give the individual a legitimate claim of entitlement to governmentally supported benefits? and (3) Does affirmative action confer "property interest rights" (rights based on government laws, statutes, and so on) or "liberty
interest rights" (civil rights common in society) on the individual based on merit?
Finally, we will analyze the policy impact that the doctrine of reverse discrimination has on the liberty and property interests of blacks.

AFFIRMATIVE ACTION AND REVERSE DISCRIMINATION

The reverse-discrimination argument rests on the assumption that the intent
of the Civil Rights Act of 1964 was to include meritocracy among those property and liberty interest rights that qualify for protection under the Fourteenth
Amendment.[7] This is evidenced in the three landmark reverse-discrimination
cases that reached the U.S. Supreme Court—*DeFunis v. Odegaard* (1974), *Regents of the University of California v. Bakke* (1978) and *United Steelworkers
v. Weber* (1979).[8] All three plaintiffs were successful in convincing the lower
courts that affirmative-action programs at their institutions violated their constitutional rights because they selected individuals on the basis of race instead of
merit.*

The question that emerges here is whether merit or performance gives the
individual protected rights to benefits. The answer to this question is no. Nothing in the civil rights law or the Fourteenth Amendment extends such protection
to the individual. The only legal standing that a white person has in advancing
a claim of reverse discrimination is to invoke the constitutionally suspect classification rule in which race must be shown to have been used as a factor in
granting a benefit.[9] This principle is laden with internal contradictions when it
is applied to whites. The original intent of the U.S. Supreme Court was to establish a rule to review government action to determine whether an entire group's
liberty interest rights or property interest rights were being deprived or restricted.[10] Since affirmative action does not purport to deprive the individual of
any protected rights, it is a contradiction to argue that affirmative action dis-

---

*The terms "meritocracy," "the merit system," "merit" and "qualifications" will be used in-
terchangeably throughout this chapter.

criminates against the entire white race (that is, deprivation of liberty interest rights), especially when whites are receiving a disproportionate share of the benefits in question.

Our discussion will be limited to examining whether meritocracy can ever be included among those rights that qualify for protection under the Fourteenth Amendment. We argue that in the absence of statutory requirements, rules or understandings stemming from government action it cannot.[11] To include meritocracy among those rights would be tantamount to giving the individual a right without a necessary remedy. This is why the argument that affirmative action "threatens the abandonment of our concerns for individual claims to consideration on basis of justice and equity" has never had any real meaning in the areas in which affirmative action operates.[12] It is simply an argument that the critics are using to anathematize affirmative action.

Another contradiction in the reverse-discrimination argument is the claim that affirmative action offends the constitutional rights of whites when less-qualified minorities are selected for benefits over more-qualified whites.[13] But the same individual's rights are not violated when less-qualified whites, or even marginally qualified whites, are selected for benefits over more-qualified whites. The policy implications in this scheme of things establishes a double standard of judicial review which allows any marginally qualified white to use the instrumentalities of the government to limit or deprive blacks of their liberty interest rights. It holds that meritocracy can be considered a protected right if, and only if, race can be shown to have been used as a factor.

AFFIRMATIVE-ACTION POLICY AND MERITOCRACY

Property and Liberty Interest Rights

Two major policy questions arise when discussing affirmative action and meritocracy. First, can meritocracy ever be considered a property interest right or liberty interest right? Second, does meritocracy in itself give individual whites legal standing to challenge the traditional managerial prerogatives of businesses and institutions?

The answer to the first question is no. This is a provisional right that the courts have erroneously given whites to challenge the managerial prerogatives of companies who have adopted an affirmative-action program. The courts have fallen victim to the critics' negative propaganda campaign to anathematize affirmative action.[14] They successfully convinced the courts to establish the principle that the racial suspect classification ruling is subject to the same standard of judicial review whether the individual is white or nonwhite. As we have seen, this ruling was originally established as a group right and not as an individual right.

Before the coining of the reverse-discrimination argument, individuals derived their property interest rights from statutes, rules or understandings stemming from government action.[15] Liberty interest rights were considered to be those civil rights that were common to society.[16] Until this time, the U.S. Supreme Court had on numerous occasions acknowledged that the "Constitution did not create rights but protected them."[17] But in the three reverse-discrimination cases that the Court reviewed, it departed significantly from this principle. This departure conferred, for the first time, on a body of people (a selection committee) the arbitrary power to create and confer property interest rights to government benefits on an individual based on merit.[18]

The meaning of property interest rights and liberty interest rights deserves some elaboration. In the *National Insurance Co. v. Tidewater Co.* (1968) case, the Court defined the boundaries within which an individual could legitimately claim that his or her liberty interest rights or property interest rights had been violated. It stated that property and liberty interest rights were indeed broad and majestic terms that the framers of the Constitution purposely left "to gather meaning from experience."[19] It held that the "Court has fully and finally rejected the wooden distinction between 'right' and 'privilege' that once seemed to govern the applicability of procedural due process rights."[20] While the Court did not define the terms "property interest" and "liberty interest," it did define the boundaries within which the Court would review government action to determine whether it violates equal protection guarantees. In *Board of Regents v. Roth* (1972) the Court said:

Property interests, of course, are not created by the Constitution. Rather, they are created and their dimensions are defined by existing rules or understandings that stem from an independent source such as state law—rules or understandings that secure certain benefits and that support claims of entitlement to those benefits.[21]

Considering "liberty" interest rights, the Court stated that in a "Constitution for a free people, there can be no doubt that the meaning of 'liberty' must be broad indeed."[22] Based on this principle, it acknowledged that the term "liberty" is not to be confined to "mere freedom from bodily restraint."[23] Under the law, it held, liberty "extends to the full range of conduct which the individual is free to pursue, and it cannot be restricted except for a proper government objective."[24] This definition also extends to government actions that impose "a stigma or other disability" on an individual or group which forecloses a wide range of "freedom to take advantage of other employment" and educational opportunities.[25]

The *DeFunis* and *Bakke* Cases

An examination of two of the major cases of reverse discrimination that reached the U.S. Supreme Court reveals that affirmative action did not discriminate against whites because it did not deprive them of any of their protected rights. The only legal standing that the plaintiffs, DeFunis and Bakke, had in seeking redress for their grievance was to invoke the racial suspect classification ruling. They argued that affirmative-action programs deprived them of their right to attend professional schools, law school and medical school respectively, because the institutions selected a certain percentage of minorities based on race rather than on merit.[26]

Before the advent of the reverse-discrimination argument, the racial suspect classification ruling was restricted to reviewing government actions that may have operated to deprive members of racial minorities of their liberty and property interest rights.[27] But the critics successfully convinced the lower courts that the racial suspect ruling protected whites from being discriminated against the same as minorities. The criteria that the courts used to determine if whites had been discriminated against was whether individuals were selected on the basis of merit.

The courts invoked the "rational basis" test[28] to justify the affirmative-action program at the University of California. However, the rational basis test was originally used to justify depriving individuals of their property and liberty interest rights. The Supreme Court stated:

All restrictions which curtail the civil rights of a single racial group are immediately suspect. That is not to say that all such restrictions are unconstitutional. It is to say that courts must subject them to the more rigid scrutiny. Pressing public necessity may sometimes justify the existence of such restrictions; racial antagonism never can.[29]

Under such restrictions the Court's review was limited to determining whether the restrictions were related to a proper government objective.[30] But in reverse-discrimination cases, the courts departed significantly from this ruling. Instead of using the rational test basis to determine whether restrictions were being placed on the entire white race, they started using this test to determine whether minority applicants were selected for benefits based solely on merit.

It must be noted at this point, however, that there is a constitutional difference between affirmative-action classifications and racial classifications which operate to deprive an entire race of their civil rights. Affirmative-action classification is nothing more than a system of protection to guarantee some members of minority groups that their group will receive a fair share of benefits. In other words, it is a system of protection to remove restrictions in their pursuit of benefits.

On the other hand, racial classifications that operate to restrict an entire race are within themselves invidious. They operate to deprive a group of their property and liberty interest rights. In both the *DeFunis* and *Bakke* cases, the affirmative-action programs were not invidious because they did not prevent all whites from attending professional schools. In fact, over 85 percent of the applicants selected were white.[31]

The critics were so effective with their negative affirmative-action campaign that they convinced the courts to accept the principle that whites had property interest rights for attending professional schools on the basis of merit. This is evidenced in the majority opinion of the California State Supreme Court written by Justice Stanley Mosk. He wrote:

Deprivation based on race is not subject to a less demanding standard of review under the Fourteenth Amendment merely because the race discriminated against is the majority rather than the minority , . . . the "compelling interest" test was to [be applied] in determining validity of the program.[32]

This marked the first time that the rational basis test was used when an individual's liberty and property interest rights were not in question. The only thing in question here was the desire of individual whites to get into professional schools. They were turned down through the regular process and attempted to argue that they would have been admitted if not for the affirmative-action programs.[33]

This brings us to the final and most critical policy question: Does meritocracy confer on an individual constitutionally protected rights in his or her desire to obtain government benefits? The answer again is no. In order to confer such rights on an individual, meritocracy has to fit within the boundaries of the definition of "property" or "liberty" interest rights.[34] Only within one of these definitions can an individual invoke (i.e., without the double standard of judicial review) the equal protection clause in a claim of reverse discrimination. Within this framework, we can approach the question of whether affirmative action deprives an individual of civil rights when the program takes an applicant's race into account instead of merely merit in selecting individuals for benefits.

However, offering special admission or preference to minority applicants does not in any way deprive whites of equal protection of the law. Equal protection can be applied only to those property and liberty interest rights that qualify for protection under the Fourteenth Amendment. Affirmative action could have deprived DeFunis and Bakke of their right to attend professional schools only if there had been a law, rule or understanding (property interest) stating that an individual shall be admitted on the basis of merit, or if by denying them admission affirmative action deprived them of their liberty interest rights. In order to deprive an individual of liberty interest rights, affirmative action must do more than offer preference to minority applicants; it must restrict the freedom of whites or disadvantage or impose on them a "stigma or other disability" so that their freedom "to take advantage of other" educational and employment opportunities in the future is limited.[35]

Since "liberty" is a sacred value for a constitution of free people, it deserves some elaboration here. Although the U.S. Supreme Court has not defined liberty precisely, it did spell out its boundaries in *Meyer v. Nebraska* (1923). It stated that the term "liberty" denotes not mere freedom from bodily restraint but also the right of the individual to contract, to engage in any of the common occupations of life, to acquire useful knowledge, to marry, establish a home and bring up children, to worship God according to the dictates of his own conscience, and generally to enjoy those privileges long recognized . . . as essential to the orderly pursuit of happiness by free men.[36]

It is obvious from this definition of liberty that affirmative action did not operate to deprive Bakke or DeFunis of their liberty interest rights to attend professional schools. An education in law or medicine does not fit the definition of "common occupations of life," nor is it "essential to the orderly pursuit of happiness."

The mere fact that these occupations are regulated by the state is *prima facie* evidence that they cannot be considered liberty interest rights. It would contravene the equal protection clause if a state was to establish rules and regulations to limit the number of persons entering a profession like law or medicine and turn around and establish another rule stating that individuals shall be selected on the basis of merit. Such a rule would constitute property interest rights where all applicants who meet the established criteria for admission would be entitled to procedural due process.[37] Once a state legislature determines that it is necessary to regulate resources or benefits, an individual's right to equal protection in acquiring such benefits ceases to be *juris privati* only.

Therefore, any restrictions placed on individuals' liberty interest rights must pass the rational basis test. The restrictions placed on the number of persons entering medical schools is undoubtedly in the best interest of the public. Such restrictions do not contravene the equal protection clause, nor do they deprive anyone of his or her property interest right to procedural due process. Regulation by the state, the Court has ruled, is within itself due process.[38]

DeFunis, Bakke and Meritocracy

From the above analysis it is clear that the landmark cases of reverse discrimination and affirmative action did not violate the civil rights of either plaintiff, DeFunis or Bakke. Neither of them had a property interest right to obtain the benefit they sought, because there was no law, rule or understanding stemming from government action which stated that benefits were to be granted on the basis of merit. The only question we can consider here is whether merit or performance can ever extend to the individual liberty interest right in a free society.

An examination of the *DeFunis* case will shed some light on this question. DeFunis filed suit claiming that the affirmative-action program at the University of Washington violated his civil rights because it selected minority applicants who were less qualified than he. He implicitly rejected the notion that he had a property interest right in attending law school. He did not cite any state law, rule or understanding which stated that students shall be admitted on the basis of qualifications. Without such a rule, he had no property interest rights. The question that emerges here is, Did the affirmative-action program deprive DeFunis of his liberty interest rights?

In order for affirmative action to deprive DeFunis of his liberty interest rights, it had to do more than prevent him from attending law school at the University of Washington. It had to disadvantage him by imposing on him a stigma or other disability in such a way to foreclose his freedom to take advantage of other opportunities to attend law school elsewhere. When he filed his lawsuit of reverse discrimination, DeFunis had been admitted to at least four other law schools. And when his case reached the Supreme Court he was in his third year of law school.[39]

The *Bakke* case was different. After being turned down for admission by the University of California Medical School, Bakke filed a suit of reverse discrimination claiming that if the minority program did not exist he would have been admitted. However, he was turned down by all the medical schools he had applied to including his alma mater, the University of Minnesota. His decision to file suit was strongly encouraged by some officials at the medical school.[40]

It has been argued elsewhere that the *Bakke* case was part of a conspiracy by the critics to have affirmative action declared unconstitutional.[41] It was a conspiracy because the minority program did not deprive Bakke of his liberty interest rights for two basic constitutional reasons. First, in order to have a liberty interest in an occupation, it has to fit the definition of "common occupation of life," or an occupation that is "essential to the pursuit of happiness."[42] But because the medical profession is regulated by the state, a medical education does not fit this definition. Second, the program did not in any way discriminate, disadvantage or penalize Bakke so as to deprive him of his protected rights. For the minority program to have discriminated against Bakke, it had to "impose on him a stigma or other disability"[43] in such a way to foreclose his freedom to take advantage of other educational opportunities. Nor did the program "invoke any regulations to bar" him from pursuing a medical education at other institutions in the state system. In fact, he applied at other schools and was turned down for reasons other than race. The question that emerges here is why Bakke did not file a suit against the other universities, including his alma mater. This question can best be answered by examining the legal standing that he used to get his case in court.

As mentioned earlier, the only legal standing that Bakke and DeFunis had was to invoke the racial suspect classification ruling.[44] But this rule was established to review government action to determine whether an entire racial group was being deprived of their liberty interest rights.[45] Since over 80 percent of all applicants admitted to the professional schools in the two landmark cases were white, it becomes absurd to invoke the racial suspect classification ruling to determine whether the entire white race is being deprived of their liberty interest rights. The statistics themselves are *prime facie* evidence.

The critics therefore used another strategy: to convince the courts that Title VI of the Civil Rights Act of 1964 was designed to protect whites as well as minorities from being discriminated against. They used the precedent that the Court established in the employment case of *McDonald v. Santa Fe Company* (1976) where the Court ruled that Title VII of the act (the nondiscrimination employment provision) was intended to prohibit "racial discrimination against white persons upon the same standards as racial discrimination against non-whites."[46] This ruling poses serious contradictions beyond the scope of this chapter. Suffice it to say that this is the precedent that Bakke used successfully to persuade the Supreme Court to establish the principle of double standard of judicial review.

Based on this double standard of judicial review, Bakke was able to convince the Court that the minority program at the University of California at Davis offended his constitutional rights because it offered "preference on the basis of race to persons, by the University's own standards, who were not as qualified for the study of medicine as nonminority applicants denied admission."[47] Implied in the phrase "by the University's own standards" and not "as qualified" is the notion that "standards" constituted "property" interest rights which give applicants a legitimate claim of entitlement to benefit based on merit.[48]

If meritocracy was the criterion for determining an individual's property interest rights, then Bakke's legal standing in court should not have been to invoke the racial suspect classification ruling but to argue that he was denied due process of law. Further, his qualifications in themselves would have given him a legitimate claim of entitlement to admission because the standards established by the medical school required that applicants be admitted solely on the basis of merit. The standard of judicial review should have been to examine the selection committee's procedures to determine whether the committee treated all applicants that were similarly situated equally.[49] This standard of review cannot be restricted simply to the minority program but to "all persons" who were admitted with lesser qualifications than Bakke. As the records show, there were "eight white students who were admitted with lower benchmark scores than Bakke and thirty-six with lower grade point averages than his."[50] It is a double standard of judicial review for the courts to hold that the minority program discriminated against Bakke because it selected applicants with lesser qualifications than his, but it is not illegal for the school to select less-qualified white applicants over him. This would appear to be an improper interpretation of the equal protection clause.

The equal protection clause requires the states to treat all persons equally who are similarly situated. Based on this principle, meritocracy extends to the individual a property interest in obtaining a benefit, so the state of California would have been obligated to grant all the applicants who met the standards of admission an opportunity to pursue a medical education. This means that if three thousand applicants qualified for admission, all applicants would have had a legitimate claim of entitlement to the benefit of a medical education.

It must be noted here that the University of California cannot sidestep its obligation of treating all applicants who meet their standards of qualification, that is, similarly situated, the same by arguing that it had only one hundred slots for its freshman class and that it would be economically unfeasible to accommodate all the applicants. If meritocracy were to extend property interest rights to the individual, as the critics are claiming, the equal protection clause would place two obligations on the state. First, the University of California would have been required to grant all applicants who met the admission criteria a place in its medical school. Second, the university would have had to establish procedural due process in which it would have had to explain in detail to each applicant why he or she was not selected. At such a hearing, the burden of proof would have rested with the state to prove that their selection was not a denial of equal protection.

The requirements for a procedural due process hearing offer further evidence that the Civil Rights Act of 1964 was not intended to confer benefits on an individual on the basis of merit. The hearing has to consist of more than simply sending a letter informing each applicant that the school regrets that he or she was not selected. Instead, the hearing must meet all the requirements of procedural due process as required by the U.S. Constitution. This includes providing all applicants with "timely and adequate notice, detailing the reason for" their not being admitted and offering each "an effective opportunity to defend" himself or herself and a chance to refute any adverse subjective materials in the files, such as letters of recommendation, the validity of the standardized test scores in predicting class performance and the ratings of undergraduate schools. In other words, once the door of procedural due process has been opened, a cannon may roll out and there will be no control over the number of litigations. Such a scheme of things would place an awesome burden on the affected institutions, but it would be the same price that states would have to pay if they wish to establish the principle that meritocracy should be the basis for granting benefits. Some critics have argued that the state could justify denying qualified applicants admission on economic grounds. But the U.S. Supreme Court has held that whenever property interest rights are concerned the Constitution requires procedural due process. The Supreme Court told the state of New York that it could not deny welfare recipients financial assistance because of a lack of funds. It held that whenever government "benefits are a matter of statutory entitlement for persons qualified to receive them then procedural due process is applicable to their termination."[51] It appears from this ruling then that there is no way to grant individuals a legitimate claim of entitlement to benefits based on merit.

This brings us to our other question: If Bakke and DeFunis did not have a protected right to attend the professional schools to which they applied, then what did they have? A medical or law education is a privilege that is granted to some individuals and denied to others. When provided by the state, they are government benefits. This method of allocation does not violate the equal protection clause of the simple reason that they are not protected rights, or common occupations of life.[52] The only legal argument that can be made here is that the method of allocating slots in professional schools places an undue burden on under-served racial groups in a population.

Within the framework of jurisprudence, neither DeFunis nor Bakke had a property interest right in attending the schools to which they sought admission. They simply had an abstract interest. In the *Roth* case, the Court made a distinction between a property interest right which gives an individual a legitimate claim of entitlement to a benefit, and simply his abstract interest in such a benefit. It stated, "To have a property interest in a benefit, a person clearly must have more than a unilateral expectation of it. He must, instead, have a legitimate claim of entitlement."[53]

It is clear from this analysis that meritocracy or performance cannot legally be used as a basis for launching the reverse-discrimination argument. Therefore, affirmative action does not discriminate against individuals because it does not deprive them of any rights that qualify for protection under the Fourteenth Amendment.

POLICY IMPLICATIONS OF THE REVERSE-DISCRIMINATION DOCTRINE

The sanctioning of the reverse-discrimination argument by the U.S. Supreme Court in the *Bakke* case raises some serious negative policy implications for blacks as they attempt to achieve their fair share of American goal values.[54] First, this doctrine has in effect established a double standard of judicial review. Marginally qualified whites can arbitrarily and capriciously use the instrumentalities of the government to challenge the managerial prerogatives of companies or agencies that have an affirmative-action program. One policy repercussion of this standard of review is that individual whites have the potential to deny and/or to foreclose the freedom of blacks to take advantage of a wide range of educational and employment opportunities in the future.

Furthermore, the reverse-discrimination doctrine allows marginally qualified whites to challenge the managerial prerogatives of companies that have an affirmative-action program, but it does not allow these individuals to question the same when companies hire other whites with lesser qualifications. Hence this double standard of judicial review encourages individual whites to challenge affirmative-action programs at will.

Shortly after the California State Supreme Court ruled that the University of California's affirmative-action program discriminated against whites, both state and federal courts were inundated with reverse-discrimination cases.[55] Although many of these cases were thrown out of court, a large percentage were held to be in violation of the equal protection clause before the dispute was settled by the U.S. Supreme Court in *United Steelworkers v. Weber* (1979).[56]

After the *Weber* decision, the number of reverse-discrimination cases began to diminish. While the Court's decision favored the defendant, it was narrowly decided, with Justices Lewis Powell and John Paul Stevens taking no part in the deliberation.[57] If either one of these justices had participated in the deliberation, the outcome might have been different. Both Powell and Stevens had previously decided in favor of Bakke's claim. Judging from the strong dissenting opinions by Justice William Rehnquist and Chief Justice Warren Burger, the Court might have ruled the same way it did in the *Bakke* case.

The *Weber* case centered around a voluntary affirmative-action agreement signed by the Kaiser Aluminum & Chemical Corporation and the United Steelworkers Union to select one minority applicant for its

training program for every nonminority applicant until the percentage of blacks in craft positions equaled the percentage of blacks in the local work force. Eligibility for the craft training programs was to be determined on the basis of plant seniority, with black and white applicants to be selected on the basis of their relative seniority within their racial group.[58]

The training program offered only nine positions in three on-the-job training programs for skilled craft jobs. Brian Weber, a white, applied for all three programs and was not selected to participate in any. The successful applicants were five blacks and four whites. Two of the blacks had less seniority than Weber. However, there was no seniority selection process before the adoption of this voluntary program; Kaiser had always filled its craft positions with outsiders. This resulted in the company's hiring all whites for the craft openings. To offset this imbalance, Kaiser adopted a voluntary program to train its production workers to fill craft openings with the proviso that "at least 50% of the trainees were to be black until the percentage of black skilled craftworkers in the plant approximated the percentage of blacks in the local labor force."[59] Because the program selected several blacks with less seniority than some whites, Weber filed a class-action lawsuit in the federal district court on behalf of himself and other whites who were similarly situated, claiming that the program discriminated against whites who had more seniority than the blacks who were selected. The complaint alleged that the program violated Section 703(a) and (d) of Title VII of the Civil Rights Act of 1964 that prohibited discrimination in hiring and selecting applicants for apprentices for training on account of race.

The district court entered a judgment in favor of Weber. It enjoined the company from further implementing its affirmative-action program on the basis that the program discriminated against some whites. The district court's decision was affirmed by the court of appeals on the basis that "all employment preferences based upon race, including those preferences incidental to bona fide affirmative action plans, violated Title VII's prohibition against racial discrimination."[60] However, this decision was overturned by the U.S. Supreme Court on the grounds that Congress did not intend for Title VII to "limit traditional business freedom to such a degree as to prohibit all voluntary, race-conscious affirmative action."[61] If Congress had intended such prohibition, the Court held, it would have used the phrase "require or permit" racial preference. Instead, Congress said that nothing contained in Title VII "shall be interpreted to require any employer . . . to grant preferential treatment . . . to any group because of race."[62] Based on the premise that Congress neglected to include the phrase "require or permit," the Supreme Court held that the Kaiser affirmative-action program was constitutional. The program did not violate the interests of whites by foreclosing a wide range of employment opportunities for the entire white race, as had been the case in past discrimination.[63]

Yet the mere fact that Weber had the privilege of using the instrumentalities of government to block an entire affirmative-action program because he disagreed with it has broad policy implications, for it places the basic human rights of blacks not on principles of law but on the goodwill of white people. This construction of the law marks a drastic departure from the principle which the Court acknowledged in *Yick Wo v. Hopkins* (1886), where it stated nearly a hundred years ago that the discrimination of personal liberty was not meant to

leave room for the play and action of purely personal and arbitrary power . . . . The very idea that one man [in this case, an entire race] may be compelled to hold his life, or the means of living, or any material right essential to the enjoyment of life, at the mere will of another, seems to be intolerable in any country where freedom prevails.[64]

But the reverse-discrimination doctrine not only allowed Weber to restrict the advancement of blacks at the Kaiser plant but also was able to foreclose a wide range of employment opportunities for blacks throughout the nation. For years many companies had been unsure of what role they should play in affirmative action because of the potential liabilities of their actions in either adopting or not adopting an affirmative-action program. As Justice Harry A. Blackmun noted, companies "on one hand . . . face liability for past discrimination against blacks, and on the other they face liability to whites for any voluntary preferences adopted to mitigate the effects of prior discrimination against blacks."[65]

The next voluntary affirmative-action case is *Fullilove et al. v. Klutznick, Secretary of Commerce, et al.* (1980).[66] This case stemmed from the Public Work Employment Act of 1977, which required that "at least 10% of federal funds granted for local public works projects must be used by the state or local grantee to procure services or supplies from businesses owned by minority group members, defined as United States citizens 'who are Negroes, Spanish-speaking, Orientals, Indians, Eskimos, and Aleuts.'"[67] Minority Business Enterprises (MBE) were assured a contract even if they were not the lowest bidder and "if their bids reflect merely attempts to cover costs inflated by the present effects of prior disadvantage and discrimination."[68]

The 10 percent set-aside was challenged by several associations of construction contractors and subcontractors on the ground that the program had caused them to sustain economic injury due to enforcement of the program and that "the MBE provision on its face violated the Equal Protection Clause of the Fourteenth Amendment, the equal protection component of the Due Process Clause of the Fifth Amendment, and various statutory antidiscrimination provisions."[69] The above allegation gets at the crux of the opponents' opposition to affirmative action and demonstrates the dire policy implications that the reverse-discrimination argument could have on the human rights of blacks. The 10 percent MBE program required only $400 million of the $4 billion allocated for the Public Work Employment Act to be set aside for a set of identified minority contractors. Embedded in this argument is the notion that any attempt to design a mechanism to guarantee equality of treatment for blacks deprives whites of benefits that they would have otherwise enjoyed on merit. But the irony of the argument, particularly in the *Fullilove* case, is that there was no evidence that small contractors would have enjoyed the benefit of a contract even if there were no 10 percent MBE program. This seriously undermines the petitioners' contention that they sustained an economic injury.

Also implied in opponents' arguments is the notion that the white contractors had a legitimate claim of entitlement to a contract. But nothing in the constitution or in civil rights laws supports such a claim. The only way they could get their case to court was to invoke the racial classification rule. As previously argued, this is a misapplication of that rule. To recapitulate, the racial classification rule was originally intended to review legislation that sought to restrict or deprive an entire racial group of its property interest and liberty interest rights. The 10 percent MBE program did not restrict the entire white race from obtaining a share of the $4 billion. It simply ensured minorities that they would obtain at least 10 percent of the benefits. Equally significant in the Court's decision to uphold the 10 percent MBE program was that it preserved Congress' power to enact "appropriate legislation." A decision in favor of the petitioners would have set a precedent whereby citizens could arbitrarily and capriciously challenge Congress' authority to promote the general welfare.

Further, if the Supreme Court had affirmed the petitioner's contention that the MBE program violated the Civil Rights Act of 1964, it would have elevated the authority of this act above the Article I, Section 8, paragraph 1 of the Constitution—Congress' spending power. The Court had repeatedly rejected any constitutional challenge to congressional authority to employ "spending power to further broad policy objectives by conditioning receipt of monies upon compliance by the recipient with federal statutory and administrative directives."[70] Although the petitioners did not succeed in having the affirmative-action program declared unconstitutional, they were able to undermine significantly the affirmative-action process. Their challenge offered many employers, including local governments, an incentive to resist implementing the program on the basis that it discriminated against whites.

Third, if the Supreme Court had sustained the petitioners' argument, it would have established a policy that any measure Congress takes to reduce unemployment among blacks would be unconstitutional. Giving individual whites the right to challenge affirmative action in the public employment sector raises serious questions of human rights violations, for it restricts the government's attempt to extend the liberty interest rights not only of black employees but also of the black community as well. In the public work sector, many agencies provide services to the black community which are necessary for the enjoyment of civil rights. Swift implementation of the MBE program would promote the general welfare by reducing the soaring rate of unemployment among blacks. Within the last ten years, the unemployment rate among whites has ranged between 6 percent and 10 percent, but the black unemployment rate has ranged between 14 percent and 30 percent for black males and 40 percent to 60 percent for black youths.

Having blacks working in state and local government serves a community function as well as an affirmative-action function. As the Senate Subcommittee on Labor and Public Welfare noted in 1972, state and local governmental agencies play a significant role in the daily lives of the average citizen of various communities. Equal employment opportunities in these agencies are essential to eliminate practices that tend to perpetuate discrimination:

Discrimination by government therefore serves a doubly destructive purpose. The exclusion of minorities from effective participation in the bureaucracy not only promotes ignorance of minority problems in that particular community, but also creates mistrust, alienation, and all too often hostility toward the entire process of government.[71]

A sense of trust between governmental agencies and the black community is essential for protecting the liberty interest rights of blacks. Yet under the principle of merit, individual whites can use the instrumentalities of the government to restrict or deprive the entire black community of their liberty interest rights. The only prerequisite for challenging this program is for whites to allege that affirmative action discriminates against whites who may be more qualified than some blacks. Based on this premise, any white can go to court and seek an injunction against implementation of any voluntary affirmative-action program. This construction raises serious questions of human rights violations, for its operative effect is to deprive an entire race of their liberty interest rights. An examination of various reverse discrimination cases in the public work sector will lend credence to this argument.

Many cases can be cited to illustrate that the civil rights of blacks have been held hostage to the goodwill of white people but the following two cases will suffice. In *Williams v. New Orleans* (1982), an attempt was made to correct the imbalance in the hiring of police officers in the New Orleans Police Department. A consent decree was sought in the U.S. district court to promote black and white officers on a one-to-one basis until blacks comprise 50 percent of the rank of all officers.[72] The decree was opposed by a group of white police officers, females and the U.S. Justice Department on the basis that the plan would hurt nonblacks who did not benefit from the practice of past discrimination. It is ironic that the Justice Department interceded on behalf of nonblacks, because these individuals had neither a property interest right nor a liberty interest right in employment. And if it were not for the misapplication of the suspect classification ruling, these individuals would not have had a standing in court. The decree did not violate the liberty interest of whites by foreclosing a wide range of their future employment opportunities in the police department. It was simply an attempt to correct a pattern of past discrimination inequalities.

In *Bratton v. City of Detroit* (1983), the city adopted an affirmative-action plan which required that black and white sergeants be promoted "in equal numbers until 50 percent of lieutenants are black."[73] The intent of the program was to redress past discrimination in the process of promotion. A group of white sergeants filed a lawsuit in federal district court, seeking to enjoin the city from implementing the program. Their basic argument was that the program violated their rights under Title VII of the Civil Rights Act of 1964 and the Fourteenth Amendment and that the program unduly stigmatized whites. The court rejected the plaintiffs' contention and ruled that neither Title VII nor the Fourteenth Amendment prohibited the city from redressing past injury by affirmative action.[74]

In sum, the courts' sanctioning of reverse discrimination on the basis of merit has grave policy implications for blacks. It removes their basic human and civil rights from the protection of law and places them at the doorstep of the good-will of white people. Hence it has the effect of depriving blacks of their fair share of the American system of economic and social benefits that are accorded to them and to whites by law.

NOTES

1. See Peter H. Odegard, *American Politics* (New York: Harper, 1938), p. 1.

2. Fringe benefits include such things as medical and dental insurance, tax annuities, retirement plans, and paid vacations.

3. This is the argument used by the Reagan administration as justification for opposing affirmative-action hiring goals.

4. See Nathan Glazer, *Affirmative Action: Ethnic Inequality and Public Policy* (New York: Basic, 1975), p. 221.

5. This argument was highlighted in the *amicus* brief submitted to the U.S. Supreme Court in *Regents of the University of California v. Bakke*, 438 U.S. 265 (1978), by the Anti-Defamation League and B'nai B'rith.

6. Glazer, *Affirmative Action*, p. 197.

7. For a discussion on the relation between property rights and the merit system, see *Bailey v. Richardson*, 86 U.S. App. D.C. 248, 182 f.d. aff'd by an equally divided court, 341 U.S. 918 (1950).

8. *DeFunis v. Odegaard*, 416 U.S. 312, 40 L.Ed.2d 164, 94 S.Ct. 1704 (1974); *Regents of the University of California v. Bakke*, 438 U.S. 265, 98 S.Ct. 2733, 57 L.Ed.2d (1978); and *United Steelworkers of America v. Weber*, 443 U.S. 193, 61 L.Ed.2d 480 (1979).

9. See *Bolling v. Sharpe*, 347 U.S. 497, 499–500 (1954).

10. See *Graham v. Richardson*, 403 U.S. 365, 374 (1971).

11. See *Board of Regents of State College v. Roth*, 408 U.S. 564 (1972).

12. Glazer, *Affirmative Action*, p. 221.

13. See Sidney Hook, "Discrimination, Color Blindness and the Quota System," in Barry Gross (ed.), *Reverse Discrimination* (Buffalo, N.Y.: Prometheus, 1977), pp. 84–87.

14. See John H. Ely, "The Constitutionality of Reverse Discrimination," *University of Chicago Law Review* 22 (1974): 388.

15. See *Board of Regents of State College v. Roth*, p. 577.

16. *The Slaughter-House Cases* 36 (1873), 16 Wallace 36.

17. See, e.g., *Bell v. Burson*, 402 U.S. 542 (1970); *Shapiro v. Thompson*, 394 U.S. 618, 627 (1969); and *Pickering v. Board of Education*, 391 U.S. 563, 568 (1969).

18. See *Regents of the University of California v. Bakke*.

19. See *National Ins. Co. v. Tidewater Co.*, 337 U.S. 582, 646 (1968).

20. *Bailey v. Richardson*, p. 248.

21. *Board of Regents of State College v. Roth*, p. 577.

22. Ibid., p. 572.

23. *Meyer v. Nebraska*, 262 U.S. 390, 399 (1923).

24. *Bolling v. Sharpe*, p. 499.

25. *Joint Anti-Fascist Refuge Committee v. McGarth*, 341 U.S. 123 (1968).

26. This seemed to be the cornerstone on which the majority opinion was written in the *Bakke* case. The opinion was written by Justice Stanley Mosk.

27. See *Hirabayshi v. United States*, 320 U.S. 81 (1943).

28. Ibid.

29. *Korematsu v. United States*, 323 U.S. 216 (1944).

30. *Bolling v. Sharpe*, p. 499.

31. All professional schools have had preferences. For example, at the University of Washington Law School "preferential policies were based on family background, which included children of alumni, athletic ability, musical skill and various other kinds of qualities for which colleges and universities were seeking. What may be new is the use of race or ethnic background as one of these factors but it's not the process of varying the standard performance criteria that's new." See Robert M. O'Neil, *The Advocates*, T.V. transcript, WTTW-TV (Chicago), PBS Network, aired March 14, 1974.

32. *Regents of the University of California v. Bakke*.

33. In *Taylor v. Beckham* the Court ruled that "it has held repeatedly and consistently that Government cannot employ 'property' and that in this particular case [property] is not a contract. We are able to perceive how it could be held to be 'liberty.' " (178 U.S. 548 [1900]).

34. See *Meyer v. Nebraska* (1923).

35. See *Schware v. Board of Bar Examiners*, 353 U.S. 232, 238 (1956).

36. *Meyer v. Nebraska*.

37. See *Yick Wo v. Hopkins*, 256 U.S. 367 (1886).

38. See *Munn v. Illinois*, 94 U.S. 113, 24 L.Ed. 77 (1877).

39. On these points, see Robert M. O'Neil, *Discriminating Against Discrimination* (Bloomington: Indiana University Press, 1975), p. 12.

40. See Allan P. Sindler, *Bakke, DeFunis and Minority Admissions* (New York: Longman, 1978), chap. 5.

41. See J. Owens Smith, "A commentary on *Bakke, DeFunis and Minority Admissions* by Allan P. Sindler," *Umoja* 4 (Fall 1980): 49–56.

42. See *Meyer v. Nebraska.*

43. See *Board of Regents of State College v. Roth.*

44. The California Supreme Court emphasized this argument in which it relied on a commentary written by Larry Lavinsky, "DeFunis Symposium" 75 *Columbia Law Review* (1975): 520–535.

45. See *Korematsu v. U.S.*

46. *McDonald v. Santa Fe Company*, 96 S.Ct. 2574 (1976).

47. See *Regents of the University of California v. Bakke.*

48. See *Board of Regents v. Roth.*

49. For further discussion on this point, see J. Owens Smith, "The Bakke Decision: A Flagrant Denial of Human Rights," *Western Journal of Black Studies* 2 (Winter 1979): 244–255.

50. On this point it has been argued that grades at various universities are computed differently. For example, an "A" at a state college may not have the same weight as an "A" at a state university. See Christopher Jencks, *Inequality: A Reassessment of Family and Schooling in America* (New York: Harper & Row, 1972), chaps. 2 and 3.

51. *Goldberg v. Kelley*, 397 U.S. 254 (1970).

52. See *Meyer v. Nebraska.*

53. See *Board of Regents v. Roth.*

54. For a discussion on these values, see Harold D. Lasswell, *The World Revolution of Our Time* (Palo Alto, Calif.: Stanford University Press, 1951), pp. 11–13.

55. See *Regents of the University of California v. Bakke.*

56. *United Steelworkers of America v. Weber*, 443 U.S. 193, 272 (1979).

57. Ibid., p. 2730.

58. Ibid.

59. Ibid., p. 2723.

60. Ibid., p. 2726.

61. Ibid., p. 2724.

62. Ibid., p. 2723.

63. Ibid., p. 2721.

64. 118 U.S. 356, 370 (1886).

65. *United Steelworkers of America v. Weber*, p. 2730.

66. *Fullilove et al. v. Klutznick, Secretary of Commerce et al.*, U.S. No. 78–1007 (1980).

67. Ibid., p. i.

68. Ibid.

69. Ibid., p. 3.

70. Ibid., p. 22.

71. *Legislative History of the Equal Employment Opportunity Act of 1972*, H.R. 1746 Senate, Subcommittee on Labor of the Senate Labor Committee on Labor and Public Welfare (H.R. 1746, P.L. 92–261), Amending Title VII of the Civil Rights Act of 1964, p. 419.

72. *Williams v. New Orleans* (DC E La. 543 F.Supp. 662) (CA5, 694 F.2d 987) (1982), p. 2414.

73. *Bratton v. City of Detroit* (CA6) 2613 (1982) *United States Law Week Final* 51 (June 1983).

74. Ibid., p. 2614.

9

James B. Stewart

Economic Policy and Black America

INTRODUCTION

Examination of the impacts of economic policy on the present and future situation of black Americans is a major undertaking. Virtually all domestic and international economic policies affect blacks to a significant degree. The particular status of blacks typically produces disproportional policy effects in comparison with society as a whole. In this analysis, attention is focused on policy arenas where the impacts on blacks are most direct and pronounced. The policies that shape the black economic experience today have important historical analogs, so we must be guided by the injunction of W.E.B. Du Bois that we can understand the present only by studying the past.[1]

Observed continuities over time can emanate from forces endemic to growth and development patterns in the U.S. economy, from consistency in the thrust of economic policies affecting blacks, or from some combination of the two. Historically, we know that selected policy instruments were specifically directed at blacks. By examining how the circumstances of blacks have changed as those instruments were modified to eliminate overt racial specificity, we can better understand the sensitivity of the economic situation of blacks to both minimal and substantial variation in selected economic policies. As an example, the minimum wage is a generalized policy instrument that affects blacks disproportionately and the institutions of chattel slavery and sharecropping contributed substantially to the present circumstances by limiting economic mobility and establishing a pattern of large-scale employment at subsistence wages.

Consideration of the implications of current policies on future configurations of the black economic experience must reflect the increasing degree of global interdependence and problems in the existing international economic order. Here historical perspectives are also useful, as illustrated by the fact that the institution of slavery was not simply a vehicle to stimulate domestic economic growth in the United States but a key ingredient of the international economic order during that particular era.

The principal thesis of this chapter is that the overall impact of economic policy on the black experience has been, and continues to be, the exploitation of black labor coupled with parallel exploitation of black consumer purchasing power.[2] The aggregate policy thrust can be seen by examining policies affecting the structure and functioning of labor markets, policies shaping the configuration of the economy and the location of economic activity, and policies affecting the acquisition of skills and general training. Because contemporary economic policy is the central topic of this chapter, the historical black economic experience will be examined only briefly. The chapter concludes with an examination of likely implications and impacts of economic policies on the future configuration of the black economic experience.

ECONOMIC CONTINUITY IN THE BLACK EXPERIENCE

The economic history of blacks can be divided into three partially overlapping epochs: the era of slavery, the era of debt peonage, and the era of wage peonage. These characterizations are meant to convey the linkage of the model black American to the economic order during each period. The components of the composite black response to exploitative economic policies across the three periods include (1) individual economic adjustment through job search, human capital investment, migration, entrepreneurial activity and so on; (2) collective organizational efforts to enhance the effectiveness of individual adjustment efforts spanning various sectors, including labor union formation, farmers' alliances, trade associations, mutual aid societies, international linkages, and so on; and (3) the use of political activity and organization to alter or eliminate adverse "system generated" policies through such actions as lobbying and boycotts.

During slavery the law and economic policy treated blacks as a functional equivalent of physical capital by official enforcement of claims of transferable property rights in human beings. The altered legal status of blacks associated with emancipation immediately transformed the optimum control apparatuses and patterns of capital accumulation, because capital could no longer be accumulated in the form of human beings. The Reconstruction era marked a brief flirtation with the idea of reversing the historical pattern through regulation and guarantee of labor contracts, an experiment ended by the infamous Compromise of 1877. New mechanisms were developed to transfer the freedmen's rights to own labor power to the planters. In the words of Charles Johnson, the majority of blacks were kept in the "shadow of the plantation" through the introduction of tenancy arrangements, for example, sharecropping.[3] Unscrupulous credit arrangements and pricing policies and the declining competitiveness of the agricultural sector made it virtually impossible to cover the debt servicing costs associated with production inputs and consumption goods. Some were able to escape the shadow of the plantation to find employment opportunities in the Northern industrial order, but wages for unskilled workers were depressed by the continuing influx of European immigrants and severe economic recessions. Further, many blacks were displaced from skilled occupations.[4]

Tables 9.1 and 9.2 show the occupations of gainfully employed blacks between 1890 and 1930. Disproportionate black concentration in agriculture and domestic service is evident, as well as the continuing impact of the geographical distribution of blacks during the slavery era. Black women remained relegated to two occupational classifications throughout this period: agriculture and domestic and personal service. These occupations accounted for no less than 90 percent of all gainfully employed during any of the three census years.

The Great Depression contributed to a drop in black employment of approximately 18.5 percent between 1930 and 1940, while total employment fell only about 5 percent. Many farm owners and nonsharecropping tenants were again reduced to sharecropping to survive. The number of black sharecroppers increased by approximately 20,000 between 1910 and 1940, while the number of nonwhite farm operators actually declined by 200,000. Although blacks were increasingly escaping the shadow of the plantation, the final death knell for the system of debt peonage was not sounded until the invention of the mechanical cotton picker in the 1950s.

Table 9.1
Occupational Distribution of Gainfully Employed Blacks and Whites, Selected Years, 1890–1930 (in percentages)

	Black			White		
Occupation	1890	1910	1930	1890	1910	1930
Total Workers (in thousands)	(3,073)	(5,193)	(5,504)	(19,542)	(32,774)	(42,584)
Agriculture, Forestry, and Fishing	57	55	37	37	30	20
Manufacturing and Mechanical	6	13	19	25	30	30
Transportation and Communication	5	5	7	16	7	8
Domestic and Personal Service	31	22	29	17	8	8
Other	1	6	9	5	25	34

Source: Bureau of the Census, *The Social and Economic Status of the Black Population in the United States: An Historical View, 1790–1978, Current Population Reports,* Special Series P–23, No. 80 (Washington, D.C.: Government Printing Office, 1979), Table 3, p. 74.

Table 9.2
Occupational Distribution of Gainfully Employed Black Workers by Region,
Selected Years, 1890–1930 (in percentages)

Occupation	South			North		
	1890	1910	1930	1890	1910	1930
Total Workers (in thousands)	(2,746)	(4,592)	(4,210)	(327)	(600)	(1,293)
Agriculture, Forestry, and Fishing	62	62	47	16	8	3
Manufacturing and Mechanical	5	9	15	9	20	30
Transportation and Communication	4	4	6	9	9	11
Domestic and Personal Service	28	18	24	63	48	43
Other	1	7	8	2	16	13

Source: Bureau of the Census, *The Social and Economic Status of the Black Population in the United States: An Historical View, 1790–1978, Current Population Reports,* Special Series P–23, No. 80 (Washington, D.C.: Government Printing Office, 1979), Table 3, p. 74.

Blacks escaped from the grips of Southern debt peonage only to run into the clutches of Northern wage peonage in what would become the shadow of the skyscraper. This conclusion is supported by the data in Table 9.3 which allows comparison of black and white occupational distributions between 1940 and 1977. For black males the massive drop in the proportion of agricultural workers between 1940 and 1960 is accounted for principally by an increase in the proportion of craftsmen and operatives, and workers whose occupation was not reported. For black women, the principal shifts in the occupational distribution were from agriculture and private household work to blue-collar, white-collar, and service industries. The occupational distributions for black and white males were remarkably stable between 1960 and 1977, while that for women remained in flux into the 1970s.

Succeeding waves of black migrants to Northern urban areas found restricted residential opportunities that limited choices to areas close to the central business district, while jobs increasingly migrated to suburban areas. Growth in employment opportunities in black-owned businesses has had little impact on black employment. Employment in black-owned firms in 1969, 1972 and 1977 was approximately 153,000, 147,000 and 164,000 respectively. Caught in the vise of restricted urban and rural opportunities, blacks increasingly chose or were forced into military service; the proportion of blacks in the military climbed steadily between 1954 and 1965 from 7.9 percent to 9.5 percent and reached

Table 9.3

Occupational Distribution of Experienced Male and Female Civilian Workers, Selected Years, 1940–1977 (in percentages)

| | MALE | | | | | | | |
| | Black | | | | White | | | |
Occupation	1940	1960	1970	1977	1940	1960	1970	1977
Total Employed (in thousands)	(2,937)	(3,642)	(4,091)	(5,058)	(30,932)	(39,462)	(43,501)	(51,112)
Farm Workers	41	11	4	3	21	8	4	4
Blue Collar Workers	38	54	53	58	42	45	43	46
White Collar Workers	5	11	17	22	30	37	40	42
Service Workers	15	15	14	17	6	6	7	8
Not Reported	1	8	12	--	1	4	5	--

| | FEMALE | | | | | | | |
| | Black | | | | White | | | |
Occupation	1940	1960	1970	1977	1940	1960	1970	1977
Total Employed (in thousands)	(1,542)	(2,455)	(3,329)	(4,435)	(9,564)	(18,549)	(25,471)	(34,324)
Farm Workers	16	3	1	1	2	1	1	1
Blue Collar Workers	7	14	17	19	22	18	16	15
White Collar Workers	6	17	32	43	52	59	61	65
Service Workers	70	57	38	37	22	17	16	19
Note Reported	1	8	12		1	5	6	--

Source: Bureau of the Census, *The Social and Economic Status of Black Population in the United States: An Historical View, 1790–1978, Current Population Reports,* Special Series P–23, No. 80 (Washington, D.C.: Government Printing Office, 1979), Table 3, p. 74.

11.1 percent in 1972. The occupational distribution of blacks in the military has mirrored the relegation to low-status occupations in the civilian sector.[5] Restricted opportunities have also contributed to disproportionate black involvement in the illicit and underground economies, with the expected effects on arrest and incarceration rates.[6]

Aggregate income comparisons generally reflect the occupational disparities described to this point, although the creation of what John Reid terms a "second class Black middle class" rapidly accelerated during the 1970s, and relative income gains were made in all segments of the income distribution.[7] Between 1949 and 1965, the index of income integration which measures the degree of overlap in the black/white median family income distribution increased from approximately .61 to .66. In 1966 the index shifted upward to .71 and remained in the .71 to .72 range through 1974. The value of the index is highest for families with two earners, generally falling into the .80 to .82 range. The ratio of median incomes between black and white male union members was .91 in 1970, compared with .82 for nonunion members. Yet the earnings of black male union members were only 98 percent of white male nonunion member earnings.

If family type is not controlled, the range of the ratio of black/white median family income was approximately .50 to .54 between 1947 and 1965, with an upward shift to the range .58 to .61 between 1966 and 1974. Between 1975 and 1981, the ratio fell from .60 to .56. One factor contributing to this trend is the differential rate of change in family composition, as the rate of increase in households headed by females among blacks far outdistanced that among whites. The median income of households headed by females as a proportion of all black households fell from 52 percent in 1964 to 43 percent in 1974, almost twice as large as the comparable decline among white families.

This pattern has obvious implications for the size and composition of the "poverty" population. In 1977, some 51 percent of all black households headed by females had incomes below the poverty level, compared with 24 percent of white families headed by females. Following a long period of steady decline, the poverty rate among both black and white families has been increasing since 1978. The overall poverty rates for black and white families in 1981 were 30.8 and 8.8 percent respectively. While 28 percent of white families with incomes below the poverty level resided in inner cities in 1976, the comparable figure for black families in the shadow of the skyscraper was 56 percent. As would be expected, patterns of receipt of various types of public assistance mirror the poverty distribution.[8]

The thesis of historical continuity takes a perverse twist when the unemployment experience of blacks is examined. The oft-quoted pun that the last time blacks experienced full employment was during slavery emphasizes that the transition to subsequent forms of control has imposed a continuing trade-off between freedom and employment security. The overall ratio of black and white unemployment rates has remained stable in the 2.0 range since 1948, when recording of official statistics by race began. Behind this stability, however, are several important trends. Generally, the unemployment rate among blacks deteriorates more rapidly than that among whites during economic downturns and recovers more rapidly during the recovery phase of the business cycle. In addition, in recent years the lowest unemployment achieved during economic upturns has been slowly creeping upward following each recession. The implications for the long-run black unemployment rate are foreboding. The data in Table 9.4 show the peak black unemployment rate and the lowest rate achieved following that peak before subsequent deteriorations for three periods. Calculating the average differentials between peaks and troughs and using the October 1982 black unemployment rate of 20.2 percent is as an estimate of the peak black

Table 9.4
Unemployment Rate for Blacks 16 Years and Over and Unemployment Rate Differentials, Selected Years

Year of Peak Black Unemployment Rate	Peak Unemployment Rate	Year of Lowest Unemployment Rate Subsequent to Peak Year	Minumum Unemployment Rate	Difference in Unemployment Rate, Peak to Trough
1950	9.0	1953	4.5	4.5
1958	12.6	1969	6.4	6.2
1975	14.7	1979	11.3	3.4
1982 (Oct.)	20.2	--	--	--
Average Differential	4.7			

Source: Bureau of the Census, *The Social and Economic Status of the Black Population in the United States: An Historical View, 1790–1978, Current Population Reports,* Special Series P-23, No. 80 (Washington, D.C.: Government Printing Office, 1979), Table 154, p. 209.

unemployment rate that will be experienced in the present downturn, the predicted minimum unemployment rate that blacks will likely experience before
the next economic downturn occurs is on the order of 15 percent. This pessi-
mistic forecast can serve as a useful backdrop for examination of the role of
economic policy in generating the patterns described above.

ECONOMIC POLICY AND HISTORICAL CONTINUITY

The New Deal and Its Aftermath

In response to the Great Depression, the New Deal instituted a new pattern
of government-market interaction. That role was influenced by Keynesian economics such that taxation policies, money supply policies, direct government
spending, and income transfers became tools to minimize economic fluctuations. Labor unions achieved full legal status in response to the continuing growth
of industrial capitalism, leading to greater rationalization of labor-management
relations. The acceptance of seniority as a means to regulate layoffs, establishment of minimum-wage guidelines, and overtime pay provisions also emerged
during this period as well as acceptance of progressive income taxation as a
means of financing governmental activities. Social support programs including
unemployment insurance and what has come to be known as the social security
system were established, and creation of housing lending agencies (including
the Federal Housing Administration) stimulated residential suburbanization and,
as a by-product, industrial suburbanization. Both processes gained additional
momentum in the 1950s with construction of the interstate highway system and
the associated beltways around central cities.

Immigration controls, previously strengthened in 1924 through the national origins system, continued to allow selectivity in matching the composition of labor supply and demand. The design of New Deal agricultural programs allowed landowners to withhold payments to sharecroppers, fueling continuing migration from the orbit of the shadow of the plantation. The demand for industrial labor generated by World War II and the disruption of immigration brought increased numbers of blacks into the shadow of the skyscraper.

The 1960s generated conditions that led to efforts to again rewrite the social contract. Efforts to construct the "Great Society" collided head on with the resource requirements of the Vietnam War. The seeds were thus sown for a pattern of continually escalating transfer payments and rampant inflation, costs offset in the short run by the squelching of social turmoil.[9] Employability of the disadvantaged was to be enhanced over time through government-sponsored training, including the Manpower Development and Training Act enacted in 1962. The legacy of that act was the Comprehensive Employment and Training Act (CETA) passed in 1973, which consolidated a plethora of fragmented programs. Over time, CETA programs were increasingly targeted toward the hardcore, structurally unemployed.

The antipoverty strategies described above are distinct from antidiscrimination mechanisms. The concept of equal employment opportunity became identified with this thrust, implemented through provisions of the Civil Rights Act of 1964. Unfortunately, the major enforcement vehicle, the Equal Employment Opportunity Commission, was not given any effective enforcement power until 1972 and consequently had to rely in the interim period on conciliation agreements. Comparable initiatives in the public sector led to an increase in the proportion of blacks employed in public administration as the percentage of total black employment rose from 5 percent in 1960 to 8 percent in 1980.

The role of public policy in relegating blacks to the shadow of the skyscraper can be seen from the examination of federal public housing policies. Public housing built during the post–World War II period through the mid–1970s was almost invariably of the high-rise variety located in existing predominantly black inner-city residential areas. An antidiscrimination thrust in federal lending activities was nonexistent until 1962, contributing to segregation in the more than 10 million upper-income and middle-income housing units constructed through government insurance programs since the 1930s. Studies of the extent to which the shifting location of jobs from central city to suburban areas, coupled with residential segregation, has adversely affected black employment have generated lively debate.[10]

The inflationary pressures generated by Vietnam-era spending patterns, combined with new inflationary shocks from rapid increase in petroleum prices, distorted the historical relationship between unemployment and inflation during the mid–1970s as simultaneous high inflation and high unemployment were experienced.

Limited evidence suggests that blacks were able to retain more gains during the 1974–1975 recession than in previous downturns, partly because equal employment opportunity policies have created a situation where black and white workers are not directly substitutable, requiring increased integration of an individual employer's work force. At the same time, discrimination practiced by fellow employees can limit gains, as studies that examined patterns of discrimination by labor unions show. These patterns have included total exclusion from unions, discriminatory seniority arrangements serving to restrict blacks to inferior job classifications, organization of black workers into separate locals, and failure to process grievances.[11] The political power of big labor has helped stifle efforts to tamper with the seniority system as a means to allocate layoffs, thereby ensuring that the "last hired, first fired" syndrome would continue to constrain relative gains by black workers.

The Humphrey-Hawkins Full Employment Bill, which as initially conceived would have mandated government employment programs if the unemployment rate exceeded a certain level, was a major casualty of stagflation. Concern with rampant inflation led to inclusion of a provision that allowed job creation only if the rate of inflation was below a given ceiling, making the legislation effectively worthless to the disadvantaged during the mid–1970s. The principal effect of civil rights laws on earnings and occupational patterns through the mid–1970s, then, was to change the configuration of discrimination rather than significantly reduce its impact on black earning and employment profiles.[12]

As stagflation persisted in the late 1970s, migration of jobs to low-wage states continued, with the impacts especially pronounced in the Frostbelt. In addition, the Frostbelt continued to lose its continuing tug-of-war with the Sunbelt for jobs as relatively lower wages, less extensive unionization, and state tax concessions successfully lured employers to relocate. Foreign competition intensified in ways that worsened the black economic experience, as shown by a recent study of recipients of trade adjustment assistance benefits which found that minorities were disproportionately represented.[13] The continued migration of jobs placed enormous pressure on state and local government efforts in the Northeast and the Midwest to maintain the quality of public services. The federal government was forced to reduce the rate of increase in social expenditures. One result of these forces was a declining rate of reduction in poverty between 1975 and 1978.[14]

Reaganomics as Economic Policy

The election of Ronald Reagan was touted as a mandate to reverse the direction of economic policy since the New Deal. Gone was Jimmy Carter's hope to institute a policy of reindustrialization to promote balanced regional growth and enhance the position of U.S. producers vis-à-vis foreign competitors. Candidate Reagan was able to convince the public that big government was the source of all domestic economic ills, and he rode to victory on promises to produce continual prosperity through the miracles of supply-side economics, reduced government intervention in the marketplace, reduction in the size of the federal government, the return of usurped authority to the states, and reduction in "entitlement" programs. Reduction in the size of the federal bureaucracy was to be accomplished by eliminating "superfluous" programs and shrinking others through reductions in force (RIFs). This program was presumably compatible with a massive military buildup. A balanced federal budget was to be achieved by 1984 while a tight monetary policy wrung the inflationary tendencies out of the economy. Problems of those wilting in the shadow of the skyscraper would be solved through the creation of "enterprise zones" within which locating employers would be given tax breaks and a partial subsidy of the wages paid to disadvantaged zone residents and through the adoption of lower minimum-wage rates for teenagers. CETA training programs were to be replaced by a smaller cooperative training approach involving the private sector, since workers could presumably easily vote with their feet. A "safety net" would supposedly protect the "truly disadvantaged" in conjunction with volunteerism and increased philanthropy as federal antipoverty efforts were severely curtailed.

The hallmark of supply-side economics was to be dramatic tax cuts targeted toward reducing marginal tax rates as a stimulus to savings and investment. Since the more affluent account for a disproportionate amount of savings, it was only logical that the tax cuts would favor that segment of the population.[15] Special tax provisions for businesses, including swapping of investment credits, were designed to produce an additional stimulus. In the short run the loss of tax revenue would be offset by reductions in government expenditures. In the longer run, the new investment generated by the supply-side cuts was to produce enough tax revenue to more than offset the initial drain on federal coffers. The disadvantaged would benefit in the long run as the benefits of prosperity "trickled down."

The overall fiscal thrust of "Reaganomics" can be seen from Table 9.5.[16] The following features are especially critical to the present analysis: (1) the desired percentage reduction in assistance to the poor through 1987 exactly matches the percentage increase between 1973 and 1981; (2) sizable increases in expenditures for "entitlement" programs serving the nonpoor; and (3) a rapid escalation in defense costs.

The magnitude and timing of the first phase of the tax cut ensured that little stimulus would be forthcoming, for they were counteracted by increases in state and local taxes and an increase in social security taxes beginning in January 1982. Persistently high real interest rates engendered by the Federal Reserve's continuing tight money policy made investment in new plants and equipment an irrational decision for businesses faced with the lowest capacity utilization rate in the post–World War II period. Instead, the increased cash flow financed a mad merger scramble as managers pursued the most profitable and lowest risk investments available.

The contradictions of Reaganomics emerged in sharp relief when Americans were exhorted to spend the U.S. economy out of the recession using tax cut

Table 9.5
Annual Real Growth Rate in Selected Categories of Federal Expenditures,
1973–1981 and 1981–1983

	1973-81	1981-83
Total Expenditures	4.8%	-0.5%
Post and Future Wars (Principally Defense Expenditures), Interest and Veterans Payments)	3.5	8.0
Income Support for the Poor (Principally Food, Public Assistance, and Unemployment Insurance)	9.3	-9.3
Income Support for the Non-Poor (Principally Social Security, Retirement Programs and Agricultural Support Programs)	6.0	2.3
National Public Goods	4.2	-17.4
Regional Public Goods (Principally Roads, Waterways, and Grants to State and Local Governments)	2.5	-18.1

Source: William Nordhaus, "The Budget: Let Them Eat Jelly Beans," *The New York Times,* February 21, 1982. © 1982 by New York Times Co. Reprinted by permission.

proceeds rather than increasing savings, originally promoted as the cornerstone of supply-side economics. Despite declining interest rates in the latter part of 1982, a healthy economic recovery remains elusive and the unemployment rate of blacks and whites remains at post–Depression highs. Despite earlier repeated entreaties to ''stay the course'' even though the ship of state was beginning to show increasing resemblance to the *Titanic*, signs are that course corrections will be forthcoming, including a pseudo $4.3 billion public-works job program. Prospects of $200 billion budget deficits have exploded balanced budget myths, and crisis in the international financial arena threatens the existing international economic order.

Reaganomics: Policy Implications for the Black Community

The impact of the Reagan program on the economic well-being of blacks must be examined in the context of the administration's current direction vis-à-vis equal employment opportunity and other relevant civil rights initiatives.[17] The Justice Department's employment discrimination policy no longer insists on or supports numerical or statistical formulas providing preferential treatment. The Civil Rights Act of 1982, which sought to standardize federal civil rights investigation and complaint enforcement resolution efforts, was opposed by the U.S. Civil Rights Commission. The commission at the time also opposed a proposal by the Office of Personnel Management which sought to eliminate the requirements and guidelines that provided for equal employment opportunity and affirmative action by state and local governments.

The obvious adverse effects of the diluted equal employment opportunity enforcement strategy, if successfully implemented, will come on top of the impacts of the overall Reagan program. When we recall that blacks benefited disproportionately from the expansion of employment in the public sector, it is obvious that the adverse effects of public-sector shrinkage will also have a disproportionate impact on blacks. The AFL-CIO has estimated that job losses for the 1982–1983 fiscal years will total 1,733,400, with half these losses associated with the elimination of CETA training programs and public service employment, and another 25 percent associated with cutbacks in the urban and housing areas.[18] In addition, an analysis of reductions in force by Representative Michael Barnes (D–Maryland) indicates that in fiscal year 1981 minority employees were RIFed at one and a half times the ratio of nonminorities.[19]

The proposed military budget will also adversely affect black employment. Jobs created by arms production go primarily to skilled, as opposed to semiskilled, workers. Moreover, regional imbalances in military spending tend to exacerbate the migration of jobs from the Frostbelt to the Sunbelt. One study has shown that the opportunity costs measured in terms of employment opportunities for blacks, associated with each $10 billion of defense spending is 13,000 jobs.[20]

At one level of analysis the impact of President Reagan's social program cuts on black economic well-being is obvious. It should be noted that transfer payments to the nonpoor have always dwarfed those targeted at the poor, yet they are scheduled for less retrenchment.[21] It is critical, however, to examine the impact in the context of the call for a "New Federalism." President Reagan's New Federalism as originally conceived would involve trading a federal takeover of Medicaid for the states assuming full fiscal responsibility for Aid to Families with Dependent Children, food stamp, and forty-three other programs. The likely results would be larger differentials in levels of support among states, and more rapidly declining levels of support of these programs than possible at the federal level because of greater possibility of voter control. Studies have shown that all states would lose through the proposed Indian-giving arrangement, and the current fiscal plight of the states has led so far to a response of "Thanks, but no thanks."[22]

As would be expected, the labor movement has thus far successfully opposed establishment of a differential minimum wage for teenage workers, although the latest proposal to institute subminimum wages during the summer months may be enacted. An earlier compromise has involved no cost-of-living adjustments in the minimum wage since 1981, serving to reduce the cost to employers in real terms, but it has not stimulated any significant job creation in the current economic climate. Those benefiting from the provisions of the Job Training Partnership Act are likely to be the most employable, with the truly hard-core unemployed left to increase participation in the underground and illicit economies. Consistent with the thesis of historical continuity, the current teenage labor market problems stem to a large extent from the decline since the 1940s of employment opportunities in the agricultural sector.

POLICY IMPLICATIONS AND THE ECONOMIC FUTURE OF BLACK AMERICANS

The major policy implication of the preceding analysis is the need for a comprehensive economic plan to address the continuing weaknesses in the domestic and international economies. President Jimmy Carter's reindustrialization strategy was a recognition of the need for a planned approach to foster economic revitalization. Without such an approach the current thrust of economic policies will have predictable effects on the economy as a whole and on the black economic experience in particular.

Despite protestations to the contrary by Reaganites, global economic transformation will in all likelihood generate lackluster economic performance throughout the decade. Even if an overly optimistic set of assumptions is employed, the overall unemployment rate is unlikely to drop below 7.5 percent during the 1980s, implying a black unemployment rate of 15 percent, as suggested previously. These patterns will be exacerbated by the stranglehold of the shadow of the skyscraper, which restricts black mobility as the military buildup fosters increased inequality between the Frostbelt and the Sunbelt. Increased displacement of the poor from the heart of the shadow of the skyscraper to its edges is likely as a result of expanded gentrification.

Much of the job creation in the civilian sector in the last half decade has occurred in small businesses. This trend is likely to continue, stimulated in part by what is termed the "new enterprise movement." Small firms are effectively exempt from equal employment opportunity requirements, a situation that could foster resurgence of older patterns of employment discrimination coupled with a continuation of the new patterns of differential on-the-job training investment.[23]

A comprehensive economic plan of the type advocated above must incorporate special provisions to reverse the historical and contemporary pattern on policy impacts of black Americans examined in this analysis. This was the thrust of the Community Renewal Employment Act introduced by the Black Congressional Caucus. Additional initiatives designed to spur economic gains could include efforts to require diminished use of the seniority system to allocate layoffs, and large-scale training and retraining programs to prepare workers for high-technology jobs and to improve the overall match of skill requirements and labor force capabilities. Existing patterns of use of overtime hours as a substitute for retraining workers during downturns, and hiring during early phases of economic recoveries, should be attacked through requiring double-time compensation for overtime hours rather than the present time-and-a-half. Expanded use of job-sharing arrangements could also help distribute unemployment more equitably. Increased support for employee ownership can also be an important element of a comprehensive program.

Blacks have a special role to play in creating the conditions whereby comprehensive economic planning is implemented. Coordination is required if efforts including boycotts and negotiated settlements pursued by Operation PUSH and the National Association for the Advancement of Colored People, the accumulation strategies of the Black United Fund, and the deliberation undertaken in connection with the Black Economic Summit are to coalesce into a momentum that will alter the pattern of historical continuity which has been examined. Achieving such coordination is the principal challenge to be met if black Americans are to make true and sustainable economic progress.

NOTES

1. W. E. B. Du Bois, "The Beginning of Slavery," *Voice of the Negro* 2 (February 1905): 104.

2. One of the earliest statements indicating appreciation of the possibilities of the black consumer market was raised by Northern abolitionist supporters of the Port Royal, South Carolina, "freedom" experiment during the Civil War. See Willie Lee Rose, *Rehearsal for Reconstruction: The Port Royal Experiment* (1964; reprint ed., New York: Oxford University Press, 1976).

3. The phrase "shadow of the plantation" is adopted from the book by Charles Johnson, *Shadow of the Plantation* (Chicago: University of Chicago Press, 1934).

4. See Lucian B. Gatewood, "The Black Artisan in the U.S., 1890–1930," *Review of Black Political Economy* 5 (Fall 1974): 19–44.

5. See Charles C. Moskos, "The American Dilemma in Uniform: Race in the Armed Forces," *Annals of the American Academy of Political and Social Science* 406 (March 1973): 94–106; and James B. Stewart and Joseph W. Scott, "The Institutional Decimation of Black American Males," *Western Journal of Black Studies* 2 (Summer 1978): 82–92.

6. Stewart and Scott, "The Institutional Decimation of Black American Males," p. 87.

7. John Reid, "Black America in the 1980s," *Population Bulletin* 37 (December 1982): 1–38.

8. See, e.g., U.S. Bureau of the Census, "Characteristics of Households Purchasing Food Stamps," *Current Population Reports*, Special Studies, Series P–23, no. 61 (Washington, D.C.: Government Printing Office, 1976).

9. Frances Fox Piven and Richard Cloward, *Regulating the Poor: The Functions of Public Welfare* (New York: Pantheon, 1971).

10. These studies are reviewed in Thomas Hyclak and James B. Stewart, "A Note on the Relative Earnings of Central City Black Males," *Journal of Human Resources* 16 (Spring 1981): 304–313.

11. Benjamin W. Wolkinson, *Blacks, Unions and the EEOC* (Lexington, Mass.: Lexington Books, 1973).

12. See, e.g., A. W. Niemi, Jr., "The Impact of Recent Civil Rights Laws: Relative Improvement in Occupational Structure, Earnings and Income by Nonwhites, 1960–70,"

American Journal of Economics and Sociology 33 (April 1974): 137–144; Alan G. King and Ray Marshall, ''Black-White Economic Convergence and the Civil Rights Act of 1964,'' *Labor Law Journal* 25 (August 1974): 462–471.

13. J. David Richardson, ''Trade Adjustment Assistance Under the United States Trade Act of 1974: An Analytical Examination and Worker Survey,'' in Jagdish L. Bhagnati (ed.), *Import Competition and Response* (Chicago: University of Chicago Press, 1982), pp. 321–368.

14. See Barry T. Hirsch, *The Antipoverty Effectiveness of Economic Growth and Transfers: Some New Evidence*, Working Paper No. 810601 (Greensboro: Center for Applied Research, University of North Carolina, 1981).

15. For documentation of the disproportionate tax benefits accruing to the affluent even after accounting for transfer payments, see Staffs of the Human Resources and Community Development Division and the Tax Analysis Division, Congressional Budget Office, ''Effects of Tax and Benefit Reductions in 1981 for Households in Different Income Categories,'' Special Study, Mimeographed (February 1982).

16. For a comprehensive analysis of Reaganomics, see John L. Palmer and Isabel V. Sawhill (eds.), *The Reagan Experiment* (Washington, D.C.: Urban Institute Press, 1982).

17. The summaries of recent developments on the civil rights front that follow are based primarily on material contained in various issues of *Civil Rights Update*, a periodical published by the U.S. Commission on Civil Rights.

18. AFL-CIO, *Reaganomics: The Second Dose* (February 1982).

19. See Michael D. Barnes, ''Impact of 1981 RIFs on Minorities and Women and Updated RIF Projections for FY82,'' mimeographed (December 1981).

20. See Marion Anderson, *Bombs or Bread: Black Unemployment and the Pentagon Budget* (Lansing, Mich.: Employment Research Associates, 1982).

21. As an example, projected federal expenditures for social security, old age and survivors insurance in fiscal year 1987 are $209.3 billion compared with $5.7 billion for public assistance payments.

22. For a comprehensive assessment of the fiscal conditions of state governments, see National Governors' Association Office of Research and Development, *Fiscal Survey of the States 1980–1987* (Washington, D.C., 1981).

23. See Edward Lazear, ''The Narrowing of Black-White Age Differentials Is Illusory,'' *American Economic Review* 69 (September 1979): 553–564.

10

Woodrow Jones, Jr.
Mitchell F. Rice

Black Health Care in an Era of Retrenchment Politics

Equality of access to health care is an important determinant of the general health of a population. The limitations of access to health care due to a low income have to some extent been compensated for by various insurance programs and a number of governmental programs. The effect has been a decline of inequities in terms of the health conditions of some members of the population. In the case of black Americans, however, significant disparities still exist when compared to white counterparts in the distribution of and access to health care. Nearly every set of health care indexes shows a substantial difference in the health care status of blacks and the dominant population group.[1] Joseph Gayles remarks that "Black people are ignored, mistreated, abused, and brutalized by the current health care delivery system in the United States."[2] The disparities are symptomatic of a lack of black input into health care policy and decision-making processes, especially in a period in which there is governmental retrenchment from social welfare programs.

Retrenchment has become the label attached to the creation of the "New Federalism" of the Reagan administration. There are two key tenets of the New Federalism. First, states have a responsibility to provide certain types of services to their citizens. However, in the movement toward the social welfare state, as epitomized by the New Deal, state governments have retrenched in providing their share of the burden and the benefits of governmental intervention. Second, in the provision of certain types of services a market approach is preferable to governmental intervention. It is assumed that removal of the government from the health care marketplace would allow development of a more highly competitive health care system.

In this chapter we assess present black/white health care disparities and examine a selected number of health conditions that demonstrate the extent of the disparities in the health status of the black population. This chapter also looks at contemporary efforts at retrenchment and their impact on the health status and health care of black Americans. A descriptive analysis of the inequities in health status experienced by blacks pays particular attention to infant mortality, acute and mental disorders, and prevention strategies. In each area we examine the differences between black health care and white health care. The conclusion suggests that retrenchment politics is making the health care system in the United States less responsive to black health care needs.

ISSUES IN BLACK HEALTH CARE

Infant Mortality

Adequate medical services begin before birth and continue with the provision of maternal care and child care. Research indicates that there is a lack of neonatal and postneonatal medical care for blacks.[3] While such contributing factors as poverty, lack of knowledge, urbanization and the debilitating effects of unemployment may be plausible explanations,[4] the exact relationship of each of these factors to the lack of neonatal and postneonatal care remains the subject of much study and inquiry.[5] The gains in reducing the impact of each of these factors are shown in Figure 10.1. From 1950 to 1978 the infant mortality rates for all races indicated decreased steadily over time. From 1950 to 1955 black

Figure 10.1
Infant Mortality Rates by Race: United States, 1950–1977
(rate per 1,000 live births)

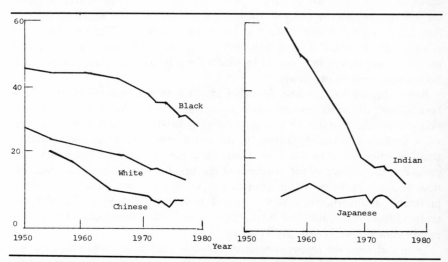

Source: U.S. Department of Health and Human Services, Public Health Service, *Health of the Disadvantaged, Chart Book II* (Washington, D.C., September 1980), p. 35, Chart 26.

infant mortality decreased slightly. From 1955 to 1960 there was a slight increase in black infant mortality, but black-white differences in infant mortality decrease significantly after 1960. This change can be attributed to the availability of care from various state and federal social programs.

Table 10.1 shows that the excess of black infant mortality rate over whites varies according to geographic area. The North-Central core provides the greatest excess, while the West has the lowest excess of black over white infant mortality. While some research suggests that the urbanization process may in part explain the decline in postneonatal deaths,[6] the geographic data in Table 10.1 seem to offer little support. Urbanization does appear to have some impact on the infant mortality rate in the West, because it increases as the size of the Standard Metropolitan Statistical Area (SMSA) increases. Other regions do not exhibit a consistent pattern suggested by the urbanization hypothesis. Outside the SMSA, there is a higher excess black infant mortality in areas not adjacent to the SMSA. Otherwise, geographic location has a differential impact on black infant mortality. The policy implications of these data are quite apparent for black infant care. There is a need for prenatal and postneonatal medical care services. Further, provision of these services in urban and rural areas is critical for the reduction in the infant mortality rate for blacks.

Table 10.1
Excess of Black Infant Mortality Rate over White Infant Mortality Rate Expressed in Percentage for Geographic Regions and Location of County of Residence: United States, 1973–1974 (rates per 1,000 births)

Location of County of Residence	United States	North-east	North Central	South	West
United States	79.3	83.2	91.2	69.5	57.9
Within SMSA	80.4	85.7	94.4	67.4	62.7
Large SMSA	85.9	86.3	96.7	73.5	65.2
Core	82.8	76.4	94.3	65.9	67.5
Fringe	82.1	96.1	87.1	80.3	29.0
Medium SMSA	75.0	90.1	95.1	62.4	70.6
Small SMSA	75.4	73.5	79.5	71.6	52.2
Outside SMSA	82.5	68.8	90.3	71.6	52.1
Adjacent to SMSA	85.2	80.8	100.5	71.7	31.9
Urbanized	99.1	86.4	100.1	90.4	35.9
Less Urbanized	77.5	*	106.0	66.8	*
Thinly populated	69.5	*	*	54.9	*
Not adjacent to SMSA	79.8	*	78.0	71.5	72.5
Urbanized	73.3	*	69.6	64.2	83.5
Less Urbanized	87.3	*	97.5	79.8	*
Thinly populated	65.7	*	*	56.7	*

Source: Based on unpublished data from the National Center for Health Statistics.

Note: Areas with fewer than 1,000 births are marked with *. SMSA = Standard Metropolitan Statistical Area.

Acute and Chronic Disorders

The economic and social conditions of the black community are manifest in the differential impact of noncommunicable diseases on blacks. Blacks have a higher death rate than whites in each of the leading causes of death (see Table 10.2). Most of the leading causes of death are related to psychological and sociological stress. George Tolbert finds that more blacks than whites develop hypertension.[7] John Reid and his associates note that a disproportionate number of older persons in the lower-income bracket have hypertension and are victims of cardiovascular stroke.[8] Ruth Deniss and Thelma Pierre implicitly argue that blacks have been unable to develop coping strategies to deal with the stress associated with inadequate resources, poor physical surroundings, and hostile climate.[9] One result of this failure is high blood pressure and hypertension. Unfortunately, high blood pressure and hypertension do not produce visible signs until it is too late for costless solutions.[10]

Studies on cancer point to the doubling of the number of black deaths as a result of cancer between 1949 and 1967. During this period, the general yearly increase for males was 7 percent for blacks and 3 percent for whites. Black females experienced a cancer death rate 1.7 times greater than that of white females. The largest increases for blacks have occurred in cancers of the lung, connective tissue, the pancreas, and the brain. The greater exposure of blacks

Table 10.2
Leading Causes of Death for Blacks at All Ages, 1974 (rates per 100,000)

MALES	
Diseases of the heart	291.0
Malignant neoplasms	173.5
Cerebrovascular diseases	89.4
Accidents	85.3
Homicide	67.2
Certain casues of mortality in early infancy	33.9
Influenza and pneumonia	32.9
Cirrhosis of liver	26.7
Diabetes mellitus	16.3
Suicide	10.2

FEMALES	
Diseases of the heart	227.9
Malignant neoplasms	117.2
Cerebrovascular diseases	92.3
Accidents	29.3
Diabetes mellitus	27.1
Certain casues of mortality in early infancy	24.6
Influenza and pneumonia	19.2
Cirrhosis of liver	14.7
Homicide	14.5
Arteriosclerosis	8.7

Source: Based on unpublished data from the National Center for Health Statistics, Division of Vital Statistics, Washington, D.C.

to environmental carcinogens and other detrimental aspects of living and working in urban areas may be primary factors in these mortality rates.[11]

Mental Disorders

The increasing urbanization and industrialization of American society has created conditions for high psychological stress and mental disorders. Despite the prevalence of mental disorders, mental health has always been underfunded and underutilized as a component of the health care system. Governmental intervention through the community mental health movement has attempted to address many of the issues on the availability of mental health services. However, Stanley Sue notes that data on the usage rate of the services by blacks and whites have not been collected in a systematic way.[12]

The rates for inpatient admissions to county mental hospitals can be used to show the prevalence of mental health problems among blacks. In Table 10.3 we find a difference in the admission rates of black males and white males in

Table 10.3
Percent Distribution, Age-Specific and Age-Adjusted Rates of Inpatient Admissions to State and County Mental Health Hospitals, by Race, Sex and Age, 1975 (per 100,000 population)

	Both Sexes	White Male	Female	Both Sexes	White Male	Female
Total admissions	296,151	190,788	105,363	83,367	53,646	29,721
			Percent Distribution			
All ages	100.0%	100.0%	100.0%	100.0%	100.0%	100.0%
Under 18	5.9	5.8	6.1	8.9	9.2	8.3
18-24	18.0	20.0	14.3	21.0	24.7	14.3
25-44	42.1	41.4	43.4	46.6	48.9	42.5
45-64	28.1	27.1	30.0	19.8	14.2	29.9
65 plus	5.9	5.7	6.2	3.7	3.0	5.0
Median age	35.2	34.2	37.3	32.1	30.0	38.0
			Percent Distribution			
Age-adjusted rates	157.6	213.3	109.9	367.3	509.4	248.5
All ages	161.1	214.2	111.2	344.2	469.5	232.2
Under 18	31.6	39.3	23.6	77.8	103.1	52.2
18-24	234.0	343.9	129.4	539.6	892.1	241.3
25-44	270.2	349.3	194.2	688.3	1032.7	406.3
45-64	213.4	276.0	155.7	414.1	414.2	413.9
65 plus	66.0	130.9	54.0	171.9	210.8	143.7

Source: Based on data from U.S. Department of Health and Human Services, Public Health Service, *Health of the Disadvantaged, Chart Book II* (Washington, D.C., September 1980), p. 81, Table 65, Chart 65.

the 45-to–65 age group. The age-adjusted admission for black males is twice that of white males and four times that of white females. The overall age-adjusted rate of admission for blacks is twice the rate for whites of both sexes. The critical period for black males is between the ages of 25 and 44. For black females, the period between the ages of 45 and 64 presents the highest probability of inpatient admission. In all age-groups there is a difference of admission rates when examining the racial characteristics of the patient. The diagnoses of patients admitted to mental health facilities also demonstrate racial differences for the same disorder. Alcoholism and schizophrenia are the leading causes of the admission of white males. Black males are admitted for the same disorders at nearly three times the rate of whites. Black women are similar to black males in that they are admitted for the same disorders and at nearly the same rate (see Table 10.4).

Outpatient care and follow-up care are important for the integration of patients into the community. However, blacks as a group are more reluctant to admit that they or a relative may have mental problems, and they are just as reluctant to admit the nature of the disorder.[13] When blacks do seek outpatient mental care they are often subjected to discrimination. In a survey of psychiatric emergency rooms, Herbert Gross and his associates found that blacks are systematically treated and discharged with little follow-up.[14] This finding lends support to an earlier study by Norman Brill and Hugh Strorrow, who found that blacks were treated less often by senior staff members and in many instances were rejected for treatment.[15] When treatment is initiated, blacks will often terminate some treatment sessions unless their symptoms become acute.[16] Table 10.5 provides some support for the assertion that outpatient services are not the

Table 10.4
Major Leading Diagnoses for Admissions to State and County Hospitals, by Race and Sex, 1975 (rates per 100,000 population)

White Male		Black Male	
Alcohol disorders	79.5	Schizophrenia	197.1
Schizophrenia	56.3	Alcohol disorders	122.0
Depressive disorders	21.7	Personality disorders	35.6
Personality disorders	16.9	Organic brain syndromes	27.0
Drug disorders	10.0	Adjustment reaction and behavior disorders of children	22.6

White Female		Black Female	
Schizophrenia	42.8	Schizophrenia	118.2
Depressive disorders	23.1	Alcohol disorders	50.1
Alcohol disorders	12.4	Organic brain syndrome	17.3
Organic brain syndrome	7.8	Depressive disorders	10.2
Personality disorders	6.6	Adjustment reaction, adult	9.8

Source: Based on unpublished data from the National Institute of Mental Health, Division of Biometry and Epidemiology.

Table 10.5
Median Number of Visits for Outpatient Psychiatric Services by Race/Ethnicity and Termination Status, 1975

Termination Status	White	Black
Total	3.8	2.8
Terminated	2.6	2.2
Not terminated	6.9	6.6

Source: Based on unpublished data from the National Institute of Mental Health, Division of Biometry and Epidemiology.

same for blacks. The number of visits before termination is less for blacks than for whites. In summary, the display of acute symptoms and the failure to respond to outpatient treatment are factors that discourage effective utilization of mental health services by blacks.

HEALTH PROMOTION AND PREVENTION ACTIVITIES

The problems of health promotion and prevention activities in the black community stem from lack of an adequate conceptualization of a public health strategy. The traditional public health approach distinguishes between three levels of prevention activities.[17] Primary prevention is directed at people who are at risk of exposure to a particular disorder. At this level, prevention programs are directed at delineating the population at risk and providing information that will help avoid occurrence of the disorder. Secondary prevention is directed at those who show signs of the disorder. Prevention programs are directed toward early treatment and containment of the disorder. Tertiary prevention effort is aimed at a reduction of the severity of the effects of a particular disorder on the population at risk. These efforts involve surveillance and rehabilitative activities to control the incidence of the disorder in the population. Each level of prevention implicitly suggests that governmental intervention can be an effective method of preventing and promoting mental health.

In the case of specific disorders, the public health approach seems plausible and gives a rationale for governmental intervention. Unfortunately, minority populations experience several disorders simultaneously from multiple causes. For example, the cumulative effects of stressful life events such as poverty, unemployment, divorce and sexual abuse are more likely to be experienced by minority populations simultaneously.[18] Thus it is probable that an individual might be exposed to several different levels of prevention activities. Furthermore, the interaction of these prevention activities and various social programs may produce conflicting results.[19]

Federal policy toward prevention in the health field has a twenty-year history. Only recently has there been a renewed effort toward making prevention an important element in the delivery of health services. The impact of presidential commissions, reports by the surgeons general, and academic literature has been to increase interest in the field as a means of reducing the ever-escalating cost of treatment. The President's Commission on Mental Health included within its recommendations an important chapter entitled "Strategies for Prevention." Despite the grandiose nature of these recommendations, federal efforts have not had an impact on the black community,[20] which can be attributed to political impediments common to black communities.

Although prevention has been accepted in principle, the actual allocation of resources to prevention activities has been meager. Instead, most medical and mental health resources are directed toward institutional and other treatment programs. Despite contradictory evidence of the effectiveness of treatment service, large-scale prevention efforts have not been evaluated as cost-effective.[21] For blacks, these findings suggest that prevention efforts may not deter the onset of mental or acute disorders. Since in the black community treatment is stigmatized and fewer treatment services are available, there is little chance for prevention and health promotion strategies to have the desired outcome. The delayed effect of the unavailability of treatment is increased hospitalization of blacks. A major goal of prevention and health promotion strategies is to reduce hospitalization of blacks.

In addition to a lack of resources, there is also no coordination of health promotion implementation strategies. While the federal government has assumed the burden of research efforts, it has not assumed effective control of the administrative process necessary for successfully implementing a prevention program. It is still the responsibility of state governments to implement any prevention strategy, but the dismal record of state governments in implementing federal policy leaves little doubt about their inability to allocate resources to blacks in any effective manner. Rather than promoting equity in the distribution process, states have been noted as the source of much of the inequity faced by the black population (e.g., medicare, Supplemental Security Income and Aid to Families with Dependent Children). For example, on the national level the recommendations of the Conference on Minority Group Alcohol, Drug Abuse, and Mental Health Issues included concern about the design of prevention materials in the local "dialect."[22] State mental health departments have not had the money or resources to perform such onerous tasks. Coordination requires resources and legitimate authority, both of which are beyond the capabilities of state and local health departments. Thus, before prevention becomes a policy option, efforts must be made to alleviate the mixture of intergovernmental conflicts that tend to undermine prevention policies.

SYNOPSIS OF THE CONDITIONS OF BLACK HEALTH

Differential health status between black and white Americans is reflected in nearly every set of health care indexes. By these same indexes blacks are less well and get less health care than white Americans. Although measures of health status show that the degree of difference between blacks and whites has decreased with time, Dorothy Newman and her associates comment, "It is more remarkable that it remains so significant."[23] Research points out that this difference has been and continues to be a product of racism in the American health care system. In other words, in the United States, patterns of racial oppression have laid the bases for differences in health status between blacks and whites.[24]

Governmental response has been to promote better access to medical care through categorical programs. From the enactment of medicare and medicaid there has been an evolution of a federal commitment to health financing and service delivery. But disenchantment with federal regulations, intervention, and intrusion into state governments has prevented further evolution. In fact, commitment toward further development of an equitable health care system ended abruptly with the Reagan administration. Consistent with prevailing political disenchantment, the administration's objective is to retrench from the commitment of federal spending, regulation, and responsibility in health care delivery.

BLACK HEALTH CARE AND RETRENCHMENT POLITICS

The Reagan administration has developed a firmly articulated set of administrative, constitutional and political defenses for the restructuring of the state-federal relationship as part of its program for economic recovery. In rethinking federalism, the administration questions the distinction between federal priorities and local responsibilities. According to Donald Moran, associate director of the Office of Management and Budget for Human Resources, the Reagan administration has clarified this distinction in the following manner: "National government is mainly responsible for defense and those matters which have any direct impact on interstate commerce . . . . A national issue [is where] . . . clearly and unambiguously everybody benefits."[25] In other words, according to John Palmer and Isabel Sawhill, the Reagan administration has "sort[ed] out public function by level of government in order to restore the 'traditional' separation of responsibilities. Federal, state, and local governments would become fully responsible for financing their own services."[26] Thus, the increasing federal involvement that has manifested itself in previous administrations has been assessed as an unacceptable intrusion into state authority. Claude Barfield observes, "The Administration has set out to reverse the trend of decline in influence and authority of the state governments."[27] Moreover, it is argued that devolution of programmatic authority would allow a better division of labor and a redelegation of decision-making to the lower levels of government. Flexibility, efficiency and decentralization would be accomplished by forcing lower-level decision makers to set priorities and to handle the political struggles that accompany them.[28]

To accomplish the goals of retrenchment, the administration for fiscal year 1982 proposed to consolidate all or part of over ninety categorical programs into a system of four block grants (two in health) to the states with a 25 percent reduction in funds. This included a proposed consolidation of twenty-five categorical health grants into two block grants. These block grants were to provide a lump sum of money to state governments according to functional area. Each state was to be responsible for the allocation of funds to local committees. Like the special general revenue-sharing bills in the early 1970s, there were to be few requirements as to how the states would implement these grants. For instance, there were to be no provisions for matching funds by the states, no earmarking of particular categories, and no requirement that the state maintain any minimum level of effort or funding for a particular program. Each grant was designed to cover a particular service area previously covered by various categorical grant programs. Programs proposed to be included in the block grants are listed in Table 10.6.

A secondary consideration was the development of a formula for the equitable distribution of resources to states and localities. No such formula has yet been developed to provide for the equity of services delivered. However, discrimination on the basis of race, age or sex is prohibited in any grant program area. Under the block grant plan, fiscal year 1982 state entitlements were to be based on what their total categorical grant funding was for fiscal year 1981 less 25 percent. Further, states were to be required to publicize their plans for spending and to provide some opportunity for public comments, thus mitigating some of the discretion of the states.

A third consideration was the overall reduction of spending for budgetary reasons. As part of the general effort to balance the budget, each block grant was to reduce the amount of governmental spending on categorical programs either by elimination or by underfunding. As specific block grant areas, it is much easier for the administration to justify programmatic cuts. Congress acceded to the Reagan block grant plan and consolidated seventy-seven categorical programs into nine block grants: four in health, one in education, and four in social services. Thus all three considerations are important for understanding the relationship between the New Federalism and black health care. Further, despite the rationale for congressional action, President Reagan's New Federalism gives the states more authority with far less fiscal support. Many programs that target minority groups will be consolidated into block grants and subsequently reduced to accomplish budgetary goals. The implications for black health care can be assessed according to the nature of the categorical programs to be terminated.

The three areas of black health care that were discussed previously are designated to be cut or consolidated into block grants. Four out of the nine block grants created for fiscal year 1982 were related to health. Maternal and child health services, nutrition for children, rehabilitation services, genetic diseases and adolescent health services were consolidated by Congress into one block grant. The fiscal year 1982 level was 13 percent below the individual categorical programs of fiscal 1981.[29] Considering the present disparities in black/white infant mortality rates, these reduced budgetary requests may lead to an increase in mortality differentials.

In the areas of mental health and health promotion, funds for staff development, drug abuse, alcohol treatment and community mental health centers were reformulated into a block grant and cut by 25 percent over fiscal 1981.[30] These budget cuts have severe consequences for black mental health and mental health promotion. One other health block grant, Preventive Health Services Block Grant, suffered a similar overall reduction for fiscal 1982. The Primary Care Health Block Grants received the same level of funding for both fiscal 1981 and fiscal 1982.[31] Concerning health, Judith Feder and her associates note that "the Rea-

Table 10.6
Programs Included in Block Grants (millions of dollars)

Programs	1981 Current Services	1982 Budget Request
HEALTH SERVICES BLOCK GRANT		
Community Health Centers:		
Primary Health Care Centers	325	
Primary Health Care	7	
Black Lung Services	5	
Migrant Health	44	
Home Health Services	4	
Maternal and Child Health:		
Grants to States	357	
Supplemental Security Income	30	
Hemophilia	3	
Sudden Infant Death Syndrome	3	
Emergency Medical Services	30	
Program Management	34	
Mental Health and Substance Abuse Services:		
Mental Health Services	324	
Drug Abuse Project Grants and Contracts	161	
Drug Abuse Grants to States	30	
Alcoholism Project Grants and Contracts	73	
Alcoholism Grants to States	50	
Program Management	57	
Total Health Services Block Grant	1,537	1,138
PREVENTIVE HEALTH SERVICES BLOCK GRANT:		
High Blood Pressure	20	
Health Incentive Grants	36	
Risk Reduction and Health Education	16	
Venereal Disease	40	
Immunization	24	
Fluoridation	5	
Rat Control	13	
Lead-Based Paint Poisoning Prevention	10	
Genetic Diseases	13	
Family Planning Services	166	
Adolescent Health Services	10	
Total Preventive Health Services Block Grant	353	260
Federal Administrative Costs		1
Total Public Health Service Block Grants	1,890	1,400

Table 10.6—*Continued*

Programs	1981 Current Services	1982 Budget Request
SOCIAL SERVICES BLOCK GRANT		
Title XX Social Services	2,716	
Title XX Day Care	200	
Title XX State and Local Training	75	
Child Welfare Services	163	
Child Welfare Training	6	
Foster Care	349	
Adoption Assistance	10	
Child Abuse	7	
Runaway Youth	10	
Developmental Disabilities	51	
OHDS Salaries and Expenses	4	
Rehabilitation Services	931	
Community Services Administration	483	
Total Social Services Block Grant	5,005	3,800
EMERGENCY ASSISTANCE BLOCK GRANT		
Emergency Assistance	55	
Hardship Energy Assistance	1,850	
Total Emergency Assistance Block Grant	1,905	1,399
Grant Total Block Grants	8,800	6,600
(Outlays)		(5,400)

Source: Based on data from Executive Office of the President, Office of Management and Budget; and Claude E. Barfield, *Rethinking Federalism: Block Grants and Federal, State and Local Responsibilities* (Washington, D.C.: American Enterprise Institute, 1981).

gan administration believes that decisions on the adequacy of service should be left to state and local governments."[32]

The response of the states to the block grant system has been mixed. Almost all states accept the ideals of increased discretion, administrative freedom and program flexibility. But the typical response has been to retain existing program categories and spread reduced funding across programs. Programs and projects that were funded directly from federal monies are continually at risk of state termination. Findings from a survey by the Urban Institute, reviewing twenty-five states' budgetary data, reveal that states are reluctant to replace federal funds lost through block grants.[33] State action to replace lost federal funds hinges on the fiscal condition of the state; a state with a surplus budget balance is more likely to replace lost funds. However, most states are under severe budgetary pressure and are making budgeting adjustments as a result.

The probability that state funds for black health care needs will be reallocated is low. Many programs for blacks are considered federal initiatives and are a low-priority item for state governments. Programs that offer broad entitlements are likely to be protected by the political appeal of beneficiaries. For example, child care programs that entitle larger segments of the population will be viewed more favorably than substance abuse programs, which have large numbers of black beneficiaries. While the above observations are warranted, the difficulty of generalizing about the total impact of retrenchment politics on black health care is compounded by the inability to predict where state service reductions will occur and their direct consequences for the black community. Nevertheless, the themes "reallocation" and "efficiency in management" do signal a curtailment of health services to blacks and other under-served groups.

CONCLUSION AND POLICY IMPLICATIONS FOR BLACK HEALTH CARE

The policy implications of retrenchment politics in health care for the black community are clear. The block grant system will not solve the problems of planning and distribution; it will only provide for accomplishment of some of the efficiency goals of the Reagan administration. States will be forced to perform much of the programmatic devolution required by federal authorities. For the black community, state authorities represent not a new health federalism but a return of arbitrary power to the state. This change may culminate in producing higher maternal deaths, higher infant mortality, and higher death rates for all blacks because of a lack of adequate health services.

Further, budget cuts will not provide the personnel and planning necessary to make conditions better. In fact, planning for personnel to implement effective care within the black community requires an equitable distribution of resources. The discriminatory practices of medical institutions and other allied health occupations result in a dependency relationship between the practitioners of medical science and the black community. Moreover, without a comprehensive health plan, there cannot be an equitable distribution of health services. Efforts to remove the regulatory aspects of health planning prevent development of a systematic means by which the black community can eradicate the present problems in the future.

In conclusion, the contemporary crisis of black health care is a direct result of the conditions of life in Black America. The cumulative efforts of poverty, unemployment, poor housing and so forth produce health conditions that are much worse than those of the white population. Although improvements in the delivery of health services have reduced some of the black/white disparities, they have not changed the basic needs for access to and availability of health care to the larger segments of the black community.

NOTES

1. See, e.g., U.S. Congress, *Background Paper: Health Differentials Between White and Nonwhite Americans* (Washington, D.C.: Government Printing Office, 1977); U.S.

Department of Health, Education and Welfare, *Facts of Life and Death* (Washington, D.C.: Government Printing Office, 1978); U.S. Department of Health, Education and Welfare, *Health Status of Minorities and Low Income Groups* (Washington, D.C.: Government Printing Office, 1979); U.S. Department of Health, Education and Welfare, *Health: United States, 1979* (Washington, D.C.: Government Printing Office, 1980); U.S. Commission on Civil Rights, *Social Indicators of Equality for Minorities and Women* (Washington, D.C.: Government Printing Office, 1978); and U.S. Department of Health and Human Services, *Health of the Disadvantaged, Chart Book—II* (Washington, D.C.: Government Printing Office, 1980).

2. Joseph N. Gayles, "Health Brutality and the Black Life Cycle," *Black Scholar* 5 (May 1972): 2–9. For a more detailed discussion of black health inequities, see Mitchell F. Rice and Woodrow Jones, Jr., "Black Health Inequities and the American Health Care System," *Health Policy and Education* 3 (October 1982): 195–214.

3. See, e.g., Dorothy K. Newman et al., *Protest, Politics and Prosperity: Black Americans and White Institutions* (New York: Pantheon, 1978); and Mitchell F. Rice, "Black Health Care: Another Look at an Old Problem," *Texas Public Health Association Journal* 33 (Fall 1981): 17–20.

4. On this point, see, e.g., George P. Tolbert, "Meeting the Health Needs of Minorities and the Poor," *Phylon* 38 (September 1977): 225–235; Lloyd Yabura, "Health Care Outcomes in the Black Community," *Phylon* 38 (June 1977): 194–202; and Evi Hang Shin, "Black/White Differentials in Infant Mortality in the South," *Demography* 12 (February 1975): 1–19.

5. See Evelyn M. Kitigawa and Philip M. Hauser, *Differential Mortality in the United States* (Cambridge, Mass.: Harvard University Press, 1973).

6. See Daniel O. Price, *Changing Characteristics of the Negro Population* (Washington, D.C.: Government Printing Office, 1969); and Reynolds Farley and Albert Hermalin, "The 1960s: A Decade of Progress for Blacks," *Demography* 9 (August 1972): 353–370.

7. Tolbert, "Meeting the Health Needs of Minorities and the Poor."

8. John D. Reid, Everett S. Lee, Davor Jedlicka and Youngshock Shin, "Trends in Black Health," *Phylon* 38 (June 1977): 105–116.

9. See, respectively, Ruth E. Deniss, "Social Stress and Mortality Among Nonwhite Males," *Phylon* 38 (September 1977): 315–328; and Thelma Pierre, "The Relationship Between Hypertension and Psycho-Social Functioning in Young Black Men," *Journal of Afro-American Issues* 4 (Summer/Fall 1976): 408–419.

10. On this point, see Richard F. Gillum et al., "Determinants of Dropout Rates Among Hypertensive Patients in an Urban Clinic," *Journal of Community Health* 5 (Winter 1979): 94–100.

11. See Jack E. White, "Cancer Differences in the Black and White Caucasian Population," *Phylon* 38 (September 1977): 297–314.

12. Stanley Sue, "Community Mental Health Services to Minority Groups: Some Optimism, Some Pessimism," *American Psychologist* 32 (August 1977): 616–624. See also Charles V. Willie et al. (eds.), *Racism and Mental Health: Essays* (Pittsburgh: University of Pittsburgh Press, 1973); and Alexander Thomas and Samuel Sillen, *Racism and Psychiatry* (New York: Brunner/Mazel, 1972).

13. On this point, see Wade W. Nobles, "Black People in White Insanity: An Issue for Black Community Mental Health," *Journal of Afro-American Issues* 4 (Winter 1976): 21–27.

14. Herbert S. Gross et al., "The Effect of Race and Sex on the Variation of Diagnosis and Disposition in a Psychiatric Emergency Room," *Journal of Nervous Mental Disease* 148 (June 1969): 638–642.

15. Norman Q. Brill and Hugh A. Strorrow, "Social Class and Psychiatric Treatment," *Archives of General Psychiatry* 3 (October 1960): 340–344.

16. This point is discussed in more detail in Anna M. Jackson et al., "Race as a Variable Affecting the Treatment Involvement of Children," *Journal of the American Academy of Child Psychiatry* 13 (January 1974): 20–31.

17. See B. L. Bloom and D. P. Buck (eds.), *Preventive Services in Mental Health Programs* (Boulder, Colo.: WICHE, 1967).

18. See V. L. Allen (ed.), *Psychological Factors in Poverty* (New York: Academic Press, 1970).

19. C. R. Payton, "Substance Abuse and Mental Health: Special Prevention Strategies Needed for Ethnics of Color," *Public Health Reports* 96 (February 1981): 20–25.

20. President's Commission on Mental Health, *Task Panel Report* (Washington, D.C.: Government Printing Office, 1978).

21. On this point, see S. E. Goldstein, "Overview of Primary Prevention Programming," in D. C. Klein and S. E. Goldston (eds.), *Primary Prevention: An Idea Whose Time Has Come* (Rockville, Md.: National Institute of Mental Health, 1977): pp. 23–41.

22. Alcohol, Drug Abuse, and Mental Health Administration's Final Progress Report, *Implementation of the Recommendations Formulated at the 1978 National Conference on Minority Group Alcohol, Drug Abuse, and Mental Health Issues* (Rockville, Md.: Office of Public Liaison, May 1980).

23. Newman et al., *Protest, Politics and Prosperity*, p. 189.

24. Richard L. Cooper et al., "Racism, Society and Disease: An Exploration of the Social and Biological Mechanisms of Differential Mortality," *International Journal of Health Service* 11 (Fall 1981): 389–414.

25. Donald W. Moran, quoted in Claude E. Barfield, *Rethinking Federalism: Block Grants and Federal, State and Local Responsibilities* (Washington D.C.: American Enterprise Institute, 1981), pp. 23–24.

26. John L. Palmer and Isabel V. Sawhill (eds.), *The Reagan Experiment: An Examination of Economic and Social Policies Under the Reagan Administration* (Washington, D.C.: Urban Institute Press, 1982), p. 12.

27. Barfield, *Rethinking Federalism*, p. 24.

28. Ibid.

29. Ibid., p. 32.

30. Ibid., p. 31.

31. Ibid., p. 33.

32. Judith Feder et al., "Health," in Palmer and Sawhill, *The Reagan Experiment*, p. 291.

33. George E. Petterson, "The State and Local Sector," in ibid., pp. 180–181.

Public Policy and Alternative
Futures for Black America

INTRODUCTION

Public policy can be viewed as a supplement or alternative to the market mechanisms or price system as a method for deciding how society's resources are to be utilized. In many cases public policy is simply an attempt to correct for market failure or the changing values and objectives of society. These objectives are expressed in four fundamental value-goals: equity, efficiency, stability and growth. Unfortunately, in pursuing one goal society is forced to forgo one or more of the others.

It would be ingenuous to assume that social policy in a socially stratified, multiracial society is entirely free of ideology, racial antipathies and class interests. After all, policymakers are expected to ensure that policy "objectives are consonant with the fundamental values of society."[1] Thus the impact of social policy designed for the "common good" may often have deleterious effects on Black America. An important example can be found in the trade-off between unemployment and inflation. The cost of pursuing price stability is often higher unemployment rates disproportionately borne by Black America. This is true even though the impacts and effects of implementing such a policy are anticipated and known to policymakers beforehand.

The purpose of this chapter is to examine long-range consequences that social policy can have on Black America in the future. We accept Alvin Toffler's proposition that "every society faces not merely a succession of probable futures but an array of possible futures and a *conflict* over preferable ones."[2] We will employ the phrase "black economic development" to mean both the long-range *objectives* of Black America and the *process* by which they are attained. The objectives could well be expressed in terms of increasing the quantity and quality of job opportunities and enhancing Black America's health, housing,

education, training and technical sophistication—in short, progress. By process
we mean an identifiable mechanism that has the effect of, or is explicitly designed for, improving Black America's socioeconomic status over a given period of time. The question is "What type of long-range black economic development is possible, and how can public policy be optimally used to obtain it?"

POSSIBLE FUTURES

The realm of possibility has multiple dimensions and is constantly changing.
What may actually be possible (that is, the outcome at any given time) is determined by a resultant "vector of possibilities" (that is, what is technically,
politically, morally, logically, economically and ideologically possible). Therefore disagreement is bound to exist about both the desirability and the efficacy
of possible futures and who is ultimately responsible. The prime example here
is the basic conflict over the extent to which the individual or society is to be
held accountable for the well-being of the individual. Are we individually cap-
tains of our fate? In Table 11.1 we compare the potential influence that the
individual and policy have over several critical factors that determine an individual's livelihood and well-being. In no case does the individual have any significant degree of influence. On the other hand, public policy could have an
influence on all of them.

Thus there are really only two approaches for devising public policy to address the problems of black economic development. The first is to locate and
eliminate undesirable and/or unplanned systemic or structural impediments to
development. The second is to devise a conscious and deliberate plan, with
timetables, objectives and resources, having a specific focus on black economic
development. The critical question—the question that makes concern for the
future of Black America more than academic—is whether Black America's own
optimistic projections into the future are compatible with the existing social system
and whether they are attainable without changing or destroying that system. From
the perspective of Black America, every conceivable image of the future (which
is based on hope rather than despair) presumes that over time it will acquire
greater leverage over the most important determinants of its physical and social
environment.

The future will certainly be different from the present, but we cannot know
precisely how different. However, certain future developments are predictable
with various degrees of accuracy.[3] "Futures studies" refers to a class of activities, employing a wide range of methodologies, designed to improve the basis
for making choices. One obvious benefit of futures studies is that it ultimately
raises questions about the efficacy of present policy with respect to its ostensi-
ble objectives and unanticipated consequences. Therefore, we can view futures
studies as an effective early warning system. Figure 11.1 captures many of the
essential, though oversimplified, features of futures studies. It employs a long-
term trend line from past to present and projects a range of possibilities on the

Table 11.1
Potential Influence of Major Factors That Determine Livelihood and Well-Being

Factors	Significant	Some	Insignificant
	Degree of Influence		
Individual Characteristics			
Age	P		I
Race	P		I
Gender	P		I
Health		P,I	
Family Class Status		P	I
Mobility (geographically)	P	I	
Education	P	I	
Motivation		P,I	
Industry Characteristics			
Local Job Market Conditions	P		I
Phase of the business cycle		P	I
Rate of technological change		P	I
Minimum Wage	P	I	
Unionization		P	I
Foreign Trade	P		I
Societal Characteristics			
Crime Rate		P	I
Environment	P		I

I = Individual   P = Policy

future. The trend line could represent, for example, data on growth rates, income, employment or other such proxy indicators of well-being from a generation ago to the present (see Figure 11.1).

It would take us too far afield to attempt a full discussion of futures studies, but we note some of its limitations because of the unpredictability of human

Figure 11.1
Simple Features of Futures Studies

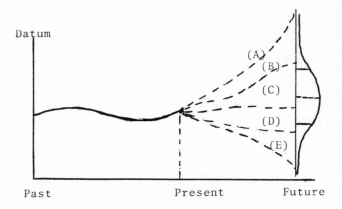

behavior. "One cannot talk prudently about a single predicted future, but rather may describe several plausible futures."[4]

Referring back to Figure 11.1, note that several conceptually simple methods can be used to fill the time gap between the present and the future state. Two methods used for guiding long-term policy formation are scenario-writing and divergence-mapping. Both require that we begin with a set of images of future states of the world not too different from reasonable projections of past trends. James Robertson points out that the future can be analytically condensed into five major scenarios that would capture what most futurologists believe to be possible:

1. Business as usual: future pretty much like the past.
2. Disaster: doomsday, nuclear war, famine, genocide.
3. Totalitarian: authoritarian regimes to prevent disasters.
4. Hyper-expansionist: new technology will overcome all impediments imposed by scarcity.
5. Ecological steady state: a human potential and planning society.[5]

Upon examination, only the last two scenarios are clearly compatible with black socioeconomic development. It is also true that each, except the last (human potential in the manner of Maslow), may have an entirely different implication for Black America.[6] Some would argue that for Black America the Business as Usual scenario implies or guarantees either the Disaster (genocide) or Totalitarian (ghetto police state) scenario.[7] In any case, we will discuss only the first and the last two scenarios.

THE BUSINESS AS USUAL SCENARIO

The history of Black America's social and economic experience in the United States hardly needs retelling. Metaphorically, it has been like the back wheels pathetically trying to catch the front wheels on a moving vehicle. A cynic might add, "And social policy has been like the traffic cop who merely monitors the speed and direction of the vehicle." If we assume that the best measures of human well-being are useful employment and stability of real income, public policy fails Black America miserably on both counts. Almost one-third of the 27 million black people in the United States live on an income below the poverty line, and these same people are also experiencing significantly higher rates of unemployment, mortality, morbidity, family instability, dilapidated housing, homicide and various forms of institutionalization.

In 1944, Gunnar Myrdal's classic study concluded that the great cleavage between the races was "not only America's greatest failure, but also America's incomparable great opportunity for the future." But he also wrote what amounts to an important political axiom that effectively defined the limits of Black America's effort in its own behalf. In Myrdal's words, "Negroes can never, in any period, hope to attain more *in the short-term power bargain* than the most benevolent white groups are prepared to give them."[8] Since the status of Black America has been traditionally determined by the work it has been allowed to perform, this axiom has its greatest relevance in terms of the number and quality of jobs allotted to Black America. Several decades after Myrdal's opus, Charles Killingsworth conducted an important study of black workers in the U.S. labor market and concluded with a statement that even now has not lost its currency:

Certain broad implications for policy are rather obvious from the conclusion of this analysis. The first is that some of the remedies most often prescribed for Negro unemployment are to yield disappointingly small results. Anti-discrimination laws, higher rates of attendance at today's schools, faster economic growth, the normal push-pull forces in the labor market . . . none of these seem to hold the promise of substantial impact on the basic source of Negro disadvantage. A second implication is that the mere passage of time without the application of powerful remedial measures will probably increase Negro disadvantage.[9]

Virtually all proposals for improving the socioeconomic status of Black America call for full employment and continuous expansion of the gross national product as the necessary condition to make it possible. This implicitly recognizes that Black America's progress is not so much contingent on an amorphous "benevolent white group" as it is on manifold forces that determine the occupational structure. Irrespective of whether we are to believe critics on the left who argue that the logic of capitalism requires unemployment, or those on the right who reject the idea of a capitalism with a mandated social responsibility, public policy has a definite role to play in creating the necessary conditions for black progress.

Two kinds of historical periods deserve special attention because they exhibit, roughly, the kind of economic or political climate deemed requisite for black advancement. The first is during war and the subsequent labor shortage. The second was in the civil rights era, especially the years 1959 to 1964, when public policy began aggressively to challenge blatant economic discrimination. Over the past twenty-five years, real income for black families has shown improvement, with the most significant gains occurring between 1964 and 1969, going from 54 percent of white family income in 1964 to 61 percent in 1969. However, these gains lacked stability, and we see that the median income (as a percentage of white income) in 1980 was actually less than the 1966 level (Figure 11.2). Between 1946 and 1963 the real income of black families, with few exceptions, fluctuated between 50 and 55 percent of white families. Then, beginning in 1963 and continuing to 1970, there was an impressive surge in the relative income of blacks, going from 55 to 64 percent. Thereafter it declined to just below the 60 percent level.

Figure 11.2
Relative Income of Blacks to Whites, 1951–1980

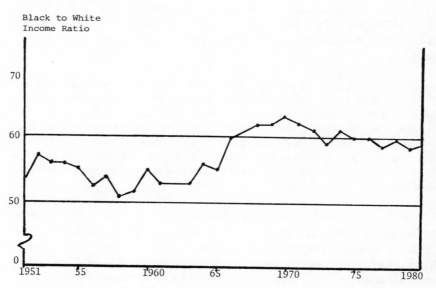

Source: Data from Bureau of the Census, *Current Population Reports,* Special Studies Series, P–23, Number 80 (Washington, D.C.: Government Printing Office, 1980), p. 69.

Note: Horizontal lines indicate that black income on the average has been 50 to 60 percent of white income. "Black" includes other non-white groups.

Education is where Black America has made its most impressive gains. Responding to the private sector's often heard lamentations—"We want to hire one, but we just can't find qualified . . . "—and aided by college outreach programs, black college enrollment increased from 129,000 in 1969 to 688,000 in 1980. By 1980, some 27 percent (down from 32 percent in 1975) of blacks aged 18 to 24 were enrolled in college.

The occupational structure of the black labor force has also undergone impressive changes over the last twenty years. For example, between 1960 and 1980 the number of black workers in professional, sales and clerical occupations more than doubled. Blacks have also registered gains, though smaller, in management and the crafts.

This nominal progress should not obscure the alarming trends of some other important indexes of black economic development. First, the relative gains blacks have made in educational achievement have not generally payed off in terms of employment. Bennett Harrison succinctly describes this situation and concludes:

The findings reported in this paper seem to call rather convincingly for a change in emphasis away from concentration on the alleged defects of the ghetto poor themselves toward the investigation of defects in the market system which constrain the poor from realizing their potential. Without a direct transformation and augmentation for the demand for their labor, significant improvement in the economic situation of ghetto dwellers is unlikely.[10]

Second, not only has black employment been very unstable and subjected to a roller-coaster effect (see Figure 11.3B), but the *relative* rate of unemployment between black and white workers remained remarkably stable (at about twice the white rate) between 1951 and 1980 (see Figure 11.3A). Between 1948 and 1980, black unemployment was below 6 percent in only four years. These instances occurred 30 years ago. In Figure 11.3B, four-year moving averages (shown as straight lines) are used to give a clearer picture of the peaks and dips. Note that in the past twenty-five years the lowest four-year average rate of unemployment (1966–1970) was a very high 7.2 percent. If these same rates were to be experienced by the entire U.S. labor force, it is not difficult to imagine labor leaders, academicians, the media and politicians using the term "crisis" to describe the situation and demanding immediate corrective measures. There exists a critical and glaring asymmetry in public policy responses in the United States which has been ignored for too long.

In doing so, the social cost, the variable most relevant to public policy formation, is becoming unacceptably high. According to Harvey Brenner's study,[11] prepared for the Joint Economic Committee of Congress, there is a strong statistical association between unemployment, and mental and physical health and criminal aggression. Thus black communities that are continuously subjected to the cumulative strains of long-term (marginal and/or periodic) unemployment

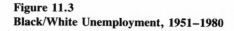

Figure 11.3
Black/White Unemployment, 1951–1980

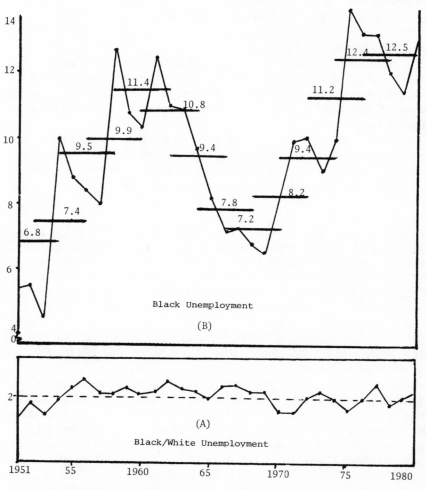

Source: Data from Bureau of the Census, *Current Population Reports,* Special Studies Series, P–23, Number 80 (Washington, D.C.: Government Printing Office, 1980), p. 69; and *Statistical Abstracts of the United States, 1980–1983* (Washington, D.C.: Government Printing Office, 1983), p. 392.

Note: Horizontal lines indicate four-year moving averages. "Black" includes other non-white groups.

in an overstimulated consumerist environment cannot realistically be expected to thrive, and the high levels of alienation and malaise found in the inner cities attest to this. These are not healthy conditions for a people to suffer for even a short period. Yet even in the best periods of economic growth and political climates over the last generation, public policies have been either remiss or ineffectual in ameliorating them.

Black economic development necessitates an allocation of the nation's resources which is fundamentally different from the existing one. This can occur in two ways. One is to redistribute shares of the existing economic pie. Another way is for Black America to receive proportionately larger slices of an ever-expanding pie. What public policy in the United States has been content to do is defer the problems of Black America's poverty and unemployment indefinitely, based on the fiction that a buoyant and rapidly expanding economy will resolve the issue painlessly. What must be recognized is that all images of the future, whether desired, feared, or expected, will influence attitudes, behavior, and decisions in the present.[12] If the nation continues a "business as usual" course, the future of Black America is certainly in question, if not in jeopardy.

THE TECHNOLOGICAL-FIX SCENARIO

By far the favorite scenario of most Americans is a rapidly expanding economy. It is the scenario that virtually all discussions of reducing the black/white socioeconomic gap is based on. This scenario is also most compatible with the inherent dynamic of capitalism, which requires a perpetual motion "growth machine" that ironically steamrolls over one of its own basic tenets, the law of scarcity. Physical limits, if they are recognized at all, will determine not only the level at which the economic system functions but, more important, how dominant ethical values may change—for example, how concepts of fairness, justice, and equity will be enunciated. In the absence of a new paradigm of work and worth, most futurists envision a very bleak society whose members engage in violent and lethal forms of "maintaining." Robert Heilbroner, for example, believes that "the problem of income distribution would post extreme difficulties for capitalism of a political as well as an economic kind. The struggle for relative position would not only pit one class against another, but also each against all."[13]

Herman Kahn is the best-known proponent of the technological fix scenario which claims that energy, food, and resource scarcities can be averted by rapid growth and wise management.[14] This calls for an exponential growth (see Path A in Figure 11.1). This means that in order just to maintain a constant rate of growth from one year to the next, the system must use a greater quantity of resources than the previous year. Another version of the increasing growth scenario, but at a decreasing rate, is shown by Path B in Figure 11.1.

A relationship between growth rates and expanding employment opportunities is expressed in Okun's Law. Using historical data, Arthur Okun developed a theoretical relationship between the rate of growth of the real GNP and unemployment.[15] It states that the U.S. economy must grow at an annual rate of 4 percent just to maintain any given level of employment. But in order to decrease overall unemployment by 1 percentage point, the GNP must grow by an additional 3.3 percent of its long-term average rate of growth. The importance of this relationship for Black America has been shown in a study by Harold Guthrie, who looked at how various rates of unemployment affected the prospect for narrowing black-white income differentials. Guthrie found that "a 5.0 percent [unemployment] rate will delay attainment of equality of income an additional 50 years compared to what might be expected at 3.5 percent rate. *A rate of 6.0 percent puts equality out of sight.*"[16] Considering the fact that "normal" unemployment is presently being defined at 5, 6 or even 7 percent, there is good reason for pessimism to overshadow most optimistic visions of a brighter and more promising future for the nation's most disadvantaged citizens being transmitted via higher growth rates. The high growth scenario, however, presents Black America with a dilemma: Economic growth does not tend to make the worse-off much better, but no growth may make things worse for those a little better off.

Are there limits to growth? Over the past few years a number of long-term forecasts for the United States have called for dramatic new thinking about the possibilities for long-term growth. The earth's resources *are* finite. Presently in the United States, resources use (particularly of nonrenewable fossil energy fuels) has reached the point that the nation, with only 6 percent of the world's population, consumes over 30 percent of the world's resources.

The arguments for limited economic growth in the future are persuasive. E. J. Mishan[17] and E. F. Schumacker[18] raise the issue of whether the real needs of human beings can be reconciled with the needs of technology and growth. In another view, Nicholas Georgescu-Roegen[19] and Jeremy Rifkin[20] argue that there are limitations to energy-based growth because of the Entropy Law. Other writers are looking not only at the physical-ecological limits but also at the ethics of growth. Herman Daly summarizes this view:

Growth in GNP in poor countries means more food, clothing, shelter, basic education, and security, whereas for the rich country it means more electric toothbrushes, yet another brand of cigarettes, more tension and unsecurity, and more force feeding through more advertising.[21]

Faced with the possibility of limits, growth can no longer realistically be looked on as the process by which Black America will reach the same level of material affluence as the rest of the nation. In any case, data suggest that neither within the United States nor in a global context has growth narrowed the gap between the rich and the poor. Thus public policy that does not have a redistributional objective within a short time frame must be looked at with a great deal of skepticism.

THE ECOLOGICAL STEADY STATE SCENARIO

The ecological steady state economy, or what James Robertson[22] and others see as the only sane alternative, will involve a radical change of direction in the development of U.S. society. It involves nothing less than a transformation of the value system of the United States. It accepts as given that the planet is not an inexhaustible cornucopia, and argues for policies that will put the world on a permanently sustainable resource-use pattern. It calls for redefining work and restructuring the work environment. It recognizes that the struggle for subsistence is not the fundamental issue for industrialized nations, but rather more a struggle with the existential question "What does the 'good life' look like?"

The ecological scenario sees the need for global balance and therefore the need to find meaning to a "just" distribution of income and wealth. It argues that most if not all public policies are misguided because they presume that the market criteria of efficiency has automatically answered the equity question. It makes a demand on us to separate our real needs from culturally determined wants (synthetic needs). Thus policy formation is to be fashioned with an economics based on a theory of human needs as developed by Abraham Maslow.[23] And it is for precisely this reason that the steady growth, human potential, ecological scenario must be seen as most relevant to Black America's quest for economic development.

Most existing images of long-range black economic development, and the expectations and demands with which those images correspond, must be redefined and made consistent with the global set of possibility vectors. For those who have been conditioned for generations to measure their worth in terms of possessions, the frugality implied by the ecological scenario must appear to be an unacceptable alternative and a cruel joke. But the great irony is that the more this attitude prevails—and the more the ethos of our society promotes it—the more economic growth will be unlikely to provide solace.

CONCLUSION

Public policy as it affects Black America has several conditions placed on it which invariably render it ineffective in addressing long-standing problems confronting Black America. The inferior economic status of Black America has not simply been the result of a series of inadvertent and disjointed policies (e.g., benign neglect), but also the result of an impersonal market system operating under institutional controls and sanctions in which one's race was considered significant. The economic weight of large corporations, and the ideological commitment to market solutions to social problems and long-ingrained racial antipathies, continue to hold sway. Public policy directed toward eliminating poverty and deprivation is currently premised on economic growth, which depends on increasing resource-use rates, which in turn is contingent on the rest of the world's going with less and yet remaining stable sources of supply.

There is little prospect of any real progress in narrowing the gap between Black America and White America without a substantive change in the economic *structure* of America. And Black America should not be tranquilized by what appears to be motion toward the objectives of black progress, for as in the so-called "infinite walk paradox"—where the objective was for a person to traverse the length of a room, but only with steps half the length of the previous step—the closest they will ever get is two steps away from the starting point, and only then with an infinite amount of time and movement. To be useful in the process of black economic development, public policy must engage in long-term planning and goal-setting, for which there is no substitute.

NOTES

1. Edith Stokey and Richard Zeckhouser, *A Primer for Policy Analysis* (New York: W. W. Norton, 1978), p. 260.

2. Alvin Toffler, *The Futurist* (New York: Random House, 1972), p. 108.

3. Edward Cornish, *The Study of the Future* (Washington, D.C.: World Future Society, 1977), pp. 103–120.

4. Willis Harmon, *An Incomplete Guide to the Future* (New York: W. W. Norton, 1979), p. 15.

5. James Robertson, *The Sane Alternative* (St. Paul, Minn.: River Basin, 1979), pp. 16–18.

6. See, e.g., Mark Lutz and Kenneth Lux, *The Challenge of Humanistic Economics* (Menlo Park, Calif.: Benjamin Cummings, 1979), pp. 10–19.

7. For more on this point, see Sidney M. Willhelm, *Who Needs the Negro* (Garden City, N.Y.: Doubleday, 1971).

8. Gunnar Myrdal, *An American Dilemma: The Negro Problem in Modern Democracy* (New York: McGraw-Hill, 1944), pp. 740, 1021, emphasis in the original.

9. Charles Killingsworth, "Negroes in a Changing Labor Market," in Arthur Ross and Herbert Hill (eds.), *Employment, Race and Poverty* (New York: Harcourt Brace & World, 1967), pp. 71–72.

10. Bennett Harrison, "Education and Underemployment in the Urban Ghetto," in David Gordon (ed.), *Problems in Political Economy: An Urban Perspective* (Lexington, Mass.: D. C. Heath, 1977), pp. 262–263.

11. Harvey Brenner, *Estimating the Social Cost of National Economic Policy: Implications for Mental, Physical Health and Criminal Aggression*, Study for the Joint Economic Committee, 94th Cong. 2d Sess. (Washington, D.C.: Government Printing Office, 1976).

12. Harmon, *Incomplete Guide*, p. 1.

13. Robert Heilbroner, *An Inquiry into the Human Prospect* (New York: W. W. Norton, 1979), p. 104.

14. Herman Kahn, *The Next 200 Years: A Scenario for America and the World* (New York: William Morrow, 1979).

15. Arthur Okun, "Potential GNP: Its Measurement and Significance," Proceedings of the Business and Economic Statistic Section of American Statistical Association, 1962, pp. 98–104.

16. Harold Guthrie, "The Prospect for Equality Under Varying Rates of Unemployment," *Journal of Human Resources* (4) (Fall, 1970): 446, emphasis added.

17. E. J. Mishan, *Technology and Growth: The Price We Pay* (New York: Praeger, 1970).

18. E. F. Schumacker, *Small Is Beautiful* (New York: Praeger, 1973).

19. Nicholas Georgescu-Roegen, *The Entropy Law and the Economic Process* (Cambridge, Mass.: Harvard University Press, 1971).

20. Jeremy Rifkin, *Entropy: A New World View* (New York: Bantam, 1981).

21. Herman Daly (ed.), *Toward a Steady State Economy* (San Francisco: W. H. Freeman, 1973), p. 11.

22. Robertson, *Sane Alternative*.

23. On this point, see Lutz and Lux, *Challenge of Humanistic Economics*, pp. 297–308.

Black Public Administrators and Opposing Expectations

INTRODUCTION

A law student once stated that most of the significant issues in civil rights had been resolved by the courts. This conclusion may be correct if it means there is a legal basis for addressing various civil rights issues, but the same conclusion cannot be made about the experiences of black public administrators in the administrative arm of government. Lawrence Howard suggests that black administrators are expected to buffer white-controlled organizations against demands from the black community.[1]* Whether one agrees or disagrees with Howard, he implies that black administrators find themselves in a difficult position. Many would agree that most black administrators make significant contributions to organizations, that is, that they do more than serve as buffers. However, the administrative experiences of blacks do include having to deal with different expectations from members of the organization and the black community.[2]

Frederick Mosher believes that resolving different expectations is the most difficult moral problem faced by public administrators.[3] This situation is further complicated when one group pursuing their interest needs government services to help alleviate the effects of racial discrimination.

This chapter will focus on how black public administrators can address the different expectations they may encounter by discussing the bases of expectations from blacks and from members of the organization. The chapter will then suggest that by minimizing different expectations black public administrators

---

* The "black community" is defined as blacks who live in a specific area in the community as well as blacks who are employed by an agency.

can concentrate on responding to the public need for government service through policy-making and program management.

THE BASIS OF BLACK EXPECTATIONS FOR THE PUBLIC SECTOR

One objective of black politics is to influence political decisions about the delivery of public benefits. Charles Hamilton points out that because black influence is limited it is necessary to resort to "demand making tactics" in order to eliminate barriers caused by a lack of political power.[4] Limited success, according to Hamilton, has led blacks to redefine the criteria for participation in the political process. Redefining the criteria for participation is important because it means (1) that blacks can claim a share of public benefits without posing a threat to other groups feeding at the public trough and (2) that blacks can alter their ability to influence government and increase their numbers in decision-making positions. The outcome is that government benefits are increased and the status of blacks is improved. Altering the relationship between blacks and the political system has one other important benefit, which Milton Morris points out in his discussion of the influence of blacks on public policy. Morris believes that blacks occupy the "untenable position of being almost entirely dependent on the beneficence of a political system that has been so clearly unsympathetic over time."[5] Changing their untenable position is a goal that seemed to have been a possibility during the 1960s and 1970s. The possibility that surfaced during those decades can be linked to several developments. Jewel Prestage points out that since 1900 blacks have been in an "uphill battle to achieve full participation in the political process."[6] Significant legal victories, such as the outlawing of white primaries in 1944 and the passage of the civil rights acts in 1957, 1960 and 1964, the anti-poll tax amendment in 1963 and the federal Voting Rights Act of 1965 are all a part of the uphill battle. This progress was accomplished through government and therefore enhances the importance of public institutions in the fight against racial discrimination. Success encourages hope that government will deliver, which is translated into expectations for public administrators who are charged with implementing as well as enforcing antidiscrimination laws.

During the 1960s and 1970s the preference for controlling institutions within the black community meant that self-government was viewed as a means of limiting, if not eliminating, the effects of racial discrimination. Even in this instance the need is for sympathetic public administrators who are supportive of the goals of black self-government. Perhaps more important than sympathetic administrators is having black public administrators who have experienced the negativeness of racism. The point is that while sympathetic white administrators can be helpful, having experienced racism provides an insight that makes the black public administrator more understanding, perceptive and willing to oppose racism.

The belief that black public administrators will be more responsive becomes the basis of accountability. When black public administrators fail to satisfy the standards of accountability, they may be reprimanded, for instance, by being accused of selling out their brothers and sisters. Such pressure can be a heavy burden for the black person who is sensitive to this kind of accusation. Adam Herbert believes that the ability of nonwhite administrators to fulfill their responsibilities will become increasingly difficult if there is a "collective perception" that minority administrators have exclusive understanding of the problems faced by people experiencing the effects of discrimination.[7]

JUDGING TACTICS USED BY BLACKS: A CULTURAL FACTOR

Michael Lipsky observes that powerless groups must operate in the political arena with little to use for bargaining.[8] Because they do not have conventional political resources, they must rely on unconventional methods when dealing with organizations. Blacks may use tactics they consider legitimate which are inconsistent with ideas of professionalism favored by public administrators. Tactics such as office demonstrations, verbal outbursts during meetings and nonverbal behavior used to intimidate administrators are viewed as "disruptive behavior characteristic of a lower-class cultural way of life."[9] Judgment of this kind suggests that different cultural values are being used to reject the validity of tactics used by blacks. The judgmental values being used can be traced to Woodrow Wilson, who advised that European public administrators should be Americanized in language, thought, principles and objectives.[10] This means simply that public administration should be compatible with American cultural values.

Individualism is an important value in American culture which has been translated into organizational responses. Deryl Hunt argues that "conventional public administration tends to execute public policies as if the clientele were composed of discrete individuals."[11] This approach contributes to an orderly process of administration which provides a basis for administrative control. Subculture values that challenge the preference for orderliness and control are judged rigidly and, if perceived as a threat, rejected.

The different perceptions about the legitimacy of tactics used by blacks brings to mind Edward Hall's conclusion that culture determines what makes sense and depends on the context where the evaluation is made. The result, according to Hall, is that "people in culture-contact situations frequently fail to really understand each other."[12] This lack of understanding may be called racism, but the labeling does not get at the purpose of this kind of behavior. To the extent that public administration reflects the dominant culture (which is significant), the purpose is to support and maintain the belief that will ensure the survival of dominant culture and professional values.

Blacks educated in public administration programs or who progressed through the ranks are familiar with professional values that may influence their organizational roles. Herbert discusses several role determinants which he believes influence minority administrators' perception of their responsibility to their employing agency and their community. Two of Herbert's role determinants most relevant to the discussion here are system demands and colleague pressure. System demands refer to organizational performance expectations that are manipulated through various rewards and sanctions. The objective is to get administrators to follow orders without questioning their validity and to conform to organizational standards of acceptable behavior. Herbert suggests that there is a pronounced effort to find suitable minorities. However, prospective candidates are subject to being weeded out if they are judged to be non-team players.

Colleague pressure involves judging whether a worker's job performance is acceptable to his or her colleagues. Herbert gives several examples of the extremes some minorities will go to in order to be accepted by their peers. For instance, minority police officers may be more forceful in order to gain the attention of their peers and get promoted; minority welfare workers will apply the rules rigidly to clients in order to be perceived as competent; and minority teachers will blame the students rather than the quality of the academic experience in order to be accepted by colleagues.[13] These examples demonstrate that blacks are subject to pressures to assume traditional roles that are compatible with dominant group organizational behavior. Resisting the pressures to conform means not responding to the dominant culture values that are the bases of organizational practices and behaviors. Carried a step further, practices and behaviors become professional standards that administrators are expected to incorporate into their value systems.

The discussion thus far has argued that black administrators may experience pressures from their colleagues and the employing organization. The pressure is to choose one or the other, which the black administrator may be unable to do without being labeled a "sellout" by blacks and a "non-team player" by the organization. This dilemma is an example of expectations that create an ethical problem for black public administrators. There is an option available which can help minimize, if not eliminate, the dilemma.

ETHICS: A DEFINITION WITH EXPLANATION

One problem in discussing ethics is first to find a suitable definition. The definition of ethics used here borrows heavily from the work of Jeremy Plant. According to Plant, ethics is " 'right conduct,' which is appropriate to particular situations."[14] It is difficult to argue against situational ethics as long as the administrator making ethical decisions realizes that ethical relativism cannot be extended into the realm of the unreasonable. Frederick Mosher's argument that "standards of ethical behavior that are applicable and sufficient to a private citizen in his private social relationships are not in themselves adequate for the public decisions of an administrator" suggests that, regardless of the situation, what is reasonable for public administrators should exceed ethical standards for private citizens.[15]

ETHICS: AN APPROACH TO RESOLVING OPPOSITE EXPECTATIONS

Resolving opposite expectations should be based on standards reflecting ethical values. Stephen Bailey's memorial essay to Paul Appleby is a starting point for a partial discussion of ethical standards. Bailey's essentials of moral behavior—mental attitudes and moral qualities—are prerequisites for ethical conduct as well as necessary qualities for all public administrators. According to Bailey, mental attitudes involve an awareness on the part of public servants of the problems caused by personal and private goals versus the public interest; of the morally ambivalent effect of public policies; of the shifting of context and values priorities, which creates administrative dilemmas; of the increasing difficulty of making ethical choices as administrators progress upward in an organization's hierarchy; of the need for flexibility in resolving administrative uncertainties that involve moral choices; and of the effect of using procedure, rules and standards nonproductively and the advantages of using them to promote fair and open administration. Bailey views these qualities as part of the essentials and turns his discussion to the moral qualities needed to practice ethical public administration.[16]

The essential moral qualities are optimism, courage and fairness, tempered by charity. Optimism is the ability to face uncertain and contradictory situations without becoming dysfunctional. Optimism is the basis for creativity in response to political conflicts that require risky solutions. Courage involves not retreating from unpopular, contradictory, and unclear situations when withdrawing is an easy solution. Administrators must not be afraid to make decisions and avoid passing the buck. Fairness tempered by charity means relying on standards of justice which encourage the exercising of power fairly and compassionately. Charity is the good quality that compensates for limited information and helps restrain the inclination for personal gain in favor of the public interest.[17] Bailey's essentials cannot be ignored, because they do emphasize moral ambiguities as well as proprose prerequisites for ethical conduct. However, Bailey does ignore what he calls the obvious virtues—honesty, patience, sensitivity, etc.—and concentrates on his essentials. In a culture-contact situation, administrators cannot ignore the obvious, because by doing so they will find themselves between groups with opposing perspectives that may seem unresolvable.

ETHICS AS OBVIOUS VIRTUES AND THE BLACK ADMINISTRATOR

The obvious virtues that black administrators can rely on are responsiveness and administrative integrity. To be responsive, black administrators must be accessible, able to communicate and, within reason, willing to share information. Responsiveness is accomplished through formal and informal interaction with members of the black community and white colleagues. For instance, through responsiveness black administrators are able to share information with members of the black community. In situations where a policy is being made, black administrators can help members of the black community understand issues and their effects. This information can be used to formulate a response. The implication here is that when members of the black community fail to act, black administrators can argue that they have been supportive and thus have lived up to their responsibility.

Responsiveness to white colleagues includes being a competent administrator who does not resort to excessive actions in order to gain a colleague's acceptance. Administrative competence is a factor that lends itself to the accomplishing side of the obvious virtues. While being an ethical person is essential, an initial requirement for being competent is that black administrators must have the knowledge and the managerial skills as well as the ability to practice these skills successfully.

Among reasonable people, administrative competence should be viewed as a basis for limiting doubts about the ability of black administrators to perform their job responsibilities. It is more important, however, that competent black administrators be perceived as having some commitment to professional standards that many administrators find acceptable. Yet black administrators must keep in mind that, while professionalism is a desirable quality, responsiveness through professionalism may adversely affect problem identification, limits decision-making and policy-making and inhibits their ability to deal with routine and nonroutine situations creatively.[18]

In situations where black administrators find they are between their colleagues and the black community, they can turn to the obvious virtue—responsiveness. Equal responsiveness to colleagues and the black community can help minimize differences. Further, being equally responsive communicates a sense of fairness, which means that one of Bailey's essential moral qualities is to be utilized. Responsiveness is an important avenue for dealing with both the black community and colleagues, but it must be accompanied by administrative integrity. Administrative integrity includes honesty, being trusted and having moral convictions. In practice, administrative integrity involves black administrators' being honest in their dealings with colleagues and members of the black community. Honesty is the basis for developing trust, which is necessary if pressure on black administrators is to be minimized.

When people experience moral conflict because they disagree with an organizational policy or practice, they must be prepared to take an ethically based position opposing the policy or practice. In order to take an ethical position, individuals must "know they possess the moral beliefs and integrity of conviction to endure and fight for their position."[19] Where black public administrators are concerned, they must have ethical convictions that are applied fairly and consistently when dealing with colleagues and the black community. This is difficult, but blacks, as well as all other public administrators, do not have the luxury of being selectively ethical.[20] Honesty, trust, and moral convictions are worthwhile qualities that black public administrators must use, qualities that provide a basis for interacting with all others. Through interaction, black public administrators can identify a basis that can be used to eliminate cultural differences that serve as barriers. By eliminating barriers, black administrators can remove the need to serve as mediators and avoid being accused of serving as buffers to protect white administrators from demands of the black community.

CONCLUSION AND IMPLICATIONS FOR POLICY-MAKING

It can be argued that all administrators experience the push and pull of interest groups and professional standards. This is true, but the race element is an additional factor that affects black administrators uniquely. The effect, as previously argued, is that black administrators find themselves having to respond to demands from white colleagues and from the black community. To respond to these demands, black administrators must become mediators.

Black administrators must realize that mediation involves devising alternatives to perceptions that their white colleagues and members of the black community have about how they should conduct themselves as administrators. It is argued that their conduct should be based on ethical administration, which means practicing the obvious virtues discussed previously. Black administrators should realize that mediation involves devising proposals that exceed the constraints imposed by demands made by members of the black community and organizational colleagues. Proposals should introduce conditions that both sides can accept and use as a basis for additional discussion. The effect is that instead of being in the middle, black administrators can assume an active role in shifting, to some degree, the focus of their activities from responding to interest-based demands to administration and policy-making. To shift from interest-based demands, black administrators must have credibility with colleagues and with members of the black community. Credibility is based on responsiveness to issues and concerns held by each side. It is the basis for each side's inclination to accept proposals as well as their willingness to engage in discussions intended to develop ideas that both groups can accept. In this sense the limitation of cultural logic is transcended and the focus can shift to problem resolution, decision-making and policy development.

In conclusion, the discussion of ethical administration—the obvious virtues—is intended to introduce a degree of consistency that protects an administrator's credibility. Ethical administration is no panacea for the conflict that can emerge in situations where there is culture based on conflict, but it does offer a dimension that is consistent with the legacy left by Martin Luther King, Jr.[21] Adam Herbert believes that minority administrators have "life experiences which give them an appreciation for certain social, economic, and political realities which they can often articulate more effectively than others."[22] Thus, if black administrators are not hampered by limitations imposed by their colleagues and the black community, they can focus on articulating these experiences in the policy process.

NOTES

I am indebted to Nancy J. Winn, John Hodges and T. McN. Simpson for their helpful and insightful comments on an earlier draft of this chapter.

1. Lawrence C. Howard, "Black Praxis of Governance: Toward an Alternative Paradigm for Public Administration," *Journal of Afro-American Issues* 3 (Spring 1975): 145.
2. On this point, see Adam W. Herbert, "The Minority Public Administrator: Problems, Prospects and Challenges." *Public Administration Review* 34 (November/December 1974): 556–563.
3. Frederick C. Mosher, *Democracy and the Public Service*, 2d ed. (New York: Oxford University Press, 1982), p. 230.
4. Charles V. Hamilton, "Racial, Ethnic and Social Class Politics and Administration," *Public Administration Review* 32 (October 1972): 638–645.
5. Milton D. Morris, *The Politics of Black America* (New York: Harper & Row, 1975), p. 281.
6. See Jewel L. Prestage, "Black Political Participation," in Bryan T. Downes (ed.), *Cities and Suburbs* (Belmont, Calif.: Wadsworth, 1971), p. 195.
7. Herbert, "The Minority Public Administrator," p. 559.
8. Michael Lipsky, "Protest as a Political Resource," in Downes, *Cities and Suburbs*.
9. For a more detailed discussion on this point, see Hamilton, "Racial, Ethnic and Social Class Politics and Administration," p. 646.
10. Woodrow Wilson, "The Study of Administration," *Political Science Quarterly* 2 (June 1887): 197–222.
11. Deryl G. Hunt, "The Black Perspective on Management," *Public Administration Review* 34 (November/December 1974): 521.
12. Edward T. Hall, *Beyond Culture* (Garden City, N.Y.: Anchor, 1976), p. 188.
13. Herbert, "The Minority Public Administrator," pp. 560–561.
14. Jeremy F. Plant, "Ethics and Public Personnel Administration," in Steven W. Hays and Richard C. Kearney (eds.), *Public Personnel Administration* (Englewood Cliffs, N.J.: Prentice-Hall, 1983), pp. 290–296.
15. Mosher, *Democracy and the Public Service*, p. 230.
16. Stephen K. Bailey, "Ethics and the Public Service," in Roscoe C. Martin (ed.), *Public Administration and Democracy* (Syracuse, N.Y.: Syracuse University Press, 1965), p. 292.
17. Ibid., pp. 293–297.
18. Mosher, *Democracy and the Public Service*, chap. 5.
19. J. Patrick Dobel, "Doing Good by Staying In," *Public Personnel Management* 2 (Summer 1982): 126–139.
20. For further discussion on this point, see Melbourne S. Cumming, "Andrew Young:

A Profile in Politico-Religious Activism,'' *Western Journal of Black Studies* 3 (Winter 1979): 228–232.

21. Peter A. French, *Ethics in Government* (Englewood Cliffs, N.J.: Prentice-Hall, 1983), p. 10.

22. Adam W. Herbert, "The Evolving Challenges of Black Urban Administration," *Journal of Afro-American Issues* 3 (Spring 1975): 177.

Selected Bibliography

AFL-CIO. *Reaganomics: The Second Dose* (February 1982).

Allen, V. L. (ed.). *Psychological Factors in Poverty* (New York: Academic Press, 1970).

Anderson, James E. *Public Policy-Making* (New York: Praeger, 1975).

Anderson, Marion. *Bombs or Bread: Black Unemployment and the Pentagon Budget* (Lansing, Mich.: Employment Research Associates, 1982).

"Appendix: Minority Owned Broadcast Properties." *Journal of Minority Business Finance*, Summer 1980, pp. 38–50.

Barfield, Claude E. *Rethinking Federalism: Block Grants and Federal, State and Local Responsibilities* (Washington, D.C.: American Enterprise Institute, 1981).

Barker, Lucius, and Jesse J. McCrory, Jr. *Black Americans and the Political System*, 2d ed. (Boston: Little, Brown and Co., 1980).

Barnett, Maguerite R., and James A. Hefner. *Public Policy for The Black Community* (New York: Alfred Publishing Co., 1976).

Bates, Timothy. "The Potential of Black Capitalism." *Public Policy* 21 (Winter 1973): 135–148.

———. "Financing Black Enterprise." *Journal of Finance* 29 (June 1974): 747–762.

———. "Trends in Government Promotion and Black Entrepreneurship." *Review of Black Political Economy* 5 (Winter 1975): 175–184.

———. "Government as Financial Intermediary for Minority Entrepreneurs: An Evaluation." *Journal of Business* 48 (October 1975): 541–557.

Binkin, Martin, and Mark Etelberg with Alvin Schexnider and Marvin Smith. *Blacks and the Military* (Washington, D.C.: The Brookings Institution, 1982).

Borjas, George J. "The Politics of Employment Discrimination in the Federal Bureaucracy." *Journal of Law and Economics* 25 (October 1982): 271–299.

Bradford, William D., Alfred E. Osborne and Lewis J. Spellman. "The Efficiency and Profitability of Minority-Controlled Savings and Loan Associations." *Journal of Money, Credit and Banking* 10 (February 1978): 65–74.

Brandon, Patricia A. "The Right of Access of the Medically Underserved to Health Care Services." *Journal of Legal Medicine* 2 (September 1981): 297–345.

Brazzel, John M., and Leon J. Hunter. "Trends in Energy Expenditures by Black Households." *Review of Black Political Economy* 9 (Spring 1979): 276–299.

Brimmer, Andrew F. "The Black Banks: An Assessment of Performance and Prospects." *Journal of Finance* 26 (May 1971): 379–406.

Brown, George L. "Invisible Again: Blacks and the Energy Crisis." *Social Policy* 7 (January/February 1977): 39–42.

Brown, Tyrone. "The Federal Communications Commission and Minority Radio Ownership: Evolving Opportunities." *Journal of Minority Business Finance*, Summer 1980, pp. 23–28.

Browning, H. L., S. C. Loperato and D. L. Poston, Jr. "Income and Veteran Status: Variations Among Mexicans, Blacks and Anglos." *American Sociological Review* 38 (February 1973): 763–785.

Bryce, Herrington (ed.) *Urban Governance and Minorities* (New York: Praeger, 1976).

Bullock, Charles S., James E. Anderson and David W. Brady. *Public Policy in the Eighties* (Monterey, Calif.: Brooks/Cole Publishers, 1983).

Butler, John S. "Inequality in the Military: An Examination of Promotion Time for Black and White Enlisted Men." *American Sociological Review* 41 (October 1976): 807–818.

————. *Inequality in the Military: The Black Experience* (Saratoga, Calif.: Century Twenty One, 1980).

Coffey, Kenneth J. (ed.). *Strategic Implications of the All-Volunteer Force: The Conventional Defense of Central Europe* (Chapel Hill: University of North Carolina Press, 1979).

Cooper, Richard L., Michael Steinhauer, William Miller, Richard David and Arthur Schatzkin. "Racism, Society and Disease: An Exploration of the Social and Biological Mechanisms of Differential Mortality." *International Journal of Health Services* 11 (Fall 1981): 389–414.

Cornish, Edward. *The Study of the Future* (Washington, D.C.: World Future Society, 1977).

Cose, Ellis (ed.). *Energy and Equity: Some Social Concerns* (Washington, D.C.: Joint Center for Political Studies, 1978).

Cose, Ellis, and Milton Morris. *Energy Policy and the Poor* (Washington, D.C.: Joint Center for Political Studies, 1977).

Curtis, James L. "Civil Rights in Medicine." *Journal of Public Health Policy* 1 (1980): 110–120.

Deniss, Ruth E. "Social Stress and Mortality Among Nonwhite Males." *Phylon* 38 (September 1977): 315–328.

Doeringer, P. B. (ed.). *Programs to Employ the Disadvantaged* (Englewood Cliffs, N.J.: Prentice-Hall, 1969).

Dye, Thomas R. *Understanding Public Policy* (Englewood Cliffs, N.J.: Prentice-Hall, 1975).

Edward, Lazear. "The Narrowing of Black-White Age Is Illusory." *American Economic Review* 69 (September 1979): 553–564.

Eisinger, Peter. *Black Employment in City Government* (Washington, D.C.: Joint Center for Political Studies, 1983).

Ely, John H. "The Constitutionality of Reverse Racial Discrimination." *University of Chicago Law Review* 41 (1974): 723–741.

Equal Employment Opportunity Commission. *Affirmative Action and Equal Employment: A Guidebook for Employers* (Washington, D.C.: Government Printing Office, 1974).

Ermer, Virginia, and John H. Strange (eds.). *Blacks and Bureaucracy: The Problems and Politics of Change* (New York: Thomas Y. Crowell, 1972).

Ernt, Robert T., and Lawrence Hugg (eds.). *Black America: Geographical Perspectives* (New York: Anchor Books, 1976).

Fisher, Frank. *Politics, Values and Public Policy* (Boulder, Colo.: Westview Press, 1980).

Fletcher, Marvin. *The Black Soldier and Officer in the United States Army, 1881–1917* (Columbia: University of Missouri Press, 1974).

Foner, Jack D. *Blacks and the Military in American History: A New Perspective* (New York: Praeger Publishers, 1974).

Garofalo, James. *Public Opinion About Crime: The Attitudes of Victims and Nonvictims in Selected Cities* (Albany, N.Y.: Criminal Justice Research Center, 1977).

Gayles, Joseph N. "Health Brutality and the Black Life Cycle." *Black Scholar* 5 (May 1972): 2–9.

Georgakas, Dan, and Marvin Surkin. *Detroit, I Do Mind Dying: A Study in Urban Revolution* (New York: St. Martin's Press, 1975).

Gillum, Richard F., R. R. Neuta, W. B. Stason and H. S. Solomon. "Determinants of Dropout Rates Among Hypertensive Patients in an Urban Clinic." *Journal of Community Health* 5 (Winter 1979): 94–100.

Glazer, Nathan. *Affirmative Action: Ethnic Inequality and Public Policy* (New York: Basic Books, 1975).

Greenberg, Edward S., Neal Milner and David J. Olsen. *Black Politics* (New York: Holt, Rinehart & Winston, 1971).

Greer, Edward. *Big Steel: Black Politics and Corporate Power in Gary, Indiana* (New York: Monthly Review Press, 1979).

Grier, Eunice S. *Colder . . . Darker: The Energy Crisis and Low Income Americans: An Analysis of Impact and Options* (Washington, D.C.: Community Services Administration, 1977).

Gross, Barry. *Reverse Discrimination* (Buffalo, N.Y.: Prometheus Books, 1977).

Guthrie, Harold. "The Prospect of Equality of Incomes Between White and Black Families Under Varying Rates of Unemployment." *Journal of Human Resources* 5 (Fall 1970): 431–446.

Guzda, Henry P. "Labor Department's First Program to Assist Black Workers." *Monthly Labor Review* 105 (June 1982): 39–44.

Hall, Edward T. *Beyond Culture* (Garden City, N.Y.: Anchor Press, 1976).

Hall, Grace, and Alan Saltzstein. "Equal Employment in Urban Governments: The Potential Problem of Interminority Competition." *Public Personnel Management* 4 (November/December 1975): 386–393.

———. "Equal Employment Opportunity for Minorities in Municipal Government." *Social Science Quarterly* 57 (March 1977): 864–872.

Hamilton, Charles V. "Racial Ethnic and Social Class Politics and Administration." *Public Administration Review* 32 (October 1972): 638–645.

Harlow, Karen, and Mark Rosentraub. *Crime Victimization and Citizens Perceptions of Safety and Police Services in Ft. Worth* (Fort Worth, Tex.: City of Fort Worth, 1978).

Harrison, Bennett. "Education and Underemployment in the Urban Ghetto." In David Gordon (ed.), *Problems in Political Economy: An Urban Perspective* (Lexington, Mass.: D. C. Heath & Co., 1977).

Henderson, Lenneal J. "Energy Policy and Socioeconomic Growth in Low-Income Communities." *Review of Black Political Economy* 8 (Fall 1977): 260–275.

————. "Administrative Advocacy and Black Urban Administrators." *Annals of the American Academy of Political and Social Science* 439 (September 1978): 68–79.

————. "The Impact of the Equal Employment Opportunity Act on Women and Minorities in Municipal Government." *Policy Studies Journal* 7 (Winter 1978): 234–239.

————. "Energy, Urban Policy and Socioeconomic Development." *Urban League Review*, 3 (Winter 1978): 34–40.

————. "Public Utility Regulation: The Socioeconomic Dimension of Reform." *Review of Black Political Economy* 9 (Spring 1979): 260–275.

————. "Energy Policy and Social Equity." In Robert Lawrence (ed.), *New Dimensions to Energy Policy* (Lexington, Mass.: D. C. Heath & Co., 1979).

————. *Administrative Advocacy: Black Administrators in Urban Bureaucracy* (Palo Alto, Calif.: R & E Research Associates, 1979).

————. "Energy Policy and Public Administration: A Social Systems Perspective." *Howard Law Journal* 24 (November 1981): 211–233.

Herbert, Adam W. "The Minority Public Administrator: Problems, Prospects and Challenges." *Public Administration Review* 34 (November/December 1974): 556–563.

————. "The Evolving Challenges of Black Urban Administration." *Journal of Afro-American Issues* 3 (Spring 1975): 173–179.

Hill, Robert B. *Economic Policies and Black Progress: Myths and Realities* (Washington, D.C.: National Urban League, 1981).

————. "The Economic Status of Black Americans." In *The State of Black America 1981* (New York: National Urban League, 1981).

Hirsch, Barry T. *The Anti-Poverty Effectiveness of Economic Growth and Transfers: Some New Evidence.* Working paper no. 810601 (Greensboro, N.C.: Center for Applied Research, University of North Carolina at Greensboro,1981).

Howard, Lawrence C. "Black Praxis of Governance: Toward an Alternative Paradigm for Public Administration." *Journal of Afro-American Issues* 3 (Spring 1975): 143–159.

————. "Civil Service Reform: A Minority and Woman's Perspective." *Public Administration Review* 38 (July/August 1978): 305–309.

Howard, Lawrence, Lenneal J. Henderson and Deryl G. Hunt (eds.). *Public Administration and Public Policy: A Minority Perspective* (Pittsburgh: Public Policy Press, 1977).

Hunt, Deryl G. "The Black Perspective on Management." *Public Administration Review* 34 (November/December 1974): 520–525.

Hunt, Deryl G., Clyde Bishop and Lawrence C. Howard. *Culture and Administration: A Black Perspective* (Pittsburgh: Public Policy Press, 1979).

Hyclack, Thomas, and James B. Stewart. "A Note on the Relative Earnings of Central City Black Males." *Journal of Human Resources* 16 (Spring 1981): 304–313.

Institute of Medicine. *Health Care in a Civil Rights Context* (Washington, D.C.: National Academy Press, 1981).

Janowitz, Morris, and Charles Moskos. "Racial Composition in the All-Volunteer Force." *Armed Forces and Society* 1 (November 1974): 109–123.

Jencks, Christopher. *Inequality: A Reassessment of Family and Schooling in America* (New York: Harper & Row, 1972).

Joint Center for Political Studies. "Blacks, Demographic Change and Public Safety." *Focus* 10 (November 1982): 2–3.

———. *National Roster of Black Elected Officials* (Washington, D.C.: Joint Center for Political Studies, 1983).

Jones, Woodrow, Jr., and Mitchell F. Rice. "Health Care, Civil Rights and the Black Community." *Policy Studies Review* 3 (August 1983): 114–119.

Keeky, John B. (ed.). *The All-Volunteer Force and American Society* (Charlottesville: University Press of Virginia, 1978).

Kim, Choongsoo, et al. *The All-Volunteer Force: An Analysis of Youth Participation, Attraction and Reenlistment* (Columbus: Ohio State University, Center for Human Resource Research, 1980).

King, Alan G., and Ray Marshall. "Black-White Economic Convergence and the Civil Rights Act of 1964." *Labor Law Journal* 25 (August 1974): 462–471.

Kitigawa, Evelyn M., and Philip M. Hauser. *Differential Mortality in the United States* (Cambridge, Mass.: Harvard University Press, 1973).

Knith, Kenneth, and Terry Dorsey. "Capital Problems in Minority Business Development: A Critical Analysis." *American Economic Review* 66 (May 1976): 328–331.

Kranz, Harry. *A More Representative Bureaucracy: The Adequacy and Desirability of Minority and Female Population Parity in Public Employment* (Ph.D. dissertation, American University, 1974).

Krislov, Samuel. *The Negro In Federal Employment: The Quest for Equal Opportunity* (Minneapolis: University of Minnesota Press, 1976).

Lekachman, Robert. *Greed Is Not Enough: Reaganomics* (New York: Pantheon Books, 1982).

Lavinsky, Larry. "DeFunis Symposium." *Columbia Law Review* 75 (1975): 520–533.

Lee, Anne S. "Material Mortality in the United States." *Phylon* 38 (September 1977): 259–266.

Levy, Mark R., and Michael S. Kramer. *The Ethnic Factor: How America's Minorities Decide Elections* (New York: Simon & Schuster, 1972).

Litt, Edgar. *Ethnic Politics in America* (Glenview, Ill.: Scott, Foresman Publishers, 1970).

Luft, Harold. *Poverty and Health: Economic Causes and Consequences of Health Problems* (Cambridge, Mass.: Ballinger Publishing Co., 1978).

MacGregor, Morris J. *Integration of the Armed Forces, 1940–1965* (Washington, D.C.: U.S. Army Center of Military History, 1981).

Morris, Milton D. *The Politics of Black America* (New York: Harper & Row, 1975).

Moskos, Charles C. "Has the Army Killed Jim Crow?" *Negro History Bulletin*, November 1957, pp. 28–34.

———. "The American Dilemma in Uniform: Race in the Armed Forces." *Annals of the American Academy of Political and Social Science* 406 (March 1973): 94–106.

Moskos, Charles C., J. S. Butler, A. N. Sabrosky and A. J. Schexnider. "Symposium: Race and the United States Military." *Armed Forces and Society* 6 (Summer 1980).

Myrdal, Gunnar. *An American Dilemma: The Problem in Modern Democracy* (New York: McGraw-Hill, 1944).

National Advisory Commission on Civil Disorders. *Report of the National Advisory Commission on Disorders* (New York: New York Times Co., 1968).

Nelson, William E., Jr. "Black Mayors as Urban Managers." *Annals of the American Academy of Political and Social Science* 439 (September 1978): 53–67.

Nelson, William E., Jr., and Philip Meranto. *Electing Black Mayors: Political Action in the Black Community* (Columbus: Ohio State University Press, 1977).

Nelson, William E., Jr., and Winston Van Horne. "Black Elected Administrators: The Trials of Office." *Public Administration Review* 34 (November/December 1974): 526–533.

Newman, Dorothy K., Nancy J. Amidei, Barbara L. Carter, Dawn Day, William J. Kruvant and Jack S. Russell. *Protest, Politics and Prosperity: Black Americans and White Institutions* (New York: Pantheon Books, 1978).

Niewi, A. W., Jr. "The Impact of Recent Civil Rights Laws: Relative Improvement in Occupational Structure, Earnings and Income by Nonwhites, 1960–70." *American Journal of Economics and Sociology* 33 (April 1974): 137–144.

Nobles, Wade W. "Black People in White Insanity: An Issue for Black Community Health." *Journal of Afro-American Issues* 4 (Winter 1976): 21–27.

O'Neil, Robert M. *Discriminating Against Discrimination* (Bloomington: Indiana University Press, 1975).

Palmer, John L., and Isabel V. Sawhill (eds.). *The Reagan Experiment* (Washington, D.C.: Urban Institute Press, 1982).

Paul, Ellen F., and Philip A. Russo, Jr. (eds.) *Public Policy: Issues, Analysis and Ideology* (Chatham, N.J.: Chatham House Publishers, 1982).

Perry, Huey L. "Review Essay on Energy, the Environment and Public Policy." *Policy Studies Journal* 11 (Fall 1982): 190–194.

Perry, Huey L., and Emma B. Perry. "Energy and Minorities: Women and the Poor." *Public Administration Series: Bibliography* (Monticello, Ill.: Vance Bibliographies, 1980).

Piven, Frances Fox, and Richard A. Cloward. *Regulating the Poor: The Functions of Public Welfare* (New York: Pantheon Books, 1971).

———. *The New Class War: Reagan's Attack on the Welfare State and Its Consequences* (New York: Pantheon Books, 1982).

Poole, Isaiah J. "Black Business: A Negative View of Washington." *Black Enterprise*, June 1982, p. 57.

President's Commission on Mental Health. *Task Panel Report* (Washington, D.C.: Government Printing Office, 1978).

Preston, Michael B. "Limitations of Black Urban Power: The Case of Black Mayors." In Louis H. Masotti and Robert L. Lineberry (eds.), *The New Urban Politics* (Cambridge, Mass.: Ballinger, 1976).

———. "Blacks and Public Policy." *Policy Studies Journal* 6 (Winter 1977): 245–255.

———. "Black Elected Officials and Public Policy: Symbolic or Substantive Representation?" *Policy Studies Journal* 7 (December 1978): 196–200.

Preston, Michael B., Lenneal J. Henderson, Jr., and Paul Puryear (eds.). *The New Black Politics: The Search for Political Power* (New York: Longman, 1982).

Pugh, G. Douglas, and William F. Haddad (eds.). *Black Economic Development* (Englewood Cliffs, N.J.: Prentice-Hall, 1969).

Rayton, C. R. "Substance Abuse and Mental Health: Special Prevention Needed for Ethics of Color." *Public Health Reports* 96 (February 1981): 20–25.

Reid, John D., Everett S. Lee, Davor Jedlicka and Youngshock Shin. "Trends in Black Health." *Phylon* 38 (June 1977): 105–116.

Rice, Mitchell F. "Inequality, Discrimination and Service Delivery: A Recapitulation for the Public Administrator." *International Journal of Public Administration* 1 (Winter 1979): 409–433.

———. "Support for Equal Employment Opportunity and Affirmative Action Among Municipal Administrators in Texas." *Public Affairs Comment* 27 (May 1981): 1–6.

———. "Black Health Care: Another Look at an Old Problem." *Texas Public Health Association Journal* 33 (Fall 1981): 17–20.

———. "Personnel Attitudes, Interminority Competition and Affirmative Action." *The Municipal Matrix* 15 (March 1983): 1–4.

Rice, Mitchell F., and Woodrow Jones, Jr. "Liberalism, Politics and Health Planning." *Journal of Health and Human Resources* 3 (August 1980): 56–66.

———. "Black Health Inequities and the American Health Care System." *Health Policy and Education: An International Journal* 3 (Fall 1982): 195–214.

Rice, Mitchell F., and William Verner, Jr. "Implementing Federal Policy: A Preliminary Analysis of Equal Employment Opportunity and Affirmative Action in Selected Texas Cities." *Urban Affairs Papers* 2 (Summer 1980): 37–54.

Rocky Mountain Region State Advisory Committees to the U.S. Commission on Civil Rights. *Energy Resource Development: Implications for Women and Minorities in the Intermountain West* (Washington, D.C.: Government Printing Office, 1979).

Rose, Harold M. *The Black Ghetto: A Spatial Behavior Perspective* (New York: McGraw-Hill, 1971).

Rose, Weinfield H., and Tiang Ping Chia. "The Impact of the Equal Employment Opportunity Act of 1972 on Black Employment in the Federal Service: A Preliminary Analysis." *Public Administration Review* 38 (May/June 1978): 245–252.

Rosenbloom, David H. *Federal Service and the Constitution: The Development of the Public Employment Relationship* (Ithaca, N.Y.: Cornell University Press, 1971).

———. "The Civil Service Commission's Decision to Authorize the Use of Goals and Timetables in the Federal Equal Employment Opportunity Program." *Western Political Quarterly* 26 (June 1973): 236–251.

———. "A Note on Interminority Group Competition for Federal Positions." *Public Personnel Management* 4 (November/December 1973): 43–48.

———. "Implementing Equal Employment Opportunity Goals and Timetables in the Federal Service." *Midwest Review of Public Administration* 9 (April/July 1975): 107–120.

———. *Federal Equal Employment Opportunity: Politics and Public Personnel Administration* (New York: Praeger Publishers, 1977).

Rosenbloom, David H., and Peter N. Grabosky. "Racial and Ethnic Competition for Federal Service Positions." *Midwest Review of Public Administration* 11 (December 1977): 281–290.

Rosentraub, Mark, and Karen Harlow. "Public/Private Relations and Service Delivery:

The Co-Production of Personal Safety." *Policy Studies Journal* 11 (March 1983): 445–457.

Ross, Arthur, and Herbert Hill (eds.). *Employment, Race and Poverty* (New York: Harcourt Brace & World, 1967).

Schexnider, Alvin J., and John S. Butler. "Race and the All-Volunteer System: A Reply to Janowitz and Moskos." *Armed Forces and Society* 2 (May 1976): 421–434.

Scowcroft, Brent (ed.). *Military Service in the United States* (Englewood Cliffs, N.J.: Prentice-Hall, 1982).

Seham, Max. *Blacks and American Medical Care* (Minneapolis: University of Minnesota Press, 1973).

Shields, Patricia M. *The Determinants of Service in the Armed Forces During the Vietnam Era* (Columbus: Ohio State University, Center for Human Resource Research, 1977).

———. "Enlistment During the Vietnam Era and the 'Representation' Issue of the All-Volunteer Force." *Armed Forces and Society* 7 (Fall 1980): 133–151.

———. "The Burden of the Draft: The Vietnam Years." *Journal of Political and Military Sociology* 9 (Fall 1981): 215–228.

Shin, Evi Hang. "Black-White Differentials in Infant Mortality in the South." *Demography* 12 (February 1975): 1–19.

Sindler, Allan P. *Bakke, DeFunis and Minority Admissions* (New York: Longman, 1978).

Sjoberg, Gideon, Richard A. Brymer and Buford Farris. "Bureaucracy and the Lower Class." *Sociology and Social Research* 50 (April 1966): 325–337.

Skolnick, Jerome H., and T. C. Gray (eds.). *Police in America* (Boston: Little, Brown & Co., 1975).

Smith, J. Owen. "The Bakke Decision: A Flagrant Denial of Human Rights." *Western Journal of Black Studies* 2 (Winter 1979): 244–255.

Stewart, James B., and Joseph W. Scott. "The Institutional Decimation of Black American Males." *Western Journal of Black Studies* 2 (Summer 1978): 89–92.

Sue, Stanley. "Community Mental Health Services to Minority Groups: Some Optimism, Some Pessimism." *American Psychologist* 32 (August 1977): 616–624.

Tabb, William K., and Larry Sawers. *Marxism and the Metropolis: New Perspectives in Urban Political Economy* (New York: Oxford University Press, 1978).

Thomas, Alexander, and Samuel Sillen, *Racism and Psychiatry* (New York: Brunner/Mazel, 1972).

Thompson, Frank J. "Civil Servants and the Deprived: Sociopolitical and Occupational Explanations of Attitudes Toward Minority Hiring." *American Journal of Political Science* 22 (May 1978): 325–347.

Thompson, Frank J., and Bonnie Brown. "Commitment to the Disadvantaged Among Urban Administrators: The Case of Minority Hiring." *Urban Affairs Quarterly* 13 (March 1978): 355–378.

Tolbert, George P. "Meeting the Health Needs of Minorities and the Poor." *Phylon* 38 (September 1977): 225–235.

U.S. Bureau of the Census. *1977 Survey of Minority-Owned Business Enterprise (Black)* (Washington, D.C.: Government Printing Office, 1977).

U.S. Commission on Civil Rights. *Social Indicators of Equality for Minorities and Women* (Washington, D.C., 1978).

U.S. Congress. *Background Paper: Health Differentials Between White and Nonwhite Americans* (Washington, D.C.: Government Printing Office, 1977).

U.S. Department of Commerce, *Public Employment in 1982* (Washington, D.C.: Government Printing Office, 1982).

U.S. Department of Health and Human Services. *Health of the Disadvantaged, Chart Book—II* (Washington, D.C.: Government Printing Office, 1980).

U.S. Department of Health, Education and Welfare. *Facts of Life and Death* (Washington, D.C.: Government Printing Office, 1978).

————. *Health Status of Minorities and Low-Income Groups* (Washington, D.C.: Government Printing Office, 1979).

————. *Health: United States, 1979* (Washington, D.C.: Government Printing Office, 1980).

U.S. General Accounting Office. *Limited Success of Federally-Financed Minority Businesses in Three Cities* (Washington, D.C.: General Accounting Office, 1973).

Utton, Albert E., W. R. Sewell and Timothy O'Riordan. *Natural Resources for a Democratic Society: Public Participation in Decision Making* (Boulder, Colo.: Westview Press, 1976).

Walters, Ronald. "Black Presidential Politics in the 1980s: Bargaining or Begging?" *Black Scholar* 11 (March/April 1980): 22–31.

Walton, Hanes. *Black Politics: A Theoretical and Structural Analysis* (Philadelphia: J. B. Lippincott Co., 1972).

White, Jack E. "Cancer Differences in the Black and White Caucasian Population." *Phylon* 38 (September 1977): 297–314.

Willhelm, Sidney M. *Who Needs the Negro* (Garden City, N.Y.: Doubleday & Co., 1971).

Williams, Eddie, and Milton D. Morris. *The Black Vote in a Presidential Election Year* (Washington, D.C.: Joint Center for Political Studies, 1981).

Willie, Charles V., Bernard M. Kramer and Bertram S. Brown (eds.). *Racism and Mental Health: Essays* (Pittsburgh: University of Pittsburgh Press, 1973).

Wing, Kenneth, and Marilyn Rose. "Health Facilities and the Enforcement of Civil Rights." *Legal Aspects of Health Policy: Issues and Trends* (Westport, Conn.: Greenwood Press, 1980).

Wolkinson, Benjamin W. *Blacks, Unions and the EEOC* (Lexington, Mass.: Lexington Books, 1973).

Yabura, Lloyd. "Health Care Outcomes in the Black Community." *Phylon* 38 (June 1977): 194–202.

Index

Contributors

LOUIS C. GREEN is Assistant Professor of Economics at San Diego State University. He holds the Ph.D. in Economics from the University of California at Berkeley. His areas of interest and publication are in international economics, labor productivity, and black economic development. He was awarded a Ford Foundation Postdoctoral Fellowship for 1980–81. He has published in the *Journal of Behavioral Economics, Inter-American Economic Affairs, New Scholar* and the *Review of Black Political Economy.*

KAREN HARLOW is Senior Project Manager at the Institute of Urban Studies at the University of Texas at Arlington. Her research interests are in the areas of social and municipal service delivery and decisionmaking in the nonprofit sector. Her most recent writings have appeared in the *Journal of Social Work, Policy Studies Journal,* and the *Southwest Review of Management and Economics.* She holds the Ph.D. in Administration and Urban Studies from the University of Texas at Arlington.

LENNEAL J. HENDERSON, JR., is currently a Professor in the School of Business and Public Administration at Howard University in Washington, D.C., and holds a Ford Foundation National Research Council (Ford Foundation) Postdoctoral Fellowship. His publications include *Black Political Life in the U.S.; Public Administration and Public Policy: A Minority Perspective* (with Lawrence Howard and Deryl Hunt); *Administrative Advocacy: Black Administrators in Urban Bureaucracies; The New Black Politics: The Search for Political Power* (with Michael Preston and Paul Puryear) and articles in such journals as the *Policy Studies Journal, Black Scholar, Public Administration Review, Journal of Afro-American Issues, Annals, Review of Black Political Economy* and the *Urban League Review.* He received his A.B., M.A. and Ph.D. from the University of California at Berkeley.

PHILIP MERANTO is a Visiting Lecturer at the University of Colorado at Denver. He holds the Ph.D. in Political Science from Syracuse University. He is the author of *School Politics in the Metropolis* and coauthor of *Electing Black Mayors* (with William E. Nelson, Jr.). His research interests are in the areas of urban politics and public policy.

LAWRENCE MOSQUEDA is Assistant Professor of Political Science at the University of Colorado at Denver. He holds the Ph.D. in Political Science from the University of Washington in Seattle. He is coauthor of *Urban Politics and Public Policy* (with Dennis Judd). His research interests are in the areas of urban and ethnic politics and public policy.

WILLIAM E. NELSON, JR., is Professor of Political Science and Chairman of the Department of Black Studies at The Ohio State University. He is coauthor of *Electing Black Mayors* (with Philip Meranto). His writings have also appeared in *Public Administration Review* and the *Annals of the American Academy of Political Science and Social Science*. He holds the Ph.D. in Political Science from the University of Illinois.

HUEY L. PERRY is Associate Professor of Political Science at Southern University, Baton Rouge, Louisiana. He holds the Ph.D. in Political Science from the University of Chicago. His research interests are in the areas of energy politics and minorities and Southern black politics. His most recent publications have appeared in the *Southern Review of Public Administration* and the *Review of Black Political Economy*. He is President of the National Conference of Black Political Scientists for 1984–85.

MICHAEL B. PRESTON is Associate Professor of Political Science at the University of Illinois, Urbana. He was previously a Visiting Associate Professor at the University of Chicago. His writings have appeared in *Public Administration Review, Urban Affairs Quarterly*, the *Journal of Health and Human Services* and *Policy Studies Journal*. He is coeditor (with Marian Lief Palley) of *Race, Sex and Policy Problems* and *The New Black Politics: The Search for Political Power* (with Lenneal J. Henderson and Paul Puryear). He is a member of the National Council of the American Political Science Association and Chairman of the Committee on the Status of Blacks in the Profession of the American Political Science Association. He also serves on the Board of Editors of the *Public Administration Review*. He holds the Ph.D. from the University of California at Berkeley.

MARK S. ROSENTRAUB is Director of the Urban and Regional Affairs Division of the Institute of Urban Studies and Associate Professor of Urban Studies at the University of Texas at Arlington. He has been involved in several studies of citizens' attitudes in the Dallas/Ft. Worth area. His works have appeared in the *American Behavioralist Scientist, Policy Studies Journal, Social Science Journal* and several edited volumes. He holds the Ph.D. in Urban Studies from the University of Southern California.

PATRICIA M. SHIELDS is Associate Professor of Political Science and Public Administration at Southwest Texas State University, San Marcos, Texas. She has written extensively on military conscription and military politics. Her most recent publications on these topics have appeared in *Armed Forces and Society* and the *Journal of Political and Military Sociology*. She holds the Ph.D. in Public Administration from The Ohio State University.

J. OWENS SMITH is President of the California Black Faculty Association and Assistant Professor of Political Science and Black Studies at California State University at Fullerton. He holds the Ph.D. in Political Science from the University of Chicago. He has taught previously at Chicago State University, the University of Wisconsin-Oshkosh, and San Diego State University. He has written extensively on the subject of affirmative action.

JAMES B. STEWART is Director of the Black Studies Program and Assistant Professor of Economics at Pennsylvania State University. He holds the Ph.D. in Economics from the University of Notre Dame. He has published in the *Journal of Black Studies, Review of Black Political Economy, South Atlantic Urban Studies* and the *Western Journal of Black Studies.*

MYLON WINN is Assistant Professor of Political Science and Director of the Public Administration Program at the University of Tennessee, Knoxville. His research interests are in the areas of ethical behavior and bureaucracy and public policy. He holds the Ph.D. in Political Science from the University of Washington at Seattle.

About the Editors

MITCHELL F. RICE is Associate Professor of Political Science and Public Administration at Southwest Texas State University. He holds the Ph.D. in Government from Claremont Graduate School. His writings have appeared in a number of academic and professional journals including the *International Journal of Public Administration, Policy Studies Review, Health Policy and Education* and *Midwest Review of Public Administration.* He has held an American Council on Education Fellowship in Academic Administration and holds a 1984–85 National Research Council (Ford Foundation) Postdoctoral Fellowship. He is a member of the Committee on the Status of Blacks in the Profession of the American Political Science Association and a member of the Executive Council of the Southwestern Political Science Association.

WOODROW JONES, JR., is Professor of Political Science at San Diego State University. He holds the Ph.D. in Political Science from the University of Oregon and recently completed a Postdoctoral fellowship in health (M.P.H.) at the University of Texas Health Science Center in Houston. He has published in the *American Politics Quarterly, Health Policy and Education, Policy Studies Review* and *Journal of Environmental Systems.* He has taught previously as a Visiting Associate Professor at the University of Houston.